PELICAN BOOKS

# INTERNATIONAL POLITICS

*Advisory Editor : Jean Blondel*

Joseph Frankel was born in Poland in 1913. He took his degrees at the University of Lwow in Poland, and at the University of Western Australia. He has a Ph.D (Econ.) from London University. Between 1951 and 1952 he held an appointment at University College, London, and from 1953 until 1962 was with the University of Aberdeen. Since 1963 he has been Professor of Politics at the University of Southampton.

Joseph Frankel is especially interested in foreign policy analysis and the theory of international relations. He has contributed to several journals and is the author of *The Making of Foreign Policy* and *International Relations*. He is married, with one daughter.

# JOSEPH FRANKEL

# INTERNATIONAL POLITICS

## CONFLICT AND HARMONY

PENGUIN BOOKS

Penguin Books Ltd, Harmondsworth, Middlesex, England
Penguin Books Inc., 7110 Ambassador Road, Baltimore, Maryland 21207, U.S.A.
Penguin Books Australia Ltd, Ringwood, Victoria, Australia

—

First published by Allen Lane The Penguin Press 1969
Published with revisions in Pelican Books 1973

—

Copyright © Joseph Frankel, 1969, 1973

—

Made and printed in Great Britain by
Cox & Wyman Ltd, London Reading and Fakenham
Set in Intertype Plantin

This book is sold subject to the condition
that it shall not, by way of trade or otherwise,
be lent, re-sold, hired out, or otherwise circulated
without the publisher's prior consent in any form of
binding or cover other than that in which it is
published and without a similar condition
including this condition being imposed
on the subsequent purchaser

0140215255

# CONTENTS

PART THREE

## INTERNATIONAL ISSUES AND PROSPECTS

# PREFACE

WAR and peace are the core of international politics and the red thread running through all the books written about it. This book is no exception although war and peace are considered here from a special angle – as the extremes of the two recurrent modes of social interaction, conflict and harmony. In recent years some cognate fields have been looked into on similar lines* but, to my knowledge, this is the first extensive attempt in the study of international relations.

This study is now rapidly advancing. It is accumulating and processing the relevant data and is developing scientific techniques and, in the process, its own specialist terminology. Being directed both to the specialist and to the general reader, this book employs the current terminology but, for the sake of clarity, it keeps it down to the minimum and it defines the terms which are not self-explanatory. No difficulties on that score arise in the main body of the argument. The reader averse to theory need not be put off by the brief survey of the discipline and its methods in Chapter 1 which, although put in as general and simple a form as possible, may not be quite easily comprehensible. This is not characteristic of the remainder of the book.

Within its limited scope, this book cannot be expected to provide a full picture of the world especially since it has been written without any assistance and from a hitherto untried angle. It discusses a broad theme within a world-wide setting and this would be impossible without resorting to generalizations which are explained in the opening chapter. It examines a broad range of international phenomena and events but only with respect to their relevance to the theme of conflict and harmony. Consequently not all important elements are discussed, some because

* cf. Maurice Duverger, *The Idea of Politics: the Uses of Power in Society*, Methuen, 1966, and Jan Pen, *Harmony and Conflict in Modern Society*, McGraw-Hill, 1960.

they are generally known, and others, such as 'national character' or the impact of personalities, because they defy generalization.

The argument is about the present but since the present is merely a point at which the past and the future overlap, inevitably it refers to all three. It is not based upon preconceived ideas about the relative significance either of conflict and harmony or of the patterns derived from the past and those seemingly pointing towards the future. It tries to explain rather than to evaluate. Only the concluding chapter can, in a way, be understood as a tract for our times; it was written as a summary and conclusion of the argument, after the book had been written and not beforehand.

May 1968                                    JOSEPH FRANKEL

## CHAPTER 1

# INTRODUCTORY

*The Meaning and Scope of International Politics*

THE starting-point of politics is the basic social fact that people have wants and needs which they cannot satisfy by individual efforts. They organize themselves into groups of various size and scope to deal with these wants and needs and, whenever this happens, there emerge persistent patterns of human behaviour concerned with authority, power, government and rule. These concepts form the hard core of all definitions of politics; precise definitions differ from thinker to thinker and, although the study of politics is the oldest of all sciences, its exact meaning remains hotly disputed.

Authority, power, government and rule are in our experience connected with the activities of states and their governments. These have legitimately been occupying the centre of political analysis to the point of excluding, until recently, interest in other political phenomena. Today, however, political scientists refuse to narrow their field of inquiry – they merely follow common parlance by distinguishing authority, politics and government in all human associations from the smallest ones right up to man-kind as a whole. Nevertheless, applying the vocabulary and modes of thinking evolved in domestic politics to international politics carries its difficulties and dangers. There is no international government or fully articulated system of international law with machinery for adjudication, enforcement and change; there is no underlying consensus among the members of international society on acceptable ends and means. States, the parts of the inter-national system, although frequently personified, bear little re-semblance to individuals as members of a state. They monopolize power and use it for the pursuit of their individual national interests – in contrast to the domination of the state over its citi-zens and their groupings in domestic systems, the international system is, as it has been put, 'subsystem-dominated'.

Although important in principle, the distinction should not be exaggerated; the differences between domestic and international politics are no longer as clear-cut as a century ago. On the one hand, some inter-state relations are now based upon consensus and are evolving suitable institutions, e.g. those within the European Economic Community or, to use older examples, relations between the United States and Canada or among the Scandinavian countries. On the other hand, the classical notions of politics scarcely describe situations within states which are chronically unstable and disturbed, as strikingly demonstrated in the cases of Indonesia or the Congo; these resemble more closely the relative anarchy of international relations than the order of the older well-established states.

The scope of international politics is immense. It embraces the foreign policies of all the 140 or so states (the figure depends upon the definition of the state) in their mutual interaction as well as in their interaction with the international system as a whole, with international organizations, and with social groups other than states; the operation of the international system; and also the domestic politics of all the states. Understanding of this complex universe is hampered by the heterogeneity of its elements. As every student of comparative government well knows, despite the great advances in the empirical study of the politics of single states no ready comparison lies between them; even the most methodologically advanced and the most highly sophisticated approaches limit themselves to groups of fairly homogeneous states and even then are not fully satisfactory in their methods.* Comparing the domestic policies of *all* states is, naturally, even more difficult. Their foreign policies are more intractable to comparative analysis since they cannot be studied singly and then compared, as domestic politics can; we have to study them in interaction with the foreign policies of other states as well as with other elements of the international system.†

It is the daily task of the diplomats to face and cope with the

* cf. Robert A. Dahl, *Political Opposition in Western Democracies*, New Haven, Yale University Press, 1966. See also the review article by Sidney Verba in *World Politics* XX(1), October 1967, pp. 111 ff.

† Even the most advanced effort in the field, *Foreign Policy in World Politics*, Englewood Cliffs, Prentice-Hall, 3rd ed., 1967, edited by

overwhelmingly large and heterogeneous world which cannot be fully grasped as a whole. Their basic method is employed also by scholars – they endeavour to classify and introduce some order into the chaos, in other words they simplify. To take the extreme example of full international involvement in the post-war period, the United States should take the whole international environment into account in all its foreign policy operations. This counsel of perfection is not, of course, attainable in practice. When the United States has an issue say with Guatemala, only Latin American politics need to be taken *fully* into account, with American relations with Russia, with her major European allies, with China, and with the United Nations, playing a much lesser role; relations with the majority of states in other regions can be reasonably ignored.

To practising diplomats, geographical location is the natural and fundamental basis for the classification of states according to the degree of their relevance for the foreign policy as a whole as well as for specific relationships and issues. Very small powers often limit their foreign policies to their region and extend them only sporadically beyond it. This classification by region is useful also for the scholar. If, say, Latin American or West African foreign policies are studied regionally, the resulting analysis reduces the number of variables discernible in the foreign policies of individual states, and the result is somewhat more amenable to cross-regional and world-wide comparison. The advance, however, is not very great and hence we are forced to look for other variables significantly affecting the behaviour of states, such as power, ideology, attitude to international order, degree of economic development; on each of these variables we can base a taxonomy and thus distinguish states great and small, communist and liberal democratic, *status quo* and revisionist, industrialized and underdeveloped. Each group is distinguished by the fact that its members share an important characteristic which allows us some degree of generalization about the group

---

R. C. Macridis, does not amount to more than a series of not fully comparable monographs. For the most comprehensive analysis of the problems involved see J. W. Rosenan, *The Scientific Study of Foreign Policy*, New York, The Free Press, 1971.

as well as its differentiation from the rest of the world. Unfortunately it is impossible to find simple and generally acceptable criteria for our categories. If we use the category of 'power', what is a 'small state' – one with less than ten million people, or five, or twenty? How much should we take into account its economic and military capabilities? Is the United Kingdom a 'Great Power' and, if so, does she belong to the same category as the two Superpowers? Obviously it all depends on definitions and no definitions are fully satisfactory. Nevertheless, although no degree of precision can be expected, the categories are not meaningless. Each has a hard core about which there is no disagreement, e.g. it is quite obvious that the Superpowers belong to the category of Great Powers (although it may be worth while putting them into a sub-category of their own) and that states like the Maldives or Chad belong to the category of Small Powers. Although the boundaries between the two categories are blurred, a certain amount of useful analysis and generalization is possible about them despite their vague definition.

When we try to analyse the whole international scene and generalize about it, obviously all these variables must be taken into account to cover a significant part of our field of interest. This would produce the following five-way matrix:

| | | REGIONS | | | | |
| | | Atlantic Region | Eastern Europe | Asia | Africa | Oceania |
|---|---|---|---|---|---|---|
| *Power* | Great Small Medium | | | | | |
| *Ideology* | Western Liberal Communist Other | | | | | |
| *Attitude to International Order* | Status quo Revisionist Indifferent | | | | | |
| *Economic Development* | Industrialized Developing Intermediate | | | | | |

This list of variables can scarcely be regarded as sufficient for purposes of general analysis: certainly for the majority of specific purposes additional variables have to be considered. No wonder that generalizations about international politics are rather vague, often not stating much more than the obvious, and have to be hedged with qualifications and exceptions. There are few propositions about international politics as a whole which need not be qualified by such words as 'almost', 'usually', 'generally', 'nearly', etc. The state 'population' of the 'universe' called 'the international system' is too small and too heterogeneous and the number of events is often much too small to allow us to apply statistical laws with any degree of significance.

Take, for instance, the most monumental piece of early comparative research, Professor Quincy Wright's *The Study of War*.* He identifies as many as 278 wars fought by important states in the period 1480–1941 and formulates a number of generalizations and hypotheses about the phenomenon of war, but how far can one apply his generalizations to the present, to a world in which nuclear weapons exist and to states which had never been involved in any war? Even when we discover considerable uniformities in the behaviour of nearly all the states, the behaviour of one of them can destroy the practical value of our 'empirical evidence'. A very high statistical probability that a state would try to ensure its survival is not very illuminating when a single state in question accepts the danger of complete annihilation instead of giving in; generalizations about nuclear strategy are obviously deficient when two nuclear powers, France and China, do not wish to abide by them. To understand reality we naturally must classify, generalize, and formulate hypotheses; if, however, as in this book, we are concerned with the reality of international life, we must face the fact not only that all rules seem to have exceptions but also that in some cases the exception may be more important than the rule.

*University of Chicago, 2nd ed., 1965. The figures are used only in this chapter to demonstrate the limitation of the techniques available and explain why they are not employed in the actual analysis.

## Introductory

### History, Theory and Empirical Investigations

The study of international relations as well as that of political science in general share with all other branches of knowledge the problem of choosing the focus of interest: whether to try to comprehend the field as a whole, at the risk of blurring its detailed elements, or to concentrate on these elements at the risk of losing sight of their relation to the remainder of the field. A certain distortion is inevitable and its nature is governed by the focus – is it preferable to lose sight of the wood for the trees or that of the trees for the wood? This is the subject of the age-old argument between the proponents of theory against those supporting empirical investigation. In fact, despite their acrimonious disputes, the dichotomy was never quite stark. Today the majority of scholars, though not all of them, are ready to accept that both the theoretical and the empirical approaches are important, that any advance in the one is relevant for the other, that there is no basis for the distinction between deduction as the major method of theory and induction as the exclusive method of empirical study. They remain divided about priorities.

Until the evolution of social sciences in this century, the two traditional disciplines concerned with politics and international relations were history and philosophy. In the nineteenth century historical analysis was extremely fruitful. While the stage of world politics was confined to Europe and the other continents were no more than unimportant peripheries, while the number of states of any standing or power was limited, and while the sources of information were scarce and the printed word had not yet reached its present volume, it was possible for an encyclopedic mind to build up a picture of world politics from detailed historical studies. Today, when the whole globe forms one field of activity, when the number of units has surpassed 140, and when the accumulation of knowledge is choking the channels of communication, encyclopedic knowledge is impossible. Moreover, while in the nineteenth century a historian well versed in French, British, or German history had a sound basis for understanding the history of Western Europe as a whole, today, traditionally diplomatic historians find themselves poorly equipped to

16

understand the foreign policies of states under communist régimes or belonging to the Third World. If history purports to record 'facts', there are simply too many 'facts' to record.

A more fundamental difficulty arises from the nature of social reality which does not divide itself naturally into single items of information which we take in. The so-called 'facts' are mere artificial constructions abstracted from complex and interwoven reality by means of arbitrary definitions and classifications. They are selected from the profusion of real life on the basis of implicit or explicit theories about what is important.* Before the days of economic and social history and of Sir Lewis Namier, historians were concentrating upon the politics of central governments. Lacking interest, they also lacked knowledge of the important economic, social and provincial 'facts' available to the historians today. If it is so difficult to select what is relevant in the realm of domestic politics, how much more is it in the more complex realm of contemporary international politics!

If 'facts' are artificial and are arbitrarily selected and arranged, we should articulate the ideas which determine our interpretation and enable us to arrange the external chaos into some comprehensible order. This is the role of theory, of philosophical speculation which has been traditionally considered as a competitor to history but has, in many respects, been complementary to it. Theory was not limited to philosophers; every great historian held, at least implicitly, a theory of history without which he could not have achieved an orderly narrative. The subject matter being, however, extremely complex, it is very difficult to articulate a coherent theory of politics and all rigorous approaches to it tend to take us right away from reality. This general tendency is even more pronounced in the field of international politics, one over which man utterly lacks control although, when speaking of it, he employs the vocabulary of domestic politics evolved in a sphere in which he has such control.

Today the age-old dichotomy between the two approaches is largely concerned with what, following the nomenclature of

---

*For a more extensive discussion see J. Frankel, *The Making of Foreign Policy*, Oxford University Press, 1963, Chapter 7, p. 327.

economics, is often called the 'macro-micro' problem. The major advance has been in empirical, 'micro' work. As the tools of social science were developed and applied to the empirical investigation of political phenomena, monographic case-studies followed in growing numbers. As information about contemporary and recent history became more freely available, the numbers of detailed historical analyses of major events and of the foreign policies of single countries likewise proliferated. As the field of interest grew through the establishment of new states, so grew the flood of literature. Although much of the literature is still monographic in form, a number of comparative studies began to appear dealing with regions or with selected aspects of international relations, some of them based on systematic collection of data and on clearly articulated hypotheses.

This great advance in our knowledge of detail does not, however, add up to an understanding of the whole field; on the contrary, the detailed information available is sometimes excessive since it chokes the channels of communication and cannot be easily digested by individual scholars or even by teams of them. Many of the contemporary empiricists are aware of the problem and endeavour to set their work within some general framework of reference and place it within a broader perspective. Unfortunately these attempts are generally unsuccessful. To start with, as a rule the empiricists are insufficiently sophisticated in theory and are often quite indiscriminate in their choices and combinations of the abounding but clashing theories and speculations; frequently all the theorizing is restricted to the introduction and the conclusion, without being incorporated into the actual work.

The real advances are made in accumulating and processing social and political data which, in the words of Professor David Singer, must be 'manipulated, rearranged, and combined in order to be theoretically useful'. The ten essays collected in the volume edited by him under the title *Quantitative International Relations*\* represent the promise and also the present limitations of the behavioural approach. They are based on a common endeavour to analyse hitherto unquantifiable phenomena by the application of rigorous methods to empirical data. The nature of

\*New York, Free Press, 1968, p. 12.

the conclusions varies from contribution to contribution; some are convincing both in the methods employed and in the hypotheses advanced; others merely manage to apply rigorous analysis to intractable problems. All are methodologically interesting. For instance, in the opening essay Professor James Rosenau uses a very sophisticated technique for trying to find out the relative potency of the role and of the individual variables in the attitudes of United States Senators to the Secretary of State. He compares the Acheson and the Dulles periods, showing their basic similarity, and carefully analyses the references made by the Senators to the two Secretaries. The conclusion is that the constraints of Party affiliation and of membership of the Foreign Relations Committee prevail over personal views. This plausible hypothesis now based upon empirical evidence can be fruitfully applied to other situations and the author's techniques offer a good guide to the methods to be chosen. The most conclusive attempts are in the field of decision-making. The findings regarding the national and the international levels are interesting though, on the whole, negative. For example, in the mid fifties there was no significant co-variation between a society's attributes and its propensity to conflict; while in this century the number of alliance commitments positively influences the number of wars in subsequent years, in the nineteenth century the relationship was nearly as strong but inverse.

Even in this joint volume the concepts and the methods are not uniform. The theoretical foundations of other empirical work are often highly idiosyncratic so that comparison is not easy. Moreover, for the time being at least, empirical work tends to be concerned more with methodological advance than with substance. The findings, usually related to isolated aspects of the field which happen to be amenable to the existing empirical methods, do not add up to a coherent picture. The position is much as in the general field of political science where, in the words of Professor Sidney Verba, 'The immediate need in political research is not for more facts or data; rather it is for adequate conceptual schemes and systematic theories into which to fit the facts we have and the facts we shall gather in the future.'

The purely theoretical literature, although not nearly as

abundant as the empirical one, is nevertheless imposing in its bulk as well as in its growing sophistication. Unfortunately it offers no clear guidance to the empiricist. The many individual efforts are highly idiosyncratic although, conceivably, they could be amalgamated into some kind of a general approach accommodating the major schools of social communication, of systems analysis and of decision-making.* The greater obstacle to their application is their predominantly abstract nature. Much of the theorizing about international politics is done in a purely formal manner, without reference to real life. An approach which aims at great precision and at logical coherence tends to lose any links with reality, and its most ardent practitioners can go so far as to present sets of logical categories rather than sets of propositions. It may be added that in defiance of scientific usage some theoreticians insist on calling 'theories' their conceptual frameworks, approaches and models, however loosely constructed, although these do not consist of propositions leading to testable predictions.

Despite the misleading pretensions of some of their practitioners and their remoteness from real life, theoretical approaches to international relations are indispensable for some organization of the overwhelming chaos of real life. It suffices if we accept theory for what it really is. We cannot aspire to 'knowledge' as attainable in natural sciences but this should not prevent us from seeking at least a subjective guide to international politics. The value of such a guide should be judged not by the stringent criteria applicable to a 'theory' but merely by our convenience, whether it helps us to organize the field and leaves out or fails to explain as few elements as possible.† If, as is likely to happen, the scholars fail to agree on whether an individual approach does actually constitute such an advance in our understanding, it can be considered as useful even when it passes the more modest test of providing the basis for a 'rational discussion'.‡

* See below, pp. 27–9.

† cf. Abraham Kaplan, *The Conduct of Inquiry*, San Francisco, Chandler, 1964, Part IX.

‡ cf. Richard E. Flathman, *The Public Interest*, New York, Wiley, 1966, Part II, and reference by Philip Green, 'Science, Government and the Case of Rand', *World Politics*, XX(2), January 1968, p. 302.

An analysis which is useful in this modest way can be pursued by the formulation of models, i.e. simplifications of reality which state explicitly the major structures expected in any mass of data. A theory claims correctness and excludes the validity of all rival theories, whereas a model is merely a convenient way of looking at things from a specific angle; the former can be considered as true if it cannot be falsified, the latter can be merely considered as convenient or useful. An important advantage of using models is that, while being able to clarify and systematize our approach, we are in no way precluded from using other models, looking at things from other specific angles and thus bringing into prominence all the elements that appear to us relevant.*

## *Levels of Analysis*

In international politics the proverbial difficulty about the wood and the trees is further augmented by the complication that we have three obvious levels of analysis: if the whole – the international system – can be likened to the wood, and the parts – the states – to the trees, we are, all will agree, also concerned with the people as individuals. It is necessary to elucidate the confusion often arising between these levels of analysis before the model employed is fully explained.

*States* are the central element in the situation and, indeed, until recently, most writings on international relations not only centred upon them but very often were limited to them. With minor exceptions, international politics is conducted by states, for states and with other states. It is conducted *by states* although ultimate decisions and action are taken by individuals because these individuals do not act as such but in roles they are playing within states, as decision-makers or executants of policies, e.g. civil servants or soldiers. It is conducted *for states* in spite of the fact that national policies are generally represented as serving the people of the country or society or nation, and

* cf. the explanation of a decision-making model in Frankel, *The Making of Foreign Policy*, Oxford University Press, 1963, Chapter 1.

not only the state which is merely a formal organization of the latter. It is conducted *with other states* because these states are the most important elements of the international environment and hence most international activities are connected with them.

*Individuals* can be legitimately considered as the ultimate end of all human activities, including international politics; it is arguable that only their good can provide a morally convincing and practicable yardstick for evaluating these activities. They are inevitably both the decision-makers and the executants of policies; they constitute public opinion which influences state policies and acts as a constraint upon them. Moreover, they conduct a growing range of trans-national transactions with other individuals which are to some extent independent of states. Nevertheless, international politics still clearly pertains to states, their objectives and their power. The independent role of the individuals has so far been too limited to forecast with any degree of assuredness that what used to be called 'the family of nations' is going to be transformed into 'a commonwealth of man'; certainly this transformation has not yet taken place.

It is a tenable although occasionally still disputed proposition that the *international system* as a whole is something different from the sum total of all the state-members and their interactions. The whole is more than the sum total of its parts, just as the whole of the wood is more than all the trees growing in it. Some, although not very much, of international politics is conducted not by states but by international organizations which act in a dual capacity – as organs of their state-members and as organs of the international community. Some, although again not very much, of international politics, conducted both by international organizations and by states, is not for states but for the international community itself.

This brief outline of the levels of analysis started with the statement that of the three main levels, that pertaining to states is central. This is a generally agreed opinion but is still only an opinion. Logically, the model evolved here centres upon states but this does not deny the usefulness of alternative models centring around individuals or the international system. Our appreciation of these elements will vary considerably according to whether they are accorded central or merely peripheral roles and we should look at them from both angles.

## Main Approaches to Study

The study of international politics faithfully reflects the explosive nature of its subject – the proliferation of new states and of international issues all lead to a proliferation of publications and to an increasing variety of approaches to and treatments of the subject. The confusion is overwhelming even for the specialist scholar to the point that the Carnegie Endowment for International Peace recently felt impelled to conduct a three-year inquiry into the 'state of the discipline'. The resulting report* contains information about materials so abundant that not many even among the experts could claim acquaintance with its full range. To compress the Report would be extremely difficult. Subsequent remarks merely endeavour to indicate the historical setting and the major directions of research and thinking in the field; they discuss motivations and objectives, methodology and the search for organizing concepts, and end with a brief outline of the approach here adopted.

In a subject as emotionally charged and as relevant to important policy decisions as international politics, we should properly ask in the case of each contributor about his motivations and objectives – does he engage in a pure scholarly scientific investigation in order to enhance knowledge or has he an axe to grind and, if so, what sort of an axe? Social investigations are too complex to allow for pure and completely objective induction; consciously or subconsciously we adopt theories, hypotheses or models, and it is important for us to know where these stem from. The dichotomy between pure and policy-oriented research as well as distinctions between research oriented towards conflicting policies are important and should be clearly articulated

*E. Raymond Platig, *International Relations Research: Problems of Evaluation and Research*, Santa Barbara, Clio Press for Carnegie Endowment for International Peace, 1967. cf. also W. J. M. Mackenzie, *Politics and Social Science*, Penguin Books, 1967, Chapter 20.

but, on the other hand, should not be exaggerated. All endeavours can be pooled up to a point. For instance, the study of communist foreign policy agencies not only should but can be identical for pure scholars as well as for both the opponents and the proponents of communism. A proper understanding of these agencies is essential not only for academic but also for policy reasons, even if the policies to be based upon them are conflicting. Likewise, the study of disarmament is becoming a major branch of defence policies and the immediate objectives of peace and defence policy researches may coincide, even though their ultimate goals may not.

Historically, it is possible to distinguish three broad approaches to the study of international politics in this century; two are concerned with policies – one with securing peace and the other, recently enhanced, with advice to government; the third is concerned with the advancement of knowledge. The three approaches interconnect and intertwine. Concern with peace can be traced to philosophical and moral speculations far back in history; the prophets in the Old Testament furnish a good example. This concern became stronger early in this century because of growing international instability. On the one hand, various 'devil' theories began to emerge, attributing this instability to class oppression, imperialism or private sales of arms, on the other hand, there evolved a belief in the possibilities of international law. However divergent the objectives of all these approaches may be, all can be legitimately subsumed under the general category of concern with peace. These 'eirenist' approaches further evolved in the aftermath of the First World War. The bankruptcy of the balance-of-power system resulted in adding 'power politics' to the list of the 'devils', while the establishment of the League of Nations and of the Permanent Court of International Justice added international organization to the list of alternatives. As a result of the Second World War and the development of nuclear weapons, concern with peace naturally grew. Numerous peace-research and conflict-resolution societies and programmes have arisen throughout the West, occasionally with an unhappily blurred boundary between them and communist-inspired and anti-American institutions.

The other policy-oriented approach is likewise time-honoured. In order to provide rational advice on foreign policy, the adviser to the ruler is forced to analyse international relations and, in most civilizations, we find some advisers systematically putting down their thoughts upon paper or some sages being asked to advise. Kautilya, Confucius, Plato, Ibn Khaldun and Machiavelli are striking examples. However, only in the contemporary United States did the process assume important dimensions: academic–governmental exchanges have been consistently growing through the farming out of government-sponsored research projects and the calling in of academics as consultants. The process has culminated in the conspicuous role of the 'Charles River Complex' of Harvard University and Massachusetts Institute of Technology in the Kennedy Administration. Although this phenomenon has so far been limited to the United States, it has had a colossal impact upon the study of international politics. Most of the work is being done in the United States because this country, suddenly confronted with the full range of the gravest international issues, can afford and is willing to spend large sums of money upon international relations research. With considerable delay and on a much lesser scale, government–university links are being established also in the United Kingdom.

Purely academic research cannot be fully divorced from the above-mentioned policy-inspirations which often provide the initiative and the resources necessary for research. Nevertheless, although to some extent linked and parallel, it has its own momentum; undoubtedly the extent of academic study and research is largely dependent upon the size and resources available to the various relevant departments and institutions. The interwar period witnessed the rapid evolution of Departments of International Relations in all American universities and colleges and their beginnings in the United Kingdom; it witnessed also the establishment of the first research institutions in the field, the Royal Institute of International Affairs in Britain and the Council on Foreign Relations in the United States. Since 1945 the American university departments and research institutes have grown beyond recognition and command colossal resources while also in British universities the study has spread and expanded. A similar development, is taking place in other Western countries but, so far at least, not under communist régimes.

## Methods and Organizing Concepts

Over the two-thirds of this century, the study has been repeatedly changing its focus. Concern with states before the First World War gave way to the inter-war concern with the international system and the ways of improving it through the evolution of international law and international organization. Since the Second World War, an undiminished interest in the international system is coupled with a renewed interest in the behaviour of states which is generally considered as more amenable to reform than the system as a whole.

Methods of approach have changed even more. The early students of the field were recruited mainly among diplomatic historians and international lawyers who generally pursued their traditional historical, legal and also philosophical methods even though proclaiming the necessity for a multi-disciplinary attack. Specialist training in international relations and in political science brought the next generation into a more direct contact with sociology and social anthropology, with psychology and economics. In the last, post-war generation, mathematics, especially applied to the theory of games, and systems-analysis have been increasingly popular. It is no accident that some of the striking formulations in this generation were made through 'importations', e.g. by a mathematician, Anatol Rapoport, and by economists, Thomas Schelling and Kenneth Boulding.

No wonder that the field is full of acrimonious debates between the 'traditionalists' who deprecate the newer contributions, claiming that these have little to add to the traditional lore of political science, history and law, and that they are fairly useless owing to the pretentiousness of their mathematical formulations and to their excessive jargon which cannot disguise paucity of creative thought. Against that, 'frontiersmen', some of whom are quite modest about the actual achievements of the new approaches, affirm that the only possible advance lies through the injection of precision, of scientific rigour and in the development and improvement of new methods.

Particularly vigorous and promising are such new approaches as the collection of data, simulation, and analysis of decision-making, especially through the application of the theory of games. We are beginning to use computers enabling us to store, retrieve and correlate various social data on a grand scale and on a cross-national basis, and to conduct quite elaborate experiments in decision-making. It would be foolhardy to believe that fuller data would give us full answers to the major political questions or even necessarily enable us to state these questions very much better. Undoubtedly, however, they will, when available, help us to check and refine our hypotheses and models, and occasionally also refute them. The computer can be used also in some simulations which consist of the manipulation of invented and gathered data and is becoming a frequent adjunct to many new approaches.

Although decision-making is too complex a process to allow for a great degree of systematization and quantification, its analysis has been popular for the last decade or so and has been considerably refined. A whole range of strategic and diplomatic situations have been subject to analysis employing the theory of economic bargaining or the theory of games and enabling us to suggest solutions and decisions which are more rational or economic within certain narrow definitions of these terms; it is possible to discuss even the economic use of violence. Although the treatment is necessarily schematic and simplifies reality and although the 'rationality' of solutions is limited to a narrow set of assumptions which cannot encompass more than a small portion of reality, such analysis can greatly sharpen appreciation and help to improve judgement. Particularly useful and popular are case-studies of decision-making in unprecedented detail and depth which take into account the full range of participants, influences brought to bear, and relevant restraints. It is extremely doubtful whether any historical event has ever been as closely analysed as the United States intervention in Korea in 1950 or the Cuban missile crisis in 1962.

Those using the new approaches tend to concentrate upon

behaviour and quantification. While the behavioural stress is less controversial except for the warnings not to forget the elements of political situations other than behaviour, quantification is very much more so. Its opponents claim that nothing significant can be quantified and that all quantifications are about insignificant matters and hence they detract from the really important issues. Its proponents do not deny the difficulties of quantification but strive for precision where this can be obtained, expecting that this precision may be gradually applied to wider and more significant fields. On the whole, it is true that there exists an inverse correlation between the significance of the matter and the degree to which it lends itself to quantification but this is by no means inevitable. Actually, in the heat of controversy the divisions are often exaggerated; possibly the field of study is quite quickly progressing towards some common understanding in which all the experts will accept a common scientific approach although some will continue working on the precise detail while others will continue to work on the non-quantified and more fundamental issues.

To achieve this highly desirable general consensus of the majority of scholars, it will be necessary to reach agreement, if not about a general theory or model, at least about some common organizing concept, a common nucleus of analysis. At the moment it is possible to distinguish at least three major contending concepts: 'power', 'social communication' and 'systems analysis'.

*Power* is a traditional concept which was the nucleus of the earliest analyses based upon the notion of 'power politics', i.e. of international behaviour which is primarily power-oriented. The actual meaning of the concept has undergone many changes. From the notion of 'power' as an essence which can be broken up into significant and comparable factors, the stress has shifted towards the subtler notion of 'power' as a relationship, as a capacity to influence others to act or desist from acting, as one desires; 'factors' of power have changed into 'capabilities' which should be operationally defined. This logically leads to the latest elegant and economic refinement – the shift of emphasis from the power of the state to the restraints which operate in the system,

the factors which prevent it from obtaining specific objectives.*
This refinement removes the major objection to the use of
'power' as an organizing concept – namely the difficulty of
accommodating the values, goals and objectives which determine
the intentions of the wielders of power and its ultimate use.

The cybernetical or *social communication* approach was first
fully articulated by Karl W. Deutsch.† It considers the flow of
communications among the actors as the basic process in international politics; power in this context means the ability to refuse to adapt or to take heed of what is communicated. *Systems
analysis* is rather closely connected. It employs analogies to and
insights from other fields in trying to comprehend the operation
of the international system as a whole, specifically being concerned with the twin problems of system-maintenance and sys-
tem-transformation. This is probably the most prolific and
promising school.‡

## The Approach Adopted

This book is not meant to contribute directly to the theoretical
or the methodological advancement of the discipline. It is devoted to the urgent task of bringing the theoretical and the empirical approaches together and, instead of trying to develop a
fully-fledged theory, it merely develops a model intended to facilitate the inclusion of the empirical work done into a coherent
framework. It refers throughout the argument to real-life experience although, in the absence of a fully articulated theoretical
framework, no 'empirical evidence' can be expected for any
proposition but merely a suitable empirical example clearly
illustrating the relation between the proposition and reality.

In order to remain intelligible to those exclusively interested

* Charles J. Hitch and Roland M. McKean, *Economics of Defense in
the Nuclear Age*, Cambridge, Mass., Harvard University Press, 1960.
† *Nerves of Government*, New York, Free Press of Glencoe, 1963.
‡ cf. especially Morton A. Kaplan, *System and Process in International
Politics*, New York, Wiley, 1957; Klaus Knorr and Sidney Verba, *The
International System: Theoretical Essays*, Princeton, N.J., Princeton
University Press, 1961.

in empirical work, and to the general reader, as much as possible the analysis conforms with common-sense notions, employs a non-specialist terminology, and avoids undue technicalities. Its focus lies in the whole of international politics and not in its details and hence it cannot achieve even the limited degree of rigour and of quantification available for some empirical work. It would be dishonest to make a pretence of precision when analysing the highly heterogeneous universe of international politics. Generalizations about the behaviour of states are somewhat more amenable to rigour and quantification than the analysis of the international system as a whole, but only at the cost of the limiting assumption that foreign policy is rational. This would take us far away from real life in which decision-makers usually react to events rather than make conscious, rational decisions, and where the sources of behaviour lie much more in tradition and in imitation than in rational deliberation.

The argument centres on the international system, the states, and their interaction, bearing in mind the roles played by other social groups and by individuals. Part One outlines the concept of the 'international system' and discusses the major historical systems; its approach falls within the school of systems analysis. Part Two deals with the international behaviour of states, employing mainly the concepts of the theories of decision-making and of social communication. Part Three discusses the interaction between the two, stressing the fact that the international system is the environment for the activities of the states but also influences them in turn.

The focus of interest lies in the two major modes of state interaction: conflict and harmony. Preoccupation with one of these extremes is the basis of the popular theories of power politics which claim that all international politics can be ultimately reduced to power relations and to power considerations. Preoccupation with the other extreme is the basis of the arguments advanced by the much less numerous eirenists or harmonists who believe that peace, harmony and cooperation are the norm and that power conflicts are a mere, unfortunately frequent, but remediable aberration. The majority agree that neither theory is fully correct, but saying that the truth lies somewhere in the middle does not take us very far – a single issue may be much better explained in terms of the one theory or the other, or possibly by some combination of both.

Hence in the following discussion neither theory is adopted nor is an eclectic one evolved which would combine the elements of both. Instead of a dogmatic theory which claims correctness, the argument merely proposes a model which, much more modestly, aspires to be a useful aid in comprehending and organizing the whole field. In fact it combines two models, one of conflict and one of harmony, and it systematically applies the alternative models to the major aspects of international politics with a view to determining what each of them explains and what it fails to explain.

Through constant reference to international practice the argument has a direct bearing upon the actual conduct of foreign policy and the treatment of the problems of power, conflict and peace; hence it can serve as a foundation for international policy prescriptions. Its contribution to theory is intended to lie in its relatively simple method of linking the major theoretical and empirical approaches. From the literature on international politics some likely lines of future scientific progress emerge fairly clearly. Before advancing generalizations about the whole field we must be able to classify the states into fairly homogeneous groups; in order to do that, it is essential to identify and to evaluate the major variables in state behaviour with some degree of precision; carefully adapted parallels to the psychology of individuals and of small groups provide a convenient starting-point and multivariate analysis provides convenient tools. An immense amount of work is being undertaken along these and several other lines but, in order to be of full use for the understanding of international politics, all this work must be linked together and brought into a meaningful relationship by means of a general model of the kind proposed here.

PART ONE

# STATES AND INTERNATIONAL SYSTEMS

CHAPTER 2

# STATES, INTERNATIONAL SYSTEMS, AND CONFLICT

## *The Nature of States*

WHEN analysing international politics we must pay attention both to the international system and to the states which are the main actors within it. The order of their discussion cannot be logically determined any better than that dealing with the proverbial chicken and egg but, at whichever end we start, some basic concepts pertaining to both elements should be explained at the outset.

We know, of course, quite a lot about states from daily life. They have the monopoly of political organization at its highest level and the monopoly of territory. Every person must live on a territory belonging to one state or another and difficulties are likely to arise for him if he is not a recognized citizen of some state. States have also the near-monopoly of force – they determine the degree of freedom or constraint applicable to the inhabitants of their territories and they determine the ultimate issues of international peace and war.

Normally it is easy to recognize a state as a state when one comes up against it. For example, a Londoner well knows that he is a British citizen living in the United Kingdom and also, as soon as he crosses the Channel or flies to Rome, Moscow or Bangkok, that he is in another state, France, Italy, the Soviet Union or Thailand respectively. Usually the identity of a state is clear but there are some exceptions. There are, for instance, the Himalayan realms, the boundaries of which have never been finally demarcated and the ultimate political control of which has given rise to serious conflicts since 1945; there are difficulties about territories under hostile occupation during a war, as most of Europe was between 1940 and 1945; there are cases of separatist movements as in Katanga in the Congo, in Eastern Nigeria, or in East Bengal, there is Southern Rhodesia since her unilateral declaration of independence. The Englishman present in one of these places during the strife could not readily decide what the *real* identity of the state might be although he might hold quite clear and strong views about its *legal* identity. Similar confusion could arise in other countries some of which, e.g. India or Canada, are endangered by strong separatist forces.

There is no ready guide to a world constantly in a state of flux and transition. On the whole, membership of the United Nations confirms the status of statehood but not decisively so, e.g. although the Ukraine and Byelorussia are members in their own right, the West entertains serious doubts about their separate statehood and prefers to talk about multiple Soviet membership. There is, furthermore, difficulty about China, one of the founder-members of the Organization and one of the Permanent Members of the Security Council. China's seat is occupied by the National Government of China whose sway is limited to the large island of Formosa (Taiwan) but this seating neither ensures this government's recognition by all other states nor denies the statehood of continental China with a population some fifty times larger. In the case of China as well as the other divided countries, Germany, Korea and Vietnam, it is possible to conceive of one state temporarily divided, or of two states, or of one state and one breakaway illegal structure.

Another difficulty arises from the heterogeneous nature of states. They differ in size from a few hundred to several million square miles, and in population from a few score thousand to over 700 million; they differ in basic ideologies, régimes and policy objectives. Obviously generalizations about all states are bound to be fairly vague and, on the whole, formal. To make them somewhat easier, discussion will be generally limited to modern states, from the seventeenth century onwards, although in respect of their foreign relations and the formation of international systems, they resemble their predecessors.

Since the state is such an overpowering and all-pervading element in our lives we may as well remind ourselves that this central concept of politics is extremely new. It arose some time early in the sixteenth century from the Latin word *status* denoting the 'position' or 'standing' of a ruler, usually at the time a monarch. The 'status' of the ruler carried two closely related characteristics jointly covered by the name 'sovereignty' – freedom from being subject to a superior in governing his territory, and freedom to enter into foreign relations. Gradually the noun 'state' began to denote the specifically political organization of territorial political societies. Within the international system which was established in Europe in 1648 with the Peace Treaty of Westphalia and then gradually spread to encompass the whole earth, the meaning of the 'state' did not change in spite of the drastic changes in the international system.

Centuries-long speculation on the nature of states by political thinkers, mainly international lawyers, eventually distilled four fundamental attributes: a people, a territory, a government, and sovereignty; on the whole, these attributes can be found in all organizations thought of as states and no organizations lacking any one of them are considered as such.

Since states are a form of social organization, the *people* are an obviously essential element. They are the aggregate of both sexes living in a community which need not be homogeneous. Jurists in the past used to agree that some minimum number of people is required in order to constitute a state, although they were unclear about its magnitude. Normally the emancipated colonies join the United Nations as full members as of right, irrespective of size, and only in 1967 did the Secretary General raise the suggestion that some associate-status may be more suitable for the smallest of them. It may be added that very small groups are generally deficient also in other elements of statehood.

The *territory* which is under the exclusive control of the state is the most important characteristic distinguishing the modern state from its medieval predecessor. This central attribute is often described as 'impenetrability' or 'impermeability' in its strategic aspects, as 'independence' in its political aspects, and as 'sovereignty' in its legal aspects. Territories, like populations, vary greatly in size.

The *government* consists of one or more persons who rule over the people and the territory and represent the state in its foreign relations. States conduct their foreign affairs through their governments and hence a modern state without a government, with an anarchic system, cannot be envisaged. So important is the government that, for a period, it can be acknowledged by other governments as representing its state in spite of the fact that it has become divorced from the other attributes of the state, its people and its territory, owing to what others consider a temporary and undesirable interference; e.g. during the Second World War several 'governments-in-exile' retained such recognition. In contrast to the great divergencies in the previous two elements, governments are fairly similar in their structures and functions as far as their foreign relations are concerned. Independently of its size, power or ideology, every state has a group of persons ultimately responsible for the conduct of its foreign policy; prominent among those are usually the head of the government and the foreign minister.

Irrespective of their power and size, in legal theory all states enjoy *sovereignty* in equal measure. 'Sovereignty' is undoubtedly a key-concept of international law. It has been appropriately described as 'the supreme political characteristic' and 'the central legal formula' of the international system. We are concerned here only with external sovereignty which means freedom to conduct foreign relations. Theoretically this freedom is absolute but an international system consisting of *fully* sovereign states is as unthinkable as an anarchist society consisting of fully free individuals. A compromise must be found between state sovereignty and a modicum of international order just as individual freedom must be reconciled with authority within the state. The nature of the compromise between the two clashing principles can be used to characterize individual international systems as it is used to characterize individual domestic political systems.

Even a cursory analysis of the four basic attributes of the state immediately shows that they do not provide a clear objective criterion for distinguishing social organizations which qualify from those which do not. It is difficult to question whether a given organization does not fall below the minimum size of population or territory when the tiny island of Nauru with a population of just over 3,000 obtained full independence in 1968. Much more serious are arguments about the identity of the government when two or more governments compete for control – e.g. in China, or over the limitations of sovereignty due to dependence upon another state.

To the four basic attributes must be added recognition by other states. Here both theory and practice differ. Some lawyers argue that a state exists as soon as the four attributes can be found and that formal recognition by other states merely recognizes this social fact; this is the normal practice of British governments. It is also possible to argue that recognition is constitutive, that a state assumes its identity as a member of international society only through being recognized; on this theory, pursued by the United States, the decision to recognize is political rather than legal and hence it can be withheld in spite of the presence of the four attributes, or granted even if they are somewhat dubious or defective.

## The Nature of International Systems

In the broadest meaning of the word, an international system can be defined as a collection of independent political units which interact with some regularity. If interaction among the independent units is neither frequent nor regularized, then we cannot speak of a system, e.g. China and the Western world were not parts of one international system in Marco Polo's day. If, on the other hand, the units forfeit important areas of their sovereignty, the system may lose its international character and may become a federation or a unitary state. The European federalists envisage such a future for the Western European communities.

The essence of an international system, as of all other systems, lies in the interaction of and some balance between the forces of unity and of diversity. Interaction among the sovereign units is sufficiently intensive to become regularized within the system; if it fails to reach the required intensity, no system comes into existence or the existing one disintegrates. Interaction is, however, insufficient to result in a form of political community which includes governmental institutions; if it does become sufficient, the international system becomes a fully integrated political system, in which the units forfeit the substance of their independence.

Although this is a discussion of contemporary international politics it will include a brief reference to the preceding international systems in order to enable us to grasp the characteristics of our own system in a broader perspective and to conceive more readily their implications and possible alternatives to them. Unfortunately it is virtually impossible to identify distinct historical international systems or the exact dates within which they operated. To start with, we do not find it easy to agree about the criteria which determine the identity of a system and its change into another; even when we do, the application of these criteria to historical events inevitably leads to serious differences of judgement. Also the systematic analysis of international systems is still in its infancy. All systems analysts agree that we must pay attention to the boundaries of the system, to its structure, particularly in respect to power, to its units, and to their interaction. In 1957 one of the first major proponents of this type of analysis, Morton A. Kaplan, found the main focus of comparison in the *number* of the major actors, but in 1963 Richard N. Rosencrance considered this number as only one of the criteria.* The criteria chosen can be quite complex and subtle† but even when they are helpful for finding out what the essence of an international system may be, they do not necessarily help us to decide when it begins or when it is replaced by another system. Political processes often spread over a long period of time without a clear-cut event which would enable us to find a temporal division; moreover, often contradictory political processes take place simultaneously, bedevilling our search for the essence.

Nothing short of a fully-fledged theory of international politics would enable us to produce a fully articulated account of the meaning of international systems. Subsequent remarks merely catalogue the major features which are of fairly obvious and generally agreed importance; they provide the elements for a

* Morton A. Kaplan, *System and Process in International Politics*, New York, Wiley, 1957; Richard N. Rosencrance, *Action and Reaction in World Politics*, Boston, Little Brown, 1963.

† Herbert J. Spiro, *World Politics: The Global System*, Homewood, Ill., Dorsey Press, 1966.

deeper-reaching analysis even though they do not attempt such an analysis. They will also assist us in comparing preceding international systems with the contemporary one.

A fundamental feature of an international system as of any other system is found in its *boundaries*. These can be conveniently defined in terms of social communications: they delimit the area on which interaction among the units has an effect upon the system, from that on which it has none. An important set of problems is created by the nature of the environment within which the international system maintains its boundaries: there may exist in it some 'barbarians' with whom it is scarcely in touch; there may exist in it other international or political systems; today the system occupies the whole globe. Unfortunately the quoted systems analysts do not deal with the environment although it seems fairly obvious that in this respect the contemporary system fundamentally differs from all its predecessors. Its boundaries are fixed and cannot expand, although they could conceivably contract. It is very doubtful whether outer space and celestial bodies provide an equivalent of the environments of the previous systems; they certainly offer little hope for further expansion or for 'the pushing of the frontier of civilization'.

Next we are concerned with the *structure* of the system. One of the major variables here is the degree of centralization and integration. In all systems there exist both a central, focal area within which interaction is intensive, and peripheries in which it is slighter. The proportion of the two and their interrelationship should not be neglected, e.g. it made a great difference to the contemporary system when the Third World, the Middle East and Latin America became integrated in the mainstream of the Cold War in the fifties.

The *membership* of the system is obviously of crucial importance. One must distinguish between a system embracing some two dozen relatively stable states, as in the nineteenth century, and the contemporary one with 140 states whose stability cannot be taken for granted. The dynamics of the situation require consideration: do the sources of instability indicate integration or disintegration of the existing units, in other words, is the number of states likely to increase or decrease?

Only a few of the members can be considered as main participants who are usually called 'Great Powers'. The actual number
of the Great Powers constitutes a crucial variable. The main
historical types are hierarchical systems with a single centre, bipolar systems with two centres, and multipolar systems.

The major *characteristics of the units* relevant for the study of
international systems are difficult to separate from the totality of
the political, social and economic life. We shall concentrate on
two: capabilities and intentions. *Capabilities* or the elements of
power constitute the basis for international stratification into
Great Powers (some of whom can be singled out as Superpowers,
World Powers, Nuclear Powers, etc.) and also Middle and
Small Powers. The criteria for stratification vary from system
to system but invariably military, economic, organizational
and prestige elements are taken into account. Capabilities are
a crucial but fluctuating variable. It is advisable to compare
each system with other systems in general terms as well as the
capabilities of the members within each system, paying attention to the span of differences between the strongest and the
weakest.

The *intentions* of the units are largely determined by their
political régimes and ideologies and are summed up by the notion
of 'national interest'. Two important aspects should be considered: the position the unit occupies in the spectrum between
the extremes of isolationism and of intensive participation, and
the position it occupies between the extremes of complete support
for the existing order, or as it is often called the *status quo*, and
that of out-and-out revisionism.

Lastly, we should distinguish the international *processes*. These
can be discussed from the angle of the system, e.g. in terms of
their regulatory, integrative and disintegrative nature. They can
also be discussed from the angle of the units; this commends itself
more since most international activities are conducted by these
units. Again the analysis of international processes is insufficiently
advanced to offer a generally acceptable list of factors and elements to be included. All scholars agree about the relevance of
'diplomatic styles' and of styles of violence and warfare although
not about their exact definitions.

The following argument centres upon one important variable in the various international systems: namely the propensity to encourage conflict and war, or harmony and peace. Hence the concepts of conflict and harmony are discussed next, while further discussion of international systems is postponed to Chapter 3.

## The Meaning of Conflict and Harmony

The essence of politics is well explained as a combination of common concern and of differences in interests, as has been repeatedly referred to. If the former is lacking, there is no community and therefore no system, if the latter, there would be no politics. In view of the varied nature of human needs and desires, the complete elimination of differences of interest and hence of politics is difficult to accept as possible; nevertheless it can be imagined. Thus Engels envisaged a communist millennium in which all fundamental clashes of interests had disappeared with the elimination of class exploitation and where consequently the state can 'wither away' since 'the government of people' can be replaced by 'the administration of things'. However reluctantly, the present Soviet rulers are nevertheless accepting the fact that serious conflicts are bound to persist.

In domestic politics it is easy to make the distinction between social consensus which is the basis of society and of the pursuit of the common good, and conflict of interests in which state and society play only the role of a moderator and see to it that no particular interest asserts itself to the detriment of the common good as defined by the community. The fact that all notions of common good are state-centred confuses the issue in international relations. Consensus or a community spirit on the international level are rudimentary, and hence conflict of interests is the predominant mode of activity since all states pursue their own 'national interests'. It is easy to simplify the issue by equating with conflict all the competing national interests and with harmony the few international interests germane to the international system and generally represented by international organizations. Such a view inevitably leads to a pessimistic picture of power politics. In fact, however, harmony and cooperation cannot be limited to the international elements; they can be found also in inter-state relations.

The other confusion stems from the equation between international conflict and violence and war. As the international system is loose and lacks a central government, the difficulties of adjustment are great and therefore violence is frequently resorted to while its threat is ever present. Some major endeavours to prevent war are based upon a somewhat far-fetched analogy with the evolution of domestic political systems. It is true that the very foundation of domestic law and order lies in circumscribing violence and in completely forbidding its most vicious forms; a parallel development would be highly desirable in international relations. Unfortunately the concomitants of the domestic limitation are lacking: there is very much less basic consensus, the clashes of interests are much more acute, and no adequate methods of non-violent adjustment have been evolved. It is arguable that all international consensus is limited to the minimum necessary for the maintenance of the international system – today all wish to avoid a nuclear war but agree on little more.

The close connections between conflict and the violent modes of its resolution and the confusion between the two have been bedevilling the peace-keeping activities of the United Nations. 'Preventive diplomacy' is aimed primarily at the prevention of open hostilities but cannot succeed in the long run without the successful adjustment of the underlying conflicts; it is possible that in fact it has been working in the opposite direction by enabling the contestants to nurse their mutual grievances while the situation is artificially frozen for the time being.

The third fundamental confusion arises from the mixture of two dichotomies: the pessimistic and the optimistic outlooks on the world and the psychological and the social approaches to conflict. Belief in the goodness or badness of human nature need not coincide with the belief in the goodness or badness of society. Thus both John Locke and Jean-Jacques Rousseau believed in the goodness of human nature but, while Locke was optimistic about the possibilities of a good society, Rousseau was convinced that interdependence breeds suspicion and incompatibility instead of accommodation and harmony. Starting from the opposite extreme, Thomas Hobbes believed in the nastiness of human nature but was not unduly pessimistic about the possibilities of curbing it by the 'Leviathan'. Jean-Paul Sartre is equally pessimistic about human nature and believes that people work together only because otherwise they would die by fighting each other. The social contract which he calls 'the pledge' (*le serment*) must be enforced by violence and terror; the capacity for the latter constitutes the sovereignty of the state.*

Conflict is one of the many social phenomena the approaches to which are sharply divided between those who believe in the primacy of man and those who believe in the primacy of society; this division obtains equally among those who undertake a scientific study and those who are concerned with policy decisions. We have thus a controversy between 'nature and nurture' in education, and between reform of man and that of social institutions in theories of development. In theories of peace, the preamble to the constitution of UNESCO concisely expressed the psychological theory: 'Since wars begin in the minds of men, it is in the minds of men that defences of peace must be constructed.' Social theories trace conflict to faulty social arrangements – frequently theories of development ascribe it to poverty and theories of education to ignorance and illiteracy. Marxism ascribes conflict to class exploitation.†

Bearing in mind that conflict is often equated with violence, the various theories about the origins of war are relevant for the appreciation of international conflicts. The man-society dichotomy already mentioned is further complicated by the social sector being subdivided into states and the international system; it is possible to attribute wars to man's behaviour, to the internal

* cf. M. Cranston, 'Sartre and Violence', *Encounter*, July 1967.

† It is, however, arguable that Marx was referring more to the nature of *accommodation* of conflict than to its very existence; he believed that peaceful, non-violent, harmonious accommodation would be feasible in a communist society whereas it is not under capitalist exploitation.

structure of states, or to the international system. None of the explanations proffered stands on its own.*

Ideas about the role of conflict in society vary. It is possible to consider conflict as an aberration or 'deviant behaviour' which should be curbed and, as far as possible, eliminated; complete elimination, however, can be expected only in a utopia such as Marx's ultimate state of communism or in H. G. Wells's *A Modern Utopia*.

It is also possible to think of conflict as a useful social device for containing within one system interests which are not fully compatible; in the absence of conflict such interests would either break away or have to be suppressed. Moreover, the elimination of conflict, if it were possible, would have socially undesirable effects since conflict is the major vehicle of social change and adaptation. Georg Simmel's cogent thinking about the subject has been recently revived by Lewis Coser.† Possibly a parallel lies here between social and biological organisms. As the latter prefer the combination of two opposites to a straightforward arrangement, e.g. combining male and female genes, hormones and anti-hormones, etc., since variety gives them a greater degree of flexibility, so a democratic, pluralist society prefers the flexibility of competing and conflicting interest groups to the rigidity of a centrally governed society in which the ruler suppresses all conflict. In the cogent analysis of Claude Lévi-Strauss, all cultural patterns can be reduced to a series of binary oppositions derived from the basic opposition between nature and culture.

We are, then, faced with a kind of dialectics underlying all human activities. This applies to their substance, since wants and desires are not straightforward but often lead in two opposite directions; it applies likewise to the modes of pursuit – either through conflict or through cooperation. A whole variety of issues among individuals can be clearly solved both ways, and individuals sway from the one mode to the other, being governed mainly by their predominant feelings of either friend-

*Kenneth N. Waltz, *Man, the State, and War*, New York, Columbia University Press, 1959.

† *The Function of Social Conflict*, New York, Free Press of Glencoe, 1956 and 1964.

ship or hostility; when the predominant mode leads to disappointment and when the possibilities offered by it appear to have been exhausted, the individual alters his attitude and changes over to the other mode. Relations among groups seemingly do not differ in this respect from relations among individuals. Theories of organization plausibly stress the tug-of-war between central and coercive powers and reciprocal or cooperative relations. Firms competing for markets have to choose some form of coexistence between the poles of a total conflict expressed in the form of a cut-throat price-war and of complete cooperation in the form of a tight cartel.

International relations are no exception: the struggle for power, conflict leading ultimately to war and the search for international order can be regarded as two sides of the same coin. Disappointment with one mode leads to increased stress upon the other. Thus the two world wars produced the two comprehensive international institutions, the League of Nations and the United Nations; the Suez and the Congo crises led to the establishment of the United Nations peace-keeping forces. Or to look at this relationship the other way around, it is possible to point out that the League of Nations' attempt at international order through cooperation reduced vigilance among the victor states and thus was directly responsible for the outbreak of the Second World War; the United Nations Emergency Force stationed on Egyptian territory for eleven years merely froze the Arab–Israeli conflict and inevitably led to the renewal of violence in 1967.

Or, to take the field of United States–Soviet relations, the Cuban missile crisis in 1962 led to a *détente* and to a partial nuclear test ban treaty; when the support for the arms race in the Middle East brought them to the brink of a direct clash in 1967, they must have considered the obvious switch-over to some form of cooperation in the region, aiming at moderating the behaviour of their respective *protégés*. Was this discussed and perhaps even agreed upon by President Johnson and Mr. Kosygin at Glassborough? Cooperation between China and the Soviet Union ended in a complete impasse by the early sixties, and led to a switch-over to the mode of conflict; a similar impasse in Arab–Israeli conflict-relations was emerging so starkly as the result of the six-days' war in 1967 that a change to a mode of cooperation began to appear possible. The examples could be multiplied indefinitely.

There is no general agreement as to how much conflict actually exists in international relations; we must here bear in mind how frequently in this connotation conflict is equated with violence. Many thinkers are struck by the apparent parallel between international politics and Hobbes's 'state of nature' in which man's life was 'short, nasty and brutish' until he remedied the situation through a 'social contract'. Quite apart from the conclusion usually drawn that an international social contract is the obvious solution, the parallel can be considered as strained: states cannot be equated with individuals – they are much less equal and much more self-sufficient. The life of states may often be nasty but it is rarely very short and never fully brutish; in fact international society exhibits certain refinements and re-straints upon behaviour that cannot be found in Hobbes's 'state of nature'; war is plausibly considered not the mark of the absence of an international society or of its breakdown, but a part of its functioning.* We can even go to the opposite extreme and conceive international society in terms of the solidarity of its members: in the sixteenth century Hugo Grotius assumed such a solidarity with respect to the enforcement of law; today it would be assumed with respect to the avoidance of nuclear war. One can think about international politics as Keynes or Galbraith think about economics, that conflict is due to myopia rather than to fundamental clashes of interest.

Thus conflicting interpretations at all levels of analysis mili-tate against accepting a clear-cut theory. There is no cogent reason against us accepting the coexistence of conflict and har-mony – they occur simultaneously in all fields of human en-deavour, although, of course, in vastly differing proportions. The suggestion made here is that there is no reason to be determinist about their proportion which is not fixed by the nature of any issue. History proves that the human attitude to conflict is fun-

*H. Bull and M. Wight in H. Butterfield and M. Wight, eds., *Diplomatic Investigations*, Allen & Unwin, 1966.

damentally ambivalent; nearly all situations can be covered by the adage 'if you can't beat them join them' and probably also by its counterpart, 'if you can't join them beat them'. For instance, the members of the European Economic Community were inclined to look with suspicion upon British policies following the three abortive attempts at forming links with the Community, first through a free trade association, and then as a full member. Despite British declarations to the contrary, the establishment of the European Free Trade Association (EFTA) was generally interpreted as a hostile reaction to the first exclusion. The strenuous nature of the efforts of the Wilson Government and of the members of the Community favouring British entry to keep the British application alive, can be to some extent explained by the widespread expectation that the British reaction to the rebuff would be hostile.

Modern practitioners of 'conflict resolution' do not unrealistically aim at completely eliminating conflicts; they are more modest and consequently more realistic in striving to achieve harmonious settlement and, if this proves unattainable, to substitute rational though not necessarily non-violent methods for the irrational use of violence. The issues at stake are, of course, often of life and death importance. Capabilities and policies effective for harmonious cooperation are generally ineffective for conflict and vice versa; they may be simply competitive, e.g. when we ask whether money is better spent on weapons which could be used *against* another state or for aid and development of trade facilities which can be used *with* it or *for* it; they can be even counterproductive, e.g. aid can strengthen a potential enemy and the development of weapons can estrange a potential friend.

Conflict resolution within the international system presents great difficulties. The fairly obvious absence of basic consensus and of suitable governmental institutions which are often quoted, are possibly remediable. In fact, however, we may be faced with a more fundamental obstacle. History can be interpreted as a process of relegating conflict from narrower to increasingly broader areas; 'in-group' cohesion is greatly strengthened by hostility to the 'out-group'. When we reach the world-wide level there is no further 'out-group' to help us out. It may be possible, as it is sometimes claimed, to shift such propensity to conflict as may exist to competition in sports, culture, etc. It is, however, difficult to see how this will ever take us away from defining our interests ultimately only in national terms, and from the resulting clashes among national interests; the identity and the size of states may change but the clashes may persist. In the terms of the theologian, Reinhold Niebuhr,* man has become moral only because he has relegated his sins to an immoral society; we seem to have stuck with our sins at state level without much hope of release.

However optimistic or pessimistic we may feel about the possibilities of conflict resolution, it behoves us to seek the most appropriate intellectual tools for analysing them. An important initial step lies in an adequate classification of conflict situations and here a commendable scheme proposed by Anatol Rapoport in *Fights, Games and Debates*† has become quite popular.

In a *fight* situation the opponent is merely a nuisance to be eliminated, subjugated, cut down to size. Fundamental religious and ideological conflicts come under this category or the Arab–Israeli and Indian–Pakistani issues, as seen by many nationals of these states.

In a *game* situation each opponent wishes to win at the cost of his fellow but they cooperate within the rules of the game, in fact they are essential for each other since otherwise, without the opponent, there would be no game at all. The assumption underlying a game relationship is that the opponent is not a fiend to be destroyed, but much like oneself, perhaps unpleasant and even very dangerous, but essentially governed by the same basic rational considerations. His possible and likely countermoves to one's own moves can be rationally anticipated and hence one's own moves should be devised accordingly. Many adherents of the 'theory of games' have been assiduously applying it to international relations. Even in 'zero-sum games', where the outcome is fixed and the share of one side must be carved out of that of the opponent, the game sometimes allows a 'saddle-point' which,

* *Moral Man, Immoral Society*, Scribner, 1933.
† Ann Arbor, University of Michigan Press, 1960.

on the assumption of rational behaviour on both sides, allows the greatest possible benefit (or smallest possible loss) to both. In the more complex 'non-zero-sum games' a harmonious, cooperative play improves the final outcome so that both sides can be better off. It would be foolhardy to expect, as a few of the adherents of the games theory do, that the theory will ever be directly applicable to the resolution of actual conflict situations which are infinitely more complex than game situations. Undoubtedly, however, the theory of games sharpens our appreciation of real-life conflicts and provides a readier frame of mind to tackle them cooperatively.

Finally in a *debate* situation, each participant reasons not only about the opponent's possible countermoves but endeavours to convince him, to obtain his consensus. This is actually a situation frequently encountered in international politics: it is the basis of inter-state negotiations as well as of some of the debates in the General Assembly of the United Nations. Thousands of international agreements are concluded every year; prolonged, laborious and acrimonious as General Assembly debates often are, even on such vast and controversial subjects as disarmament, human rights and national self-determination, they have resulted in a limited degree of effective persuasion embodied in some international agreements and declarations.

Conflict is not uniformly grave in all the various relations between any two states and hence the total behaviour of the two will never fall within one single class. To take the extreme of a 'fight' like the Second World War, even then both sides engaged in 'game' behaviour when trying to anticipate the likely countermoves of the adversary and refraining from the use of poison gas or the grossest forms of maltreatment of prisoners-of-war. On the other hand, such staunch allies as the United States and Great Britain during the period of an undoubted 'special relationship' in the Second World War generally treated the issues on which they were in conflict as issues of 'debate' – they tried, admittedly sometimes unsuccessfully, to use persuasion, and 'fight' between them was unthinkable. When, however, their specific interests were clashing beyond the possibility of persuasion, they also employed 'game' tactics. This was the case with independence for British colonies, with spheres of interest in Eastern Europe, or with the question of the siting and timing of the Second Front.

In a slightly different but compatible terminology, in April 1967 the Under-Secretary of State, Katzenbach, advised that United States–Soviet relations should be considered not only in terms of the evident grounds for *confrontation* but also in terms of the areas of *common interests* (e.g. re non-proliferation or trade exchange), *complementary interests* (e.g. space exploration where the Americans could profit by the Russian experience of landing spacecraft on land while the Russians could use the American global tracking system) and *compatible interests* (e.g. foreign policy conducted within the understood respective spheres of interest of the two Superpowers).

To sum up, although the distinction between harmony and conflict is of crucial importance in judging concrete international issues or relationships between any sets of states, an issue or relationship can as rarely be classified as falling exclusively within one of the two categories as an individual can be classified as entirely good or entirely bad. Our appreciation of the incidence of the two elements in any specific aspect of international politics can be sharpened by elaboration of scalar diagrams, as shown below:

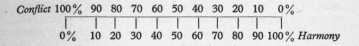

We must, however, bear in mind that in most cases the formulation of suitable quantitative indices for conflict and harmony would involve a simplification of a degree making the exercise fairly pointless.

## CHAPTER 3

# EVOLUTION OF THE INTERNATIONAL SYSTEMS

## *Pre-history*

MODERN international society is a very recent phenomenon which most writers date back only to the mid seventeenth century. The three centuries of its history is only a small fraction of the more than 7,000 years of recorded history of man and a proportionately smaller fraction of his biological history which the archaeologists are now extending further back than half a million years.

Something approaching international relations can be read into the social behaviour of animals. Groupings of animals are determined by considerations of biological survival; they must secure food and breeding-grounds and hence they are capable of fierce intra-species conflicts which generally revolve around the exclusive use of territory and the exclusion of trespassers. It is, however, difficult to regard 'international relations' of any species of animals as anything like a political system; they are too sporadic and also it would be difficult to credit the animals with much purposive rather than instinctive behaviour.

The evolution of international systems by man is explained in its broadest historical perspective by Aristotle's celebrated saying that man is by nature a political animal. This can be interpreted as being optimistic, as a postulation of harmony. At all stages of social development people have needs and wants which they cannot realize alone, and hence they form groups. A problem facing all such groups is that of delimitation, the drawing of boundaries, or of finding the size of the group best suited for its main purposes. Plato and Aristotle discuss it in their analyses of the Greek city-states; modern sociologists are concerned with it whether they develop theories of social communication or of 'areas of loyalty' or of relations between the 'in-group' and the 'out-group'. On the other hand, it is also possible to argue from a pessimistic view of human nature that man joins political organizations only to avoid the 'short, nasty and brutish' existence in the state of anarchy, that he carries his propensity to conflict and anarchy into these organizations which must effectively curb it.

Archaeologists penetrate further and further back into the obscurities of pre-history and refine our understanding of primitive man. Unfortunately, evidence is limited to physical remnants and these, until the development of writing, cannot give us direct evidence about politics. We are thus forced to speculate and all that the archaeologists can provide us with is a gradually improving picture of the physical framework within which the political processes took place. Naturally our speculation remains rather far-fetched; it is based upon the assumption that there exist some permanent patterns of social behaviour which we can extrapolate from our own time and place into such environments as we can reconstruct for the past.

It is not unreasonable to assume, by analogy to the social behaviour of animals, that the size of the first social groups established by man was determined by his biological needs, and also that relations among these groups were marked by avoidance and hostility based upon the institution of territorial boundaries. With growing numbers and with denser population, avoidance became more difficult and increasing sophistication increased contacts – the biologically desirable out-marriage could be more readily based upon an exchange of gifts than upon raids, and sporadic exchanges of gifts led to the idea of mutually advantageous trade, wherever suitable conditions obtained. Although set much later in history, the book of Genesis presents a plausible picture of the mixture between cooperative and hostile elements in the relations among semi-nomadic herdsmen. Jacob went to another tribe to find a wife, was exploited before he got her, and eventually left with wives and accumulated cattle for other pastures. Territorial conflicts could be settled by avoidance as long as population was sparse. Thus when 'the land was not able to bear' both Abraham's and Lot's herds and flocks, they peacefully separated as sufficient unoccupied green pastures were in sight.

The first revolutionary step in the development of civilization took place more than 10,000 years ago with the beginning of agricultural settlements. Here cooperation and harmony were the necessary basis even more so than among the more primitive groupings of hunters and herdsmen since agricultural tasks are continuous and the division of labour necessarily greater. At the same time the new settlements required protection against the herdsmen-nomads; the biblical Cain–Abel conflict was to continue right up into the nineteenth century when agricultural settlers almost eliminated the natives of North America and Australia.

Settled agriculture enabled men to take the next step – to build cities, as that of Jericho which in all likelihood dates to a period before 3000 B.C. Agricultural surpluses were the basic condition for the establishment of cities and for their continued existence. It is difficult to assume that these surpluses could be secured without coercion.* At first coercion may have been religious, exercised by priests exploiting religious beliefs; then physical, military coercion by the king and his army, became the rule; often the kings and the priests joined forces. It is unlikely that the pre-historic societies ever saved food surpluses much beyond a quarter of the average annual production. Hence it is plausible to assume that no more than a quarter of their populations could be fed in the cities and the armies; the remainder had to continue in agricultural pursuits.

The economic foundations of these political structures were necessarily weak; food surpluses sufficient for any length of time were rare and starvation was usually an imminent danger. In some cases, and on a minor scale, starvation could be averted by obtaining food from another unit, as Jacob did when he sent his sons to ask for it in Egypt. The obviously more promising prudent action was to broaden and stabilize the food-basis. It is no accident that the earliest centres of civilization can be found in the basins of great rivers in warm climates where large-scale publicly organized and maintained irrigation works laid the foundation for more consistent food supplies by freeing the crops

---

*This is admitted even by the great proponent of harmony and peaceful conflict resolution, Kenneth Boulding, in *The Meaning of the Twentieth Century*, Allen & Unwin, 1965, pp. 4–5.

from the vagaries of rainfall. Some 8,000 years ago such societies were formed in the river basins of the Nile and of the Euphrates and Tigris, somewhat later along the Indus River, and probably around 1500 B.C. also along the Yellow River in China. It is reasonable to assume that the harnessing of the population to the exacting tasks of building irrigation systems and to the necessity of constant maintenance caused societies to be organized rather stringently and tightly. It is plausible to accept that in such situations the needs of the resulting 'hydraulic societies' were the origin of autocratic régimes, as claimed by Karl Wittfogel* although not necessarily in all the historical instances he quoted.

We may add another expedient for securing constant food supplies which could be used on its own or in conjunction with irrigation, i.e. the accumulation and storing of food surpluses during good seasons to tide societies over bad ones. On a large scale, this too could be done only centrally, by the state, giving rise to great administrative problems. The most substantial instance recorded is the provision of Joseph of Egypt during the 'seven fat years' for the expected famines of the 'seven lean years'. This expedient was undertaken by Pharaoh's existing autocratic government which, through selling food to the population during the famine, acquired all the lands and subjected their tillers to a rent amounting to 20 per cent of their crops. Incidentally it is unlikely that similar long-term storage would have been equally successful in climates less dry than the Egyptian one.

We should not, however, jump to hasty conclusions from our speculations. If the origins of stable civilizations inevitably involved coercion, this does not mean that these civilizations were based upon conflict. Even though forced to work hard, bullied and economically exploited by the cities and the military, the humble peasants benefited from the new order; at least they could be reasonably assured of a minimum of law and order in which they could retain a proportion of the food produced. Usually governmental exactions and administrative injustices were more than compensated for by their being freed from uncontrolled private exactions and from the dangers of foreign attacks. A government often gave to the population a reasonable *quid pro*

* *Oriental Despotism*, New Haven, Yale University Press, 1952.

*quo* for what it was exacting from them; instead of a stark conflict between the peasant and the city-dweller or the government, the relationship was a mixed one, where harmony of interests played some part, although greatly differing from time to time and from place to place. Whenever the harmonious part dwindled below the acceptable limit, one may reasonably assume that all people would have developed some equivalent of the Chinese notion of the 'withdrawal of the mandate from Heaven' from the ruler; whether a revolution would break out or the irrigation system break down, a system based on coercion alone would eventually crumble.

## Early History

In the first millennium B.C. we come to a situation which resembles much more closely modern international systems. The earlier systems were geographically limited by the difficulties of communication and were generally confined to river-basins or similar geographically well-defined areas within which the evolution of integrated political systems was feasible. Now, when these separate political systems began to interplay, man was faced for the first time with the perennial dilemma of international relations in its fully articulated form: when the group is no longer self-sufficient, when some of its regular, sometimes vital needs can be satisfied only by exaction from or cooperation with the outside, is it preferable to rely upon conflict or upon harmony? Is it preferable to subjugate others or to ensure their cooperation and assistance? The choice between war and peace was painful since both carried their risks; the former a heavy cost and dangers of defeat and, even after victory, the difficulties of extending administrative responsibilities; the latter, uncertainty and impermanence due to the unstructured and anarchic international setting. Although the scanty written records provide at least some straw for our speculative bricks, we are still reduced to speculation. The records indicate that military conquest, the simpler of the two methods, was the rule. We must, however, allow for the likely tendency of these records to refer to the spectacular military feats of the rulers rather than to the less spectacular flow of peaceful intercourse such as international trade.

The theory of social communication is a convenient starting point for investigating relationships between established political systems. Distance, barriers to communication, density of population, economic incentives, appear among the most powerful factors determining social communication and hence political relations and systems-boundaries. It stands to reason that where communications among states or systems have not been inaugurated or are only sporadic and feeble, in spite of any mutual awareness, states continue to lead separate existences and do not in effect constitute an international system. Thus the Western European and the Chinese systems remained separated and did not belong to a common international system right up to modern times.

To investigate the incidence of conflict and harmony we should first consider two extreme situations in social communication. When communication barriers preclude intensive social communication and hence the establishment of a common international system, exchanges may not be altogether excluded. Thus harmonious trade exchanges arise in exotic and valuable goods, as the silk trade in the Middle Ages between Western Europe and China; cultural and ideological influences and exchanges took place between India and China in the eighth to fourteenth centuries A.D. Conflict, especially conflict involving physical violence through the use of military forces was impossible across the formidable communication barriers.

The other extreme is found in a network of social communications based upon solid economic foundations which leads to intensive political relations, intensifying both conflict and harmony. China under the Ch'in dynasty at the end of the third century B.C. provides a striking example of the unification of a centralized agricultural empire, where great irrigation works were built, bureaucracy replaced earlier feudalism, communications were expanded, the Great Wall was erected to provide a clear boundary, and written language was standardized. Similar feats were performed about the same time by the Persian Darius and by the Indian Chandragupta Maurya. It is characteristic of all these empires that they were not everlasting. The Chinese empire was the most long-lived: it lasted some four centuries and it repeatedly re-integrated in spite of three prolonged partitions. Whatever our theory of political integration may be, it is obvious that China had more solid foundations than the other two empires – a better evolved and integrated economy, communication system, and culture. An integrated 'hydraulic civilization' spread its increasing population over the territory of China and delimited itself, for a while fairly successfully, from the outsiders; the other empires were operating in less advantageous conditions and hence their successes were more short-lived. In terms of conflict-harmony, one may express the difference by saying that better economic and social foundations in China provided an opportunity for a more harmonious and therefore further-reaching and longer-lasting unity.

In real life, international systems arise in situations in between these two extremes. In some areas with a widespread network of social communications, integrative forces were too weak to prevail completely but were sufficiently strong to ensure reasonably regular intercourse. In situations of that nature, e.g. during some periods of Mesopotamian, Indian and Chinese histories, there arose the first clear precursors of the modern systems: systems of interaction among independent units governed by their separate self-interests, partly cooperating and partly conflicting. These international systems were never permanent or stable for any length of time. They were clearly interim solutions, stages in the progress towards full political integration of an area and sometimes in the partial regression to a more self-contained existence of the units.

In the course of time, the political or international systems within river-basins or other geographically clearly defined areas advanced sufficiently to come into contact with one another. Conflict across distances is difficult and in its military form often impossible and hence one may presume that the first sporadic contacts were harmonious, involving trade and cultural exchanges. The usual pattern seems to be as follows: as soon as man has learnt to overcome distances and barriers to the point of being able to move armies, some ambitious ruler arises and introduces military conflict in order to enlarge his empire at the cost of others. The Old Testament records the example of the repeated clashes between the Assyrians and the Egyptians as seen by one of their victims, the ancient Hebrews; the Persian attacks on the Greeks are another example.

History is full of examples of the foundations existing in various times and places for international systems based upon harmonious cooperation, usually with cultural and trade inter-mediaries playing a focal role, such as in their times did the Island of Rhodes or the Bactrian Kingdom, or the Phoenicians or the Arabs. Nevertheless the conflict-pattern seems to have been dominant on the political-military side; except in culturally integrated areas such as river-basins, the idea of pluralism, of co-existing independent units, was never acceptable unless these units agreed to fairly stringent over-all political control. Since it is difficult to see how they could be persuaded, they had to be threatened and eventually forced.

Thus so far we can discern only a limited range of international systems in the full contemporary meaning of the word, as a mid-way station between political unity and complete absence of unity. The inter-relationship between conflict and harmony and social communication in this period is not linear but can be best expressed by some form of an S-curve. Great barriers which pre-clude physical clashes allow mainly for harmony although only to a limited extent; when more intensive communications make troop movements possible, conflict intrudes; further in-tensification of communications allows for cultural integration in which harmony can grow parallel with conflict and even prevail, as happened in China and in other riverine civilizations.

Somewhat paradoxically, conflict arising in what we may call in modern terminology international 'threat systems' based upon fear is accompanied by growing harmony with others who share the same fear. This was expressed with admirable clarity in the theory of 'mandala' by the Indian Kautilya in the third century B.C. We may call it the 'bad neighbour policy'. Neighbours are 'naturally' enemies and therefore if one imagines a row of states, A, B, C, D, etc., it is natural that alliances against common enemies are formed by A and C as well as B and D. The situation of other neighbours, contiguous to the enemies A and B, is fluid and requires the cultivation of scientific statecraft which Kautilya expounds. This is one of the many cases in which conflict with the 'out-group' leads to the enlargement and consolidation of the 'in-group', where conflict on one level leads to increased cooperation on another.

## *The Classical Period*

The Greek system, particularly in the fifth and fourth centuries B.C., which is the first one to be reasonably well documented, shows a greater resemblance to the modern system. Greek historians analysed the intricate interaction between conflict and harmony both within the individual units, the city-states, and among them. The Greeks evolved an international system because they could not resolve the perennial dilemma of politics, whether to choose unity or diversity; they tried to enjoy both. On the one hand they responded to geographical proximity and to community of language, religion and culture by becoming conscious of Hellenic unity; on the other, they retained the independence of the units and refrained from developing effective common political institutions; neither the Amphictyonic Council nor the Olympic Games can be considered as such. Here the argument among scholars often becomes circular. It is possible to claim that the absence of such institutions prevented the evolution of effective cooperation and hence ultimate political unity, but also that the absence of sustained cooperation prevented the evolution of such institutions.

Possibly the Greeks had a chance of retaining and developing pan-Hellenic cooperation evolved during the Persian Wars but, once the basis of this cooperation, the conflict with the dangerous out-group, the Persians, had been removed, they returned to the pattern of limited, city-state loyalties. Plato and Aristotle fully agreed that these were the ultimate community-units although they did not agree about their optimum size. Within the then existing state of human attitudes, technology and economics, they were possibly right. The short period of unity was followed by a prolonged internecine struggle for hegemony between Athens and Sparta in which the Greek system gradually decayed so that it was eventually conquered by a near-barbarian outsider, Philip of Macedon.

To apply the categories outlined in the previous chapter, the Greek system clearly shows the importance of the concept of boundaries. Its hard core was the Greek Peninsula and the neighbouring islands but it was continuously extending and adjusting its boundaries all around the shores of the Mediterranean where the individual city-states were founding colonies, as well as in the north of the Peninsula where mountain tribes were brought under Greek cultural influence. The international environment from the Greek point of view included only 'barbarians', i.e. people with inferior cultures and political organization. Some of these barbarians were weak and therefore easy game, others, like the Persians, were strong and involved the Greek system in interaction and in repeated conflicts to the point of enabling us to contend that in a way they were forming a joint international system within which the Greek system was a subsystem. There were also other strong 'barbarian' units with which the Greeks were involved in nearly continuous trade although not conflicts.

The structure of the Greek system strikingly adumbrates in many respects the post-war international system. Throughout a major period of its existence its power structure was bipolar, with Athens and Sparta as the two Superpowers while other Greek city-states and colonies ranked as Middle and Small Powers. While interaction on the Peninsula was always intense, in the islands and colonies it was more intermittent and often peripheral. The units were reasonably stable. Their capabilities, even those of the two Superpowers, were generally extremely limited but the differences between the strongest and the weakest were great. The city-states were divided in their desire to isolate themselves (which they were often incapable of doing) or to participate intensively, as well as in their support for and opposition to the *status quo*. The international processes in the Greek system included a wide gamut of diplomatic and warfare behaviour but, with the exacerbation of the conflict during the Peloponnesian War, the harmonious elements diminished: diplomacy served an increasingly narrow range of harmonious decisions and warfare became increasingly less restrained.

The Greek example seems to confirm the previously advanced hypothesis about the mixed origins of political systems emerging from the analysis of earlier history: political systems come into being through conflict; harmony alone does not suffice for their establishment. Conflict and coercion alone do not, however, offer a lasting basis; the stronger the harmonious elements underlying the system, the greater its chances of survival.

The decline of the Greek system was soon followed by Alexander's short-lived 'Eurasian' world empire. Alexander started with the traditional string of conflicts and conquests, but tried to consolidate them by introducing harmonious cooperation and Hellenistic cultural influence. He died too young to consolidate his empire which promptly disintegrated, leaving in its trail confused and disturbed international relations among his epigones.

Rome succeeded where Alexander failed – it became an empire encompassing the whole 'civilized' world. The Roman Empire was probably the most long-lived and successful form of human organization. It remained in being for a thousand years to which another thousand can be added if we take into account the lifespan of its Byzantine offshoot as well as the political reality of its lingering memories in the West. At its largest expanse, during the reign of Trajan 98–111 A.D., the Empire stretched from the Caspian Sea and the Persian Gulf to the centre of Scotland, and from Rumania to the Sahara; it was inhabited by some 100 million people. No political system of comparable size was achieved before the nineteenth century.

The Roman Empire was not, however, an international system; it was a unitary political system, an experiment in world government. The Romans did not recognize other political units as independent equals with whom they could maintain relations but merely as 'barbarians' to be included in their Empire. The boundaries of the Empire stretched far, leaving out only few neighbours of much consequence, e.g. the Parthians, the more remote Germanic tribes and the Scots. The Hindu and Chinese empires were too remote to be brought into regular contact.

Although not an international system, the Roman Empire is well worth considering in this context. How can this example of large-scale order be repeated today? Could it possibly be secured by a pattern of *international* politics similar to the Roman one, or does the Roman example indicate that the balance between unity and particularism, which is the essence of international systems, is too precarious and too difficult to maintain, and that only complete unity, fully-fledged world government is possible in the long run? Whichever answer seems more plausible, the major elements of Rome's success as well as the reasons for her ultimate failure require a brief analysis.

Interpretations of Roman history differ widely. It is possible to stress, as Montesquieu does, the rigour of punishment and the cruelty of the system which induced Simone Weil to liken the Romans to the Nazis. Certainly the Empire was built upon a centuries-long series of conquests of the traditional type and the Romans were quite ruthless in their methods. The success and the duration of the Empire cannot, however, be explained otherwise than by its harmonious basis. Once in command, the Romans tried to minimize the conflicts and to make membership of the Empire attractive. They were tolerant to cultural divergencies and their law accorded justice to all citizens; their military prowess and supremacy ensured protection from foreign attacks and their great administrative skills, adequately supported by an extensive network of roads, ensured law and order. The advantages of being part of the Empire heavily outweighed its disadvantages.

Although on several occasions during their history the Romans were mortally threatened by rival political organizations, they managed to defeat all of these and to remain supreme over many centuries. Historians usually explain their decay and ultimate breakdown by domestic social difficulties rather than by the chafing of subjected people and by the inroads of unconquered barbarians. On this argument Rome could have coped with foreign challenges had she resolved the conflicts between the ruling class and the slaves, the tenant farmers, and the urban proletariat. Possibly, however, as Professor A. H. M. Jones of Cambridge argues, the increasing strength and aggressiveness of external enemies were, after all, decisive.

## CHAPTER 4

# MODERN INTERNATIONAL SYSTEMS

## The Period until 1939

ALL international systems of which records have been preserved are worth studying not only for their own sakes but in order to enable us to understand better the nature and the operation of international systems in general. In fact the more exotic and strange such systems appear to us, the greater may be the light that they are likely to shed upon those features of our own system which are so ingrained in our traditions that they blind us to possible alternatives. If this argument now jumps across thirteen centuries and concentrates upon modern Western Europe, this is not to deny the relevance and importance of such other systems as the Far Eastern, which was continuous throughout this period, or the Indian, or those in pre-Columbian America, or that of medieval Europe, the bridge between the Roman Empire and the modern system. Hypotheses and models formulated upon the basis of the study of our own modern Western system can be fruitfully checked against them and probably considerably refined and improved. Undeniably, however, the European state system which was formally established by the Peace Treaty of Westphalia in 1648 was the nucleus of the present world international system.

The time-span of modern history can be started and ended at various dates, and can be divided into several distinct international systems. The final shape of the modern international systems had to await the advent of the industrial revolution, the spread of nationalism following the French Revolution, and the great overseas expansion, all of which were not completed till the beginning of the twentieth century. The essential features of the system were, however, established in the seventeenth century when the statesmen, chastised by the inconclusive religious wars, finally accepted that it would be futile to continue struggling for political unity in the image of the Holy Roman Empire, that the political organization of Western Europe would remain plural, divided into a multitude of sovereign units. Since this argument has a contemporary focus, it devotes more attention to the recent period but the evolution of the major features of the system is considered from its very inception in 1648 up to 1939.

The *boundaries* of the system were continuously expanding. Having repelled repeated Moslem attacks, the international system which grew up on the traditions of the realm of Western Christianity also incorporated outsiders as the major members: Russia, a partly Asian state, and also the Ottoman Empire, some time before its formal admission to the Concert of Europe in 1856. Ever since the voyages of discovery had begun at the end of the fifteenth century, some members of the system founded empires overseas – the Spaniards, the Portuguese, the Dutch, the English and French, and belatedly also the Germans and the Italians. By the end of the period nearly the whole globe was encompassed in one international system, although not integrated in it in equal measure. Events in Manchuria and Abyssinia in the nineteen-thirties profoundly affected international politics but events in the colonial realms or in Latin America did not, and the centre of gravity remained decisively in European events.

Non-European political structures which came under European rule were not considered as states; they were merely objects and not subjects of international politics. Their involvement was passive and also limited to the imperial Powers directly concerned with them. The situation began to change with the successful rebellion of the Thirteen Colonies in North America which formed the United States in 1776. Latin America became emancipated from her colonial masters in the 1820s, though the new states came under strong United States influence; the emancipation of the British 'colonies of settlement' began in 1867 with Canada and concluded in 1910 with South Africa, but the newly established Dominions did not gain full formal independence until the inter-war period. Nationalism and the concomitant desire for independence penetrated to Asian dependencies only in the last decades of the nineteenth century and to some, but by no means many, African dependencies only in the inter-war period.

They were to make their full impact only during and after the Second World War.

Although by the twentieth century the system had become world-wide, its *structure* was highly Europe-centred. Undoubtedly colonial expansion led to rivalry and struggles: between the Spaniards and the Portuguese, the Portuguese and the Dutch, the Dutch and the British, and the British and the French. All these struggles were, however, clearly peripheral; the major wars were fought in Europe and peace settlements were determined by their outcomes. In fact, owing to the peripheral nature of colonial issues, instead of considering them as a source of conflict, many historians interpret them as a safety-valve for European expansionism; the imperial Powers could pursue their ambitions without direct cost to their neighbours and rivals, colonies served as convenient 'compensation' for changes in the balance of power in Europe. This interpretation is particularly plausible for the period of 'the scramble for Africa' in the third quarter of the nineteenth century. Thus, while it is difficult to pronounce a straight-out judgement upon the effects of the world-wide expansion, since it led both to conflict and harmony, it seems that the lack of complete integration of the international system, the presence of substantial peripheries, was an element conducive to harmony.

The *number of members* was subject to great fluctuations. Only few contemporary states are historically continuous, as Britain, France, Spain, Sweden or Russia. In the wake of the disintegration of the Holy Roman Empire, there were at first established hundreds of independent and semi-independent principalities which gradually amalgamated into larger units. The process continued in Germany and in Italy when the driving force of nationalism added its impetus in the nineteenth century. At the same time, however, once nationalism became the established principle of state-making, it became also a major factor in the disintegration of large multi-national structures. It grew in the geographically isolated Spanish, Portuguese and British settlements overseas which became independent during the nineteenth and twentieth centuries. It eroded also the multi-national empires of central and eastern Europe: by the end of the First World

War the Ottoman and the Austro-Hungarian Empires had been broken up and the nations on the western outskirts of the Russian Empire had become emancipated. This meant a multiplication of units. Europe became 'balkanized' and overseas states became firmly established – the two growing Great Powers, the United States and Japan, and also the twenty Latin American countries and the British Dominions.

Undoubtedly these fluctuations were all connected with conflict. Neither amalgamation nor the breaking up of units is a simple and easy process and both usually require the heat of struggle to be achieved. With good reason many observers early in the nineteenth century were struck by the then unusual cases of the disappearance of states – the recent three partitions of Poland and the obliteration of Venice by Napoleon. At the same time, the substantial social changes following the Napoleonic Wars could not be readily accommodated within the existing units and the international system managed to accommodate them only because its membership was reasonably flexible. Thus, far from being a cause of conflict, fluctuations in the identity and the number of units can be more justifiably considered as its result, as one of the methods for its accommodation.

*International stratification* and the *power structure* of international society changed from a relatively simple arrangement throughout the nineteenth century to a much more complex one in the twentieth. After the Napoleonic wars, international stratification reverted to the pre-war pattern of a few Great Powers, distinguished by larger military forces based upon relatively large populations and well evolved economies, which operated within a delicate system of balance of power. The identity of the five Great Powers remained unchanged throughout the century: the Austrian Empire (Austro-Hungary since 1867), France, Great Britain, Prussia (Germany from 1871), and Russia.

By the beginning of the twentieth century stratification became somewhat confused. Two overseas states won their spurs as Great Powers by the traditional method of winning victories over other Powers, the United States over Spain in 1898 and Japan over Russia in 1904–5, but they remained largely outside the European system. The economic and military capabilities of one of the five European Great Powers, Germany, grew so much more rapidly than those of the others that Germany could challenge the whole system with a fair expectation of success. She lost the First World War mainly owing to a late, but by no means inevitable, United States intervention.

The 1914–18 war did not end the confusion; on the contrary, it increased it. The actual post-war power structure was dangerously out of line with the potential power structure. The United States, the economically and militarily most powerful unit, immediately withdrew into isolation. Three European Great Powers were eliminated, Austro-Hungary for good, while the other two were ostracised and excluded: Germany owing to her defeat and Russia owing to her new bolshevik régime. The ensuing international system was precariously incomplete, depending on France and Great Britain, neither in agreement with the other, with the peripheral participation of Italy and Japan. In the League of Nations the Middle and Small Powers attempted, for a short while, to play a larger part in the running of the international system than ever before, but without much success.

Some scholars attribute the relative stability of the Concert of Europe to the number of the Great Powers participating in it. Admittedly, five Powers make the operation of a balance-of-power system logically easy. Three is a notoriously unstable number since two of them tend to club together against the third, while four tend to break into two rigid alliances; five seems to be the minimum number required for flexibility. The number may have been an essential but it was not a sufficient condition. Perhaps equally or even more important were three other factors obtaining in the nineteenth century: that no Great Powers were left outside the system, that capabilities did not drastically change, and that the objectives of states' policies were moderate, at least to the point of their firm intentions to maintain in existence both the international system and all its major participants. All three were sadly lacking from the beginning of the twentieth century. It has already been mentioned that the system was no longer comprehensive because not all Great Powers directly participated in it. The two other changes pertain to capabilities and intentions.

To turn now to the *constituent units*. During the nineteenth century the capabilities of the Great Powers were by no means equal, e.g. Britain was the first Power to develop a modern industrial base and enjoyed a naval supremacy undisputed till the last part of the century, while Prussia and Russia had much greater armies than the others. Nevertheless, capabilities were at least in the same category, of a similar magnitude, so that no Great Power could reasonably expect to win preponderance within the system. Some Great Powers were conservatively inclined and wished to preserve the existing order whereas others were revisionist and wanted to adjust it in their favour. None of them, however, wished to do away with the system altogether. There were no fundamental clashes of beliefs and objectives of the nature experienced during the previous religious or revolutionary wars, or the subsequent twentieth-century ideological struggles. Particularly important was the moderate and moderating foreign policy of Great Britain, a Power which appeared to be both able and willing to prevent any other Power from upsetting the equilibrium, as she had managed to do during the Napoleonic period.

As with most social phenomena, the causal nexus between capabilities and intentions is by no means clear. A sudden change in the balance of power through the rapid development of the capabilities of one Power became distinctly possible with the growth of technology and industry in the last decades of the nineteenth century; at the same time intentions disruptive to the system arose, particularly in Germany. Some circularity can be detected in the matter. It is possible to argue that Germany's rulers conceived these disruptive intentions partly as the result of having realized their latent capabilities, but also that they developed these capabilities largely as the result of their disruptive intentions. Whatever the answer, there appears to be a close connection between the disequilibria in both fields and the conflicts which emerged towards the end of the nineteenth century.

In the inter-war period the imbalances both in capabilities and in intentions grew even further. The pre-war stresses were intensified and there was added to them also an ideological split. Again, without attempting to determine the causal nexus between all these, we shall start with capabilities. The most striking differences between the post-war and the pre-war situations were the great improvement in industrial and organizational techniques, and the colossal discrepancies among the capabilities of the Great Powers. It was difficult to grasp at the time the full implications of each of these differences and even less so their interconnection. Repayments of heavy war debts owed to the United States by wartime allies, especially by France and Britain, were possible only as long as Germany maintained some reparations payments, and these were possible, in turn, only as long as United States capital was being transferred to Germany. Before the process came to a halt through the Great Depression, Germany managed to rebuild and fully modernize her industry, forging ahead of other European Powers and laying a solid industrial foundation for speedy rearmament in the thirties. Less rapid, but equally surpassing expectations, was the industrial advance of the Soviet Union in the thirties, despite her relative lack of technological tradition, the scanty assistance from outside, and the ravages suffered during the civil war and the social upheavals following the Revolution.

The sudden hastening in technological processes which made possible the building up of industrial and military power within a short period obviously endangered the stability of the international system which was marked by a great gap between actual and potential capabilities. Whereas the actual military and industrial power of France and of Great Britain was the greatest in Europe, potentially the power of Germany and the Soviet Union was even greater. This would have led to serious international tension even without any ideological implications, since Germany and the Soviet Union would have insisted upon changes in the post-war settlement once the power balance had swung in their favour.

The growth of ideologies further aggravated the tension: instead of demanding changes within the existing system, the two revisionist Powers opposed the system altogether. Ever since the October Revolution in 1917, the communist rulers of Russia favoured a revolution of the proletariat in all countries which would overthrow the existing governments and the existing international system. Their hopes for a world revolution were matched by fears among others and although both these hopes and fears diminished in the late twenties, they lingered on, bedevilling international politics. Likewise Hitler, in power in Germany since 1933, was not concerned with preserving either the international system or its major members. The Nazi ideology was more than revisionist, claiming the removal of the 'dictate' of Versailles; it was revolutionary. The triangle between Western democracies, communist Russia, and the fascist bloc led by Germany, permitted no stability in the international system. All three were fundamentally at loggerheads and combinations between any two of them, whenever attempted, were bound to prove ephemeral.

Thus, improved technology and industrial organization, discrepancies between actual and potential power, and conflicting ideologies all contributed to conflicts which eventually led to the Second World War.

Changes in the *international process* went in both directions, towards increased conflict but also towards increased cooperation. On the conflict side of the ledger must be entered the gradual disappearance of the internationalism obtaining in the dynastic states; rulers and public servants differing in their nationality from that of the majority of the people became extremely rare. Western Christianity as well as the Enlightenment and Rationalism, all traditions supporting internationalism, weakened under the impact of nationalism. The cross-national ideologies of the twentieth century did not remedy the situation since they led to very selective, divisive types of internationalism.

The international diplomatic understandings, the common Western eighteenth-century diplomatic style based upon a community of culture and language and regularized after the Napoleonic Wars, developed in the nineteenth century into 'the Concert of Europe', a system of diplomatic consultation to solve cooperatively the major issues arising with a view to preventing the traditional resort to war. The 'Concert' was not, however, capable of dealing cooperatively with the rapid succession of serious crises early in the twentieth century and ground itself to a halt already before the outbreak of the 1914–18 war. In the inter-war period, the cultural unity of diplomacy was irretrievably lost owing to the rise of hostile ideologies and to the coming of age of non-European Powers. With the evolution of mass-media and the growing influence of public opinion, instead of negotiating and striving for agreement, 'the new diplomacy' often resorted to propaganda, to direct appeals to the people of other states.

The nature of warfare changed, too. Starting with the French Revolution, citizens' armies raised by conscription began to replace the small professional armies of the eighteenth century. The new forces were constantly growing in size and the rapid pace of industry enabled governments to equip these armies with weapons of ever-increasing hitting power. Instead of being a violent but rational method of solving conflicts which could not be otherwise resolved, by 1914–18 war became increasingly devastating and 'total', involving more people, more armaments and consequently more losses and damage. Although it remained politically important to win a war rather than lose it, the manpower and material losses were so grave on both sides that it almost became a misnomer to speak about 'victory'.

At the same time, growing international interaction was not limited to exacerbated conflict; it included also an unprecedented amount of growing harmonious cooperation. From the second half of the nineteenth century international bureaux were established to cater for a growing range of human needs which could be best satisfied internationally. This 'functional' cooperation thrived best in technical fields, in proportion to their remoteness from the central issues of power, especially in the fields of communications and of the administration of international rivers, i.e. rivers flowing through the territories of several states. Both the promise and the limitation of this new type of cooperation are neatly demonstrated by the staggering contrast between the great success in organizing the strategically unimportant postal turnover through the Universal Postal Union, and the poor results in coordinating the strategically important telecommunications. At the turn of the century the first serious although not very successful attempts were made to introduce cooperation into the mainstream of power politics by providing for improved methods of pacific settlement of disputes, for the enlargement and codification of the laws of war, and, completely unsuccessfully, also for disarmament.

The League of Nations and the Permanent Court of International Justice were the institutional alternatives to violent conflict devised as the result of the First World War. Members were supposed to see to a peaceful settlement of international conflicts; to the traditional strand of conflict in the political-strategic domain there was added a parallel strand of harmony in the form of 'collective security', a collective guarantee to maintain peace, which was meant to replace traditional power politics. In historical perspective, the failure of the grand plans seems inevitable owing to the disagreement among the Great Powers: Britain and France were sceptical and endeavoured to use the League for their national ends which, to make things worse, were contradictory; the United States, the main proponent of the League, did not join it. The League of Nations failed in its major collective security activities and did not become a centre of the international system, although in the mid twenties it gave some promise of success. The Permanent Court of International Justice did not, likewise, help to introduce a 'rule of law' into international life. Major political conflicts proved intractable to legal solution; the only such conflict which came before the Court, the case of Austria's proposed customs union with Germany, resulted in the judges splitting nearly evenly, their legal views following the national interests of their countries of origin. Nevertheless, the League proved unexpectedly successful in its inconspicuous 'functional' activities and the Court helped to consolidate international law within its existing political limitations. When both went into suspension during the Second World War, nobody planning for the post-war period thought that they should be abolished.

### The Post-war Period

The world since the 1939–45 war appears to be sufficiently different in its essentials from that preceding it to make many of us speak about the emergence of a new international system. The most conspicuous changes are: greater integration of the system; greatly increased membership owing to the process of 'decolonization', now nearly completed; altered stratification with two Superpowers emerging as a class on their own and China appearing as a possible runner-up; invention of nuclear weapons and missiles which have completely altered the scale of military capabilities; and the ideological split which colours the intentions of states.

It has been pointed out that the *boundaries* of the international system had become world-wide already before the war. In the post-war period the stratosphere, outer space, the sea-bed, and even the moon have been penetrated and the planetary system may soon follow suit. All these are potentially extremely important for strategy and power relations but they do not offer opportunities for expansion similar to that in the nineteenth century. Moreover, states are beginning to realize this and to draw the obvious conclusions. It is true that conflict and competition similar in their nature to 'the scramble for Africa' are now taking place in an even more dangerous form in recently emancipated territories, such as Vietnam or the Congo. Against that, the Superpowers, at least, seem to have realized the dangers of continuing traditional conflicts in the hitherto not appropriated peripheries of the system. They felt, therefore, impelled to conclude treaties regulating the régimes of Antarctica and outer space. These exclude appropriation by any states and the possible resulting conflicts, and lay foundations for cooperation.

In contrast to the pre-war situation, the *structure* of the system has become much more centralized and integrated. In the first post-war decade it was still possible to think of a focal area in Eurasia in which the Cold War prevailed, with major theatres in Germany and in the Far East. The Western system and Latin America were then under firm United States leadership, the communist system was subjugated to the Soviet Union, the independence movements in the colonial world were relatively autonomous. By the mid-fifties, the autonomy of the subsystems was lost, the Cold War permeated the whole world and the concept of a central area and of peripheries became increasingly blurred. It is true that Berlin and Germany are still more important than some of the more obscure new states, but it is by no means an accident that the most violent post-war conflicts took place in Korea and Vietnam, two countries hitherto completely outside the mainstream of international politics.

The widespread tendency for local or regional conflicts to become enmeshed in the global conflict is usually called 'escalation'. Unfortunately 'escalation' of harmonious and cooperative issues is not nearly as simple as that of conflict and cannot be taken for granted, but it does take place. International concern for the survival and welfare of all people, wherever they may live, does now exist, although it works somewhat selectively and its scope should not be exaggerated. Instead of the previous limited and sporadic aid sent to relieve the victims of major disasters, international aid is now flowing steadily and though, especially after its recent curtailment by the United States and Britain, it is quite inadequate for its purposes, it is of incomparably greater magnitude.

The world is much too large a stage to allow this integration of the world-wide international system to proceed very evenly or very far. Significant regional subsystems deal with a variety of regional and local issues without bringing them into the orbit of the world-wide international system. Just the same the autonomy of the regions cannot be taken for granted even since the mid sixties, when the grip of the Superpowers on their spheres of influence and the all pervading influence of the Cold War had considerably abated. The Superpowers, balancing each other, often allow regional and local conflicts to play themselves out without their intervention, but nobody can ever be sure that these conflicts will not be suddenly swept into the mainstream of the Cold War. Hence every issue of any import requires consideration not only within local and regional contexts but also within the world context.

Two major influences have come to bear upon the identity and the numbers of participant states: the colonial self-determination movement and the Cold War. The former has resulted in an unparalleled rise in numbers following the emancipation of colonies. The latter has caused the splitting of several states: Germany,

China, Korea, Vietnam; this has given rise to the tricky problem whether we should consider the split states as potential wholes, or both parts as separate units, or recognize only the part to which we are more favourably inclined. The process of 'balkanization' noted earlier in Europe, has now spread to other continents, especially Africa. As in the previous period, the multiplication of independent states can be considered more fruitfully not as a source of conflict but rather as a method of conflict resolution: colonial emancipation could not be contained within the old colonial empires, neither could the communist or the American bloc accept the possibility of one of the divided countries passing fully into the orbit of its rival. At the same time, however, many of the new states are small and weak and their capabilities fall far below those enjoyed by the majority of older states; many of them are politically unstable, inviting intervention from abroad. Unification drives in the divided nations, particularly nations as powerful as China or Germany, give rise to the possibility of the most dangerous international conflicts while divided Korea and Vietnam became involved in the two major post-war wars, one of which is still being fought. No ready solution seems possible for the conflicts arising from the clash between nationalism and the divisive boundaries based exclusively upon the power politics of the Cold War.

*International stratification* and the *power structure* have now undergone a transformation much more fundamental than that which had taken place early in this century. The United States and the Soviet Union have emerged from the war with distinguished characteristics that put them in a category of their own. These Superpowers, justifiably named, are singled out primarily by their costly and sophisticated nuclear weapons systems which no other states can afford to emulate. They possess also other important attributes which no other state fully shares: their populations are exceptionally large, in the range of 200 million, surpassed only by China and India; both have evolved well organized and highly productive industrial societies; both profess ideologies with some international appeal, which enable them to claim leadership of their respective blocs.

In the early post-war years, the international system had only two significant centres of power, in Washington and in Moscow. The bipolar system was still fairly loose, since the Third World was not controlled by it and, even within the two opposing blocs, Superpower control was not firmly established. For a while, however, it seemed quite possible that all the states might eventually be forced or persuaded to join one of the blocs and that the control of the Superpowers over these would increase to the point of establishing a 'tight' bipolar system, under complete Superpower domination. This was not to come. The Third World refused to toe the line and join either camp; by the mid fifties the policy of 'nonalignment' which had prevailed among it became recognized as respectable by both Superpowers. Also within the existing spheres of influence of the two Superpowers national resistance prevailed. The Soviet bloc was first challenged by Yugoslavia which had broken away in 1947, then it faced serious challenges in Hungary and Poland in 1956, and in Czechoslovakia and Rumania in 1968. The rapidly deepening rift between China and the Soviet Union became public in the later fifties and considerably exacerbated since, encouraging independent foreign policies by the Eastern European members of the bloc. Simultaneously, as the danger of a Soviet attack against Western Europe was diminishing, NATO suffered a great weakening of purpose which was exploited by France to challenge American leadership.

While the two Superpowers remain supreme and unsurpassable in their mentioned attributes of power, their nuclear supremacy is locked up in mutual deterrence allowing other, lesser Powers to compete with them. Outside the 'balance of terror' between the United States and the Soviet Union, stratification is scarcely clear. China, with her population surpassing 700 million, has been successfully organized by its present communist rulers to form a powerful rapidly industrializing society; she has even begun to develop nuclear weapons over and above colossal land forces. China's unity has survived the impact of the powerful centrifugal forces unleashed in the 'Cultural Revolution' between 1966 and 1969, and she could become not only a runner-up to the two Superpowers, but a third Superpower.

No clear-cut criteria are available to distinguish other Great

Powers from among the rest. The United Nations Charter has singled out such a group of five designated as 'Permanent Members of the Security Council' who enjoy in it the power of veto. Apart from the Superpowers and China (which, until 1971, was paradoxically represented by the National Government ruling Formosa and not by the Central People's Government ruling the mainland), this group includes two traditional European Great Powers, the United Kingdom and France. It is interesting to note that these are, as it happens, also the only possessors of nuclear weapons apart from the Superpowers and communist China; the pre-nuclear Charter thus anticipated the rise of the class of 'Nuclear Powers' and invested these with a special rank.

In fact, however, neither possession of nuclear weapons on a limited scale nor the permanent membership of the Security Council automatically bestow Great Power status. The weapons do, undoubtedly, testify to a high degree of technological achievement and confer some prestige, but it is doubtful whether this prestige either in the eyes of the Superpowers or of the others is very significant. As military weapons, the nuclear capacities of Britain and even more of France appear unimportant. Both the United Kingdom and France lost most of their empires by the end of the fifties. Their present world roles entail more responsibility and cost than tangible political advantage; both countries suffer heavily from the heritage of their imperial past which renders them scapegoats for the many ills of their ex-colonies and precludes them from world-wide leadership. Although de Gaulle's France has used bold and enterprising diplomacy to overcome this disadvantage by severing herself in the sixties from the United States, and although she has managed to retain control over the international behaviour of the majority of her ex-colonies, her standing as a Great Power is no greater than that of Britain with her orthodox diplomacy and completely uncontrollable Commonwealth.

France has one solid advantage over the United Kingdom in that she has become the political leader of the Western European Community. In recent years, however, France has been overshadowed by the economic strength of the Federal Republic of

Germany and she can no longer be regarded as an undisputed leader of the Community. Nevertheless, being one of their main founders and having shaped them to suit her interests, she is in a much stronger position within them than Britain which is only a late applicant for admission.

The two traditional Great Powers continue to enjoy a form of Great Power status although of a somewhat uncertain, some would say rather vestigial, character. Their case indicates the logical expedient for overcoming the gap between the Superpowers and others – to amalgamate and to establish regional blocs. So far, however, only Western Europe seems to have the chance of becoming another Superpower if its states amalgamate politically. All other attempts at a full union of states have failed – notably in the cases of the United Arab Republic, Mali, Ghana-Guinea. No regional organization has been really successful in the political management of the region but, while some of them have served as tools of Superpower policies, others have been used as convenient instruments for the attempts by other states to obtain Great Power status.

Ideological revolutionary leadership which is acceptable to other states has now become a major element in raising the status of a state. The two Superpowers lack it. The Soviet Union had here at first a definite advantage through the appeal of communism as a recipe for the economic development of really backward countries, and through her uninhibited support for anti-colonial movements. She has, however, forfeited nearly all this advantage owing to successful competition by the far more radical brands of revolution propagated by China and Cuba. Moreover, neither Superpower is particularly enterprising or skilful in its diplomacy. Hence the avenue seemed open to other claimants for leadership.

The reason why all the numerous attempts at revolutionary leadership have been unsuccessful seems to lie in the inadequate capabilities of the states involved. China is the only exception. Not only as an Asian state can she successfully appeal to the racialist and anti-colonialist sentiments of the Third World, but she combines a radical revolutionary appeal with a seemingly successful recipe for economic development and is sufficiently powerful to intimidate her neighbours by her military power as well as to offer small amounts of foreign aid. However, her arrogant and aggressive diplomacy and her grave domestic disturbances between 1966 and 1969 seriously undermined her position. It remains to be seen to what extent China will be successful in her subsequent attempt to regain international influence from a background of restored domestic stability. At the end of 1971 she opened a dialogue with the United States which opens the likelihood of China assuming a world role also in the Superpower relations. India, second only to China in her population, failed in her endeavours to become a leader of Southern Asia and of the Third World as a whole. Her creed was insufficiently revolutionary and she was afflicted by economic and political weaknesses and by a continuous struggle against Pakistan; in 1962 she suffered a humiliating reverse at the hands of the Chinese. The disintegration of Pakistan in 1971 following the Bangla Desh rebellion and the successful Indian intervention have secured India dominance over the South Asian subcontinent but her internal weaknesses persist and her future depends upon continuing Soviet support.

Several 'charismatic' leaders used the springboards of relatively weak states in their attempts at personal international leadership which would have involved also the upgrading of their states to Great Power status; two of them, Sukarno of Indonesia and Nkrumah of Ghana, were forced into retirement; Nasser of Egypt suffered another humiliating military reverse at the hands of the Israelis; Tito of Yugoslavia became the arch-conservative among the communists and hence insufficiently radical to appeal; Castro of Cuba and Boumedienne of Algeria had greater ambitions than achievements since their appeals are not backed by solid power. Admittedly all these states have played and some are still playing larger roles in international relations than others with much greater capabilities, but just the same not one of them, except China, can be considered as clearly belonging to a separate category of Great Powers.

Turning now to the characteristics of the *constituent units*, one is struck by the immense growth in the *capabilities* of states.

Not only has the national product grown everywhere but the governments have assumed control over a large proportion of the increase, even in the United States where this contravenes the prevailing ideological beliefs. Governments command unprecedented economic resources and advanced industrial technology has supplied them also with hitherto unthinkable military resources. The capabilities have not, of course, grown evenly. The discrepancies between the states which are best and worst endowed have greatly increased; the rate of economic growth in most underdeveloped countries is very much lower than the rates in more advanced countries.

Nevertheless all the states, independently of their capabilities, share one problem, although admittedly not quite to the same degree: all possess capabilities short of their needs. The problem of the scarcity of resources, the dilemma of the choice between guns and butter, are, of course, traditional. The rapid growth in resources has not, however, ameliorated the situation; on the contrary, the growth of international demands and foreign policy needs have been even more rapid. Evaluation of this phenomenon gives rise to acrimonious disputes. It is possible to argue that foreign policy needs are purely conventional, lacking as they do a clear biological basis such as that underlying the needs of the individual. In other words the discrepancy between the capacities and the needs can be simply solved by scaling down the needs which are only arbitrary. On the other hand, these conventional needs involve the very survival of the state, are ultimately a matter of life and death, and hence may be considered as necessities.

Simultaneously with foreign policy needs have grown also domestic demands. Starting from diametrically opposed ideologies and greatly divergent standards of living, all states are faced with substantially increased and insistent demands for social welfare and for increased consumption. In 1967, despite protestations to the contrary by President Johnson, even the United States began to face the situation that the nation was not producing quite enough to satisfy both urgent domestic and foreign policy needs. The pressures upon the Soviet Government to divert some of their defence expenditure to domestic expenditure are even greater.

The Superpowers feel constrained to spend enough on nuclear and rocket technologies to avoid falling any distance behind the rival either in weapons technology or in space exploration which seems to carry high prestige. But the military expenditure of all states with any pretence to an international status is very heavy, particularly in the case of the other three Nuclear Powers, Britain, France and China. Moreover, states with a reasonably high standard of living are now expected to contribute considerable sums to foreign aid; this is particularly true of the two Superpowers and the ex-colonial Powers.

It may well be true, as some critics claim, that if some of the money devoted to foreign policy were spent domestically, it would benefit the states involved much more by strengthening them economically and socially. Nobody, however, can be quite certain that more limited defence may not spell mortal danger, and more limited foreign aid, significant political advances by rivals and opponents. The governments continue spending on what it is customary to spend and in more or less customary magnitudes. Short of an unlikely international understanding on curtailing foreign policy expenditures, alterations in them are considered too risky to be contemplated unilaterally on a large scale.

The majority of the new states are poor and extremely short of resources not only for economic development but also for minimum current consumption needs. Some of them are locked in political conflicts which result in absolute priorities upon high defence expenditure – this is the case of India and Pakistan and of the Middle Eastern countries. Many African states which do not feel threatened keep no armies at all, but they are all very poor. The capabilities of the Third World states are generally so low that they permanently depend upon outside aid, both economic and military. At a very much lower level of expenditure, they are pressed, on the whole, even harder than the more prosperous states.

Thus paradoxically, although the capabilities of states have grown beyond measure, they have also become increasingly inadequate. As years went by, more and more states experienced this in a variety of situations. Thus having won the war and finished with an unrivalled land-force and in occupation of all the enemy capitals, the Soviet Union found herself defenceless against American nuclear bombs; having enjoyed a short-lived monopoly of nuclear weapons, the United States was caught by the unexpectedly rapid development of nuclear technology in the Soviet Union and also in China; neither bonds of ideology nor military and economic resources secure allies, as both Super-powers have learnt from bitter experience: the futile concentration of the American military effort in Vietnam is only a pronounced example of the general limitation of military power; the lavish economic aid dispensed since the war secured little friendship for the donors and, with the notable exception of Western Europe, little economic growth for the recipients. Examples could be added indefinitely. The only obvious conclusion is that states are now highly inadequate for the traditional range of their objectives, starting with national security and ending with economic welfare.

This rather paradoxically disappointing inadequacy of the capabilities of states must be fully taken into account when analysing their *intentions*. Again, as in the inter-war period, three major ideologies can be distinguished, only the Western one favouring the *status quo*. The other two, however, although revisionist, are much less hostile to the international order than communism and Nazism had been until 1939. The major communist state has now reached a rather enviable condition of economic development, one which is well worth preserving against the dangers of a nuclear war. It is possible to say that the Soviet Union has now become a 'have' state, or that the communist ideology in Russia has mellowed with age and become less disruptive, or that the Russians have accepted the realities of the world and the fact that they would not be able to win a war against the United States, or all these explanations can be combined. It is clear that Soviet communism is much less revisionist; for some purposes, the Soviet Union can be considered as having come firmly on the side of the *status quo*. This greatly lessens the disruptive impact of the radical variety of communism embraced by China, possibly an emerging Superpower, but one still far behind the two existing ones and moreover now facing considerable difficulties.

The other great change is constituted by the disappearance of Nazism and the emergence of the compound ideologies of the Third World centring upon decolonization, non-alignment, and economic growth. They are fundamentally revisionist since they claim fundamental revisions of the international system, but the point must be stressed that the *status quo* camp has, although often very reluctantly, accepted their demands. Decolonization has taken place, non-alignment has become respectable, assistance has been given for development although not in a very effective manner. Despite some vicious and violent conflicts which had arisen prior to the demanded changes, the major colonial conflicts are now a matter of the past and have been generally replaced by some form of cooperation between the new states and the ex-imperial powers; only the problem of white-dominated Southern Africa remains acute. Foreign aid had often started as an instrument of the Cold War but, arguably, its competitive, conflict characteristics are now being replaced by more cooperative, humanitarian as well as economic considerations.

Thus, despite such vicious conflicts as those between the Arabs and Israel or India and Pakistan, despite the savage fighting in Vietnam and the uncertainty about China's ultimate intentions, it is likely that, on the whole, the intentions of the states are less disruptive than in the interwar period. Moreover, these intentions must take into account the palpably inadequate capabilities available. This is likely to have made the states reluctant to pursue policies aiming at the complete upsetting of the international system and the elimination of some of its members. Realizing their own vulnerability, states are likely to support a stable international system even if they are unhappy about some of its features. The implications are discussed in the concluding chapter.

In the *processes* of the international system, diplomacy has continued in the same direction, departing even further from the traditions of its golden age in the nineteenth century, while quite new phenomena have appeared in the domain of warfare. The striking characteristics of the post-war diplomatic practice have been the multiplication of states and the growing numbers of states unwilling to pursue traditional practices. Even for states with well-established diplomatic services it has become impossible to continue them in the same fashion. The number of outposts necessary abroad has multiplied requiring a much larger personnel; also the range of foreign policy functions has grown, creating a difficult problem of integrating specialists into the traditional service. The most striking example is found in the United States, the country most afflicted by the problem as the result of the rapid growth in its international responsibilities. Foreign aid and Central Intelligence Agencies all over the world often caused great trouble when their activities contravened the line adopted by the Department of State.

By and large it is true that all the states which are unenthusiastic about the international order are likewise unenthusiastic about the existing diplomatic practices. This applies in the first instance to communist states, which have suddenly grown in number. When the Soviet Union and the Eastern European countries became less antagonistic to the order and to its traditions, communist China became more violently opposed to both. The new states which had obtained their independence find it, on the whole, uncongenial to respect the traditional practices established in another continent and century by the very imperial powers they had expelled. This ideological dislike is reinforced by the lack of personnel versed in traditional diplomatic lore. The niceties of diplomatic protocol have been abandoned and the *mores* regarding the treatment of foreign diplomats have become increasingly cruder. Bad behaviour is both imitated and retaliated against; after relatively harmless demonstrations and slight damage to diplomatic buildings, physical attacks on diplomats and large-scale destruction of diplomatic property sometimes took place, particularly in the last years of the Sukarno régime in Indonesia and in the later sixties in China. Diplomatic outposts have in many cases completely changed their social roles. When the host country is hostile, instead of being a possible bridge, as in the past, the outpost becomes a symbol of the adversary and a convenient target for pent-up feelings. The attacks, as well as the frequent severance of diplomatic relations on the slightest provocation, are the result. Thus while the sending states had always used diplomats sent abroad as instruments not only of cooperation but also of conflict, for spying and for propaganda, these diplomats are now frequently used also by the recipient states for purposes of conflict.

A signal development in diplomacy has been the growing importance of the United Nations in this field. This occurred despite the failure of the organization's major concern with the maintenance of peace. During the first two decades of its existence, the United Nations was generally restricted to the minor conflicts while the major issues of the Cold War were dealt with directly by the Superpowers. Nevertheless, it has gradually succeeded in what the League had not, namely in becoming the undisputed diplomatic centre of international politics. In the first instance, many new states conduct much of their diplomacy through their Permanent Missions in the United Nations simply because they lack adequate representation and senior diplomatic personnel in other countries. Second, despite their hesitation and reluctance, the two Superpowers find it often more convenient to use the United Nations rather than by-pass it. A striking example is furnished by the Special Session of the General Assembly in 1967 to deal with the Middle Eastern crisis arising from the Israeli–Arab war. Although ineffective in finding a solution, the meeting was helpful in clarifying the attitudes of the Superpowers and of other states as no other type of diplomatic negotiations could possibly have done. If permanent peace is some day achieved in the Middle East, the Special Session will be considered as the preliminary peace conference.

The Second World War was a clear-cut watershed in the history of warfare. It was much more 'total' than its predecessor, in view of the much larger armies equipped with much more powerful weapons, as well as of the much greater involvement and suffering of the civilians. Moreover, its last stage served as an occasion for the use of the newly evolved nuclear weapons. Violence 'escalated' beyond bounds, and in post-war development its instruments escalated even further. The largest nuclear bombs now available are sufficiently powerful to destroy large cities with a single blast; if all of them were unleashed and hit separate targets, life on earth could be obliterated.

The paradoxical result has been that hope was born out of

fear and despair, and cooperation and possibly harmony out of stark conflict. Nuclear weapons have not been used again, despite severe crises and acute fighting since 1945. The Americans refrained from using them during the period of their monopoly and then a 'balance of terror' was established between them and the Russians. Although it might be expected that the most powerful instruments of destruction would be conducive to exacerbation of conflicts between the two Superpowers, in fact they have furnished one of the most important occasions for cooperation expressed in the partial test ban treaty in 1963 and the non-proliferation treaty in 1968. The common interest in avoiding mutual annihilation, the poisoning of the atmosphere, and the spread of nuclear weapons to other states, are an important and solid basis for American–Russian cooperation.

Harmony and cooperation based upon fear of common enemies form the pattern of operation in such regional and defence organizations as NATO, the Warsaw Pact, SEATO, ANZUS, the Arab League. In contrast to the American–Soviet cooperation in nuclear matters, this type of cooperation is directed against an outsider and is conditioned by the degree of hostility encountered from him. It is a definitely secondary phenomenon conditional on this conflict remaining in existence; with its diminution, cooperation weakens, as has recently happened in both NATO and the Warsaw Pact.

The first two decades of the post-war world were marked by a new state of international politics which was neither peace nor war, and which is usually called the 'Cold War'. It means a condition of severe, fundamental conflict between the Superpowers in which violence is used but never directly between the two Superpowers, always with much restraint, and never in its nuclear form. The Cold War was occasionally quite hot and resulted in great bloodshed. First of all, various subversion movements encouraged by communists arose in many new states and were then suppressed. Second, the two major struggles in Korea and in Vietnam, although they were not officially called that, were no less than full-scale wars; the latter is still going on. The scale of violence is great in terms of the troops deployed and the weapons used as well as the sufferings of the civilian population. For the Koreans and the Vietnamese war has remained as total as it had been between 1939 and 1945, despite the nuclear restraint.

Violence was often used also in conflicts not connected with the Cold War. Colonial independence movements resorted to it, to a varying extent, before they could force the Metropolitan Powers to withdraw; violence seems to be the only means by which territories south of the Sahara can hope to bring to an end the white rule over them. Violence was used in Kashmir and in Palestine in 1947, and the delimitation followed the lines at which fighting had come to a standstill; it was used by the Israelis in 1956 and again in 1967 against the Arabs; it was and is being used in domestic wars in several new states with unsatisfied regional and national claims, for instance in Indonesia, the Congo, Nigeria, and Pakistan.

While the United Nations Charter sets as its major goal the 'maintenance of international peace and security', the organization has merely been able to assist in the ending of hostilities after the clash of arms has to a large extent spent itself. It has been even less successful in the more fundamental goal of assisting states to solve their problems by peaceful means. Conflicts and clashes of vital interests as well as the fact that states can and do back them with massive violence, are unfortunate facts of international life. Despite the provisions of the Charter, and despite the reasonably successful further development of 'functional cooperation', the United Nations has been unable to substitute cooperation and harmony for conflict. If such cooperation, however, arises, as to a limited extent it has already done between the Americans and the Russians, the United Nations may still play an important role in the difficult transformation.

# PART TWO

# STATE BEHAVIOUR

## CHAPTER 5

# VALUES, IDEOLOGIES AND OBJECTIVES

## *Values**

IN the study of political behaviour, whether domestic or international, it is easy to become so preoccupied with what people do, with the instruments they employ and the institutions they organize, as to forget to inquire what all this political activity is about. This frequent error of political scientists is shared by political practitioners who get even more preoccupied with these very elements so that they likewise forget what their activity is really about. It is a recurrent phenomenon of politics that ideals and long-range values recede in political action and are replaced by intermediate or short-range values, that means become ends. As in the life of the individual the pursuit of money, fundamentally a means for securing other values, often degenerates into an end in itself, so in international behaviour a similar phenomenon occurs in the pursuit of power – a means for defence and self-preservation and the attainment of other objectives – which likewise often becomes an end in itself.

To start with, what does the term 'values' mean? It denotes something that people want, an element inside them which influences their action. Men do not merely react to environmental influences – they bring to bear upon their environment this inner element which, in any situation, can be equally or even more important. There is little agreement not only about the relevance of this inner element, but also about its nature and scope. Many terms are confusingly employed to define it: ideologies, doctrines, values and valuations, utilities, policies, commitments, goals, objectives, purposes, ends, programmes, interests or the good (national, of the country, of the people), aims, ethos, way of life, etc. etc. Definitions and schemes of inter-relationship differ from thinker to thinker and clarification is difficult,

*This section paraphrases part of Chapter 8 from the author's *The Making of Foreign Policy*, Oxford University Press, 1963.

especially in view of the social taboos which protect values from rational analysis, whether these taboos are explicit as in totalitarian societies, or implicit as in democratic ones.

Without indulging in a futile addition to the voluminous controversies, we may try to follow common usage realizing, of course, that it is not logically fully satisfactory. When we say a man pursues values in social action, we describe the purposive element of action, that he wants to achieve something, be it positively or negatively, directly or indirectly, explicitly or implicitly, perhaps even consciously or subconsciously. We generally also assume that all men hold values and that they combine these, however loosely, into value systems or ideologies. It is important to insist upon the distinction between the aspirational and the operational levels, between values held and values pursued; the latter are usually distinctively called objectives or goals. Only if the holder of the values were omnipotent, only if he were free from all environmental restraints, only then could he transform all his values into concrete political objectives. In fact we accept most values only as guides for the direction of our action, as elements of our vision of the good life to which we aspire and towards which we try to progress, but which is never fully attainable.

Declaratory policies must not be equated with actual policies for the simple reason that their upholders may deliberately or subconsciously mislead others and perhaps even themselves about their reality. If a communist says that he wants to communize the world or an anti-communist that he wants to rid it of communism, we must first ask the question how genuine their declarations are and then how far they intend to implement their values, if genuine. Objectives and policies follow professed values but not necessarily so.

All people hold many conflicting values and hence find it hard to reconcile and organize them. For instance, however much we may be aware of the old truth that 'we cannot have it both ways', that 'we cannot have our cake and eat it', we find it virtually impossible to formulate a rational value calculus to profit from these simple insights. Values are not quantifiable, it is impossible to aspire to mathematical precision in their specification and comparison; it is hard even to decide on priorities. One may, for example, think that the preservation of the life of the individual or of the existence of the state could be considered supreme. Usually it can, but there are situations in which individuals may sacrifice their lives, e.g. when they fight for their country or when they try to save other people's lives, or when they refuse to betray their beliefs, or when they decide to commit suicide. Similarly, in a way the policy of deterrence may be thought to defy the preservation of the state since it declares that in certain, not clearly specified conditions, the state will use its nuclear weapons in the knowledge that the opponent would do likewise. The result may be bordering upon suicide but does not dispose of the avowed preference 'better dead than red' or its equivalent on the communist side.

Even 'ranking' of values – putting them in order of preference – is very difficult. The preservation of territorial integrity is obviously one of the major national values and has caused many wars in history. Nevertheless, territories have changed hands in the past not only to forestall attacks which could possibly have been resisted although at a great loss of life and wealth, but also to secure friendship, trade or financial benefits and compensations. In other cases costs are incurred which appear to outsiders as grossly excessive. Thus India became involved in an armed struggle with China in 1962 over the large but completely unpopulated and barren territory of Ladakh for which the Indians had no use whatsoever whereas the Chinese had constructed across it an important road to Tibet. Territory has a high symbolic value and the Indians insisted that they had clear titles to it although the Chinese disputed this.

No discussion of the political implications of values is complete without taking into account the identity of those who hold them. Values can, of course, be held both by individuals and by social groups, beginning with the smallest and ending with mankind as a whole. We need not in this context consider the crucial question whether the individual or the community is the ultimate yardstick of all values. On either view, both the influence of the group in which the individual takes part and plays a role, as well as his own contribution, must be considered.

Of great significance is the phenomenon of 'multivalence', the simultaneous existence of several, sometimes conflicting systems of values applicable to the various roles the individual may play in life. Since the family and the nation are the sources of origin of the major values, clashes between them are of the greatest political importance in most political systems. A conflict of this sort arises when the statesman has to weigh his own life or that of a close relation against the welfare of his state; less dramatically, he faces a conflict when family loyalty demands actions opposed by the state, e.g. patronage unjustified by merits, or protection of relatives from the due process of law.

The two major sources of value orientation, which takes place during the upbringing of children and their later education, are the family and the educational system. The modern state makes good use of the opportunities offering to inculcate the supremacy of national values: education is usually operated by the states or by state-controlled agencies or is at least supervised by them. They thus supersede the role of the family as an alternative agent of social upbringing. Since the educational network embraces an increasingly larger proportion of the population for an increasingly longer period of life, the balance is swinging in favour of the state. The role of the family has remained relatively greater in the well-established liberal Western states where values originating in the family and in the state tend to coincide. In collectivist communist states, especially in China, deliberate and stringent policies aim at reducing the role of the family in order to avoid the danger of frequent value clashes. Even in the West, however, we are so indoctrinated that, when faced with a clash of national values with another value originating in the family or another sub-group, we tend to start with the assumption that national values *should* prevail, especially in times of national crisis. Within the context of the state this is a definite element of harmony, a guide to value priorities. Needless to say, people do not always act according to these priorities but they tend to acknowledge them as being right, perhaps not always in relation to their own behaviour, but at least in relation to that of others.

The acknowledged supremacy of national values becomes, however, a potential element of conflict when applied to other values within the international context. The national values of one state are inevitably confronted with the national values of other states. It is, admittedly, not inherent in the nature of international relations that all these confrontations should result in conflict; in many cases the confronting value may be complementary or permissive, but in some cases conflict does arise. It is impossible to eliminate these conflicts entirely but we may still profitably try to reduce the amount of violence employed and to substitute game relationships for direct fights.

Another situation relates to a clash between national and what may be termed 'cross-national' values. While an individual is normally a citizen of only one state (the cases of dual nationality are exceptional), some of the sub-groups to which he belongs may have international affiliations. An issue on which the sub-group values are opposed by national values may be relatively unimportant, e.g. sportsmen, actors or chess-players may feel thwarted by a national policy which precludes exchanges of visits with 'unfriendly' countries. A few of them may feel really strongly about the issue but the majority will either accept the national view of ideological purity and stop supporting the objectionable international links, or try to influence national policy and meanwhile abide by it. Whichever the behaviour, the conflict is unlikely to be serious. It becomes so when the international link is more intimately connected with hostility to one's state. It stands to reason that all communist front organizations and, even more so, communist parties would propound values opposed to those of a Western liberal state and likewise that a Western-sponsored organization, such as the Congress for Cultural Freedom, would propound values opposed to those of communist states. Although membership of the latter is illegal in communist countries as adherence to communist parties is in some Western countries, it is reasonable to assume that both have their sympathizers. The clash of values is here direct and it is rather obvious why the state sometimes intervenes by prohibiting or strongly resisting its rivals, although rarely with full success.

## Ideologies

Although there are as many definitions of ideology as writers about it, practically all of them stress two essential elements: a system of beliefs, and its relationship to political action. There is, however, no general agreement about the significance of ideologies in politics. They may be considered of secondary importance, as being the reflection of economic, social and psychological conditions or as the rationalization of secret desires; they can also be considered as a primary, guiding principle. Undoubtedly this is a question of fundamental importance in international politics – for instance our appraisal of the behaviour of communist states will greatly differ according to how relevant we consider the communist ideology. One cannot escape the difficulty by simple reference to observed international behaviour since the conclusions we draw from it depend on a prior interpretation of the role of ideology; this is proven by the violent disputes among the Sovietologists concerning the possibilities of an East-West understanding in 1945, after 1953 and since 1962. The only generally acceptable generalization is trite – that ideologies and social conditions interact, that there is some sort of an interplay between them.

Historical analogies do not help us much in understanding ideologies which are a modern phenomenon. The closest parallel is with religion when it constituted the dominant element in human lives, and indeed some writers call ideologies secular or political religions. There are, however, fundamental differences between ideologies and religions both in the nature of beliefs and in the characteristics of the historical international environments within which they predominated, say the fifteenth and the twentieth centuries.

### NATIONALISM

Since ideologies play a central part in the issue of conflict and harmony, the major ideologies of our times and their interrelationship require discussion. We shall start with that of nationalism which, ever since the French Revolution, has been the major spiritual and emotional force in international politics and also the main principle of state-formation.

Nationalism is, of course, a powerful foundation for harmony and cooperation within the national group but some of its characteristics constitute it also as one of the most powerful elements of international conflict and strife, particularly dangerous owing to its association with the state, the holder of physical force.

A nation is never a completely clear-cut entity. When we start probing even into a well-established national group, we are immediately confronted with uncertainties and problems. Undoubtedly the Russians are one of the oldest nations in Europe but how does one distinguish them from other Soviet nationals who amount to nearly half of the population of the Soviet Union? If one goes by ethnic origin, there are many mixed marriages; if one goes by culture, many non-Russians have become fully assimilated into the Russian culture. The French create relatively few doubts although in their case the repatriated 'Frenchmen' from North Africa included many individuals of Italian or part-Italian origin. Is the English nation co-terminous with the British nation and, if so, what about the Celtic fringe? To which nation belong the Indians living in East Africa who travel on British passports and are not Indian, Pakistani or local citizens? The American nation is relatively young and has scarcely completed the 'melting-pot' process in which individuals of foreign origin were subjected to an assimilation process and integrated. On the whole, this takes a full three generations and has been ineffective in the case of the Negroes. Are the latter members of the American nation?

A nation can be defined by certain elements such as common government, certain size and closeness of contact, territory, common characteristics, especially language, common interests, and finally, some think decisively, national consciousness. Not many nations partake of all these characteristics and the resulting uncertainties give rise to a whole range of insoluble conflicts. An example from central Europe, the cockpit of nationalist strife, may show how intricate the problems can be. Take the area around the town of Klagenfurt in southern Carinthia which lies on the border of the historical confrontation between the Teutons and the Slavs. In the last two centuries much of the original Slav population has been replaced by German-speaking Austrians or assimilated, often without trace. Some Slavs, however, have retained a consciousness of being different and feel that they have remained members of the Slovene nation, one of the nations of the Federal Republic of Yugoslavia, the southern neighbour of Carinthia. These nationally conscious Slovenes are entitled to an internationally guaranteed minority status under the State Agreement of 1955 but since they are living in a German-speaking state, the time and effort devoted in the schools to their national language and culture is, by the nature of things, taken from the time available for the normal curriculum. Do the riches of national culture compensate for the loss? Is it true that bilingual education is valuable as training although the Slovene language has practically no commercial application? While the nationally conscious Slovenes desire 'parallel but equal' educational facilities, the assimilated and more economically oriented Slovenes have their doubts about them and do not oppose the government which prefers gradual assimilation. Should a majority in an individual parish have the right to compel the minority to partake or not to partake of training in the Slovene language? Anyway, how does one define a Slovene? Should the historical element be taken into account that so many members of the nation have been forcibly assimilated to the German-speaking Austrians? Should therefore their children be given the opportunity to become de-assimilated by introducing them to their paternal culture? The problems have been put in the form of questions because no clear answers are available.

Boundaries between nations are generally blurred, giving rise to complications with the institution of the territorial state. Existing political, state boundaries often do not coincide with historical, economic or strategic boundaries. They never fully coincide with national boundaries: no state encompasses only one nation and no nation is wholly encompassed in one single state.

The historical relationship between nation and state varies: in Western Europe states preceded nations which slowly evolved later within their existing boundaries; in central Europe nations preceded states and were instrumental in building them; again in contemporary Africa, states have preceded nations and nation-building is one of their most urgent and arduous tasks. Also the stage of evolution of any given nationalism should be taken into account. There is a general tendency for young nationalism to generate the heat of fanaticism, while mature, satisfied national-ism generally becomes more tolerant and less prone to conflict. The dynamism of change varies greatly from period to period and from continent to continent, and within them, in each single case.

Nationalism is an ideology which has caused many inter-national conflicts of a very serious nature but most of these arise from the inter-relationship between the nation and the state and could be, with some justification, ascribed largely to the institu-tion of the state. One source of conflict arises when a nation seeks statehood. Here the cases of German and Italian unification come to mind; conflicts over *terrae irredentae* and national min-orities were one of the basic themes of European politics from the third quarter of the nineteenth century until the Second World War. Now the problem has been greatly reduced. Physical elimination and great shifts of population unprecedented in size and in inhumanity, have brought state boundaries in Europe into much greater conformity with national boundaries. Some terri-torial disputes nevertheless persist and remain potentially grave: the German claims to the territories east of the Oder-Neisse lost to Poland; Austrian claims to South Tyrol; Rumanian-Hungarian differences over Translyvania. Even issues now apparently dormant could revive, such as the Yugoslav claims to parts of southern Austria or the Polish claim to the territories lost to the Soviet Union. On the other hand, the Alsace-Lorraine issue, for a long time a major obstacle to friendly French–German relations, seems to be finally settled.

Multi-national states and empires are today few. In the greatest of them, the Soviet Union, the non-Russian nationalities are becoming assimilated to an all-embracing Soviet nationalism but it is impossible to evaluate the length to which this process has gone until it is subjected to the test of a major political crisis. Admittedly in more difficult circumstances, the communist régime in Yugoslavia had pursued since 1945 an enlightened nationalities policy and had voiced the conviction that, with the elimination of nationalist oppression, the constituent nations had merged into the Yugoslav nation. In fact nationalist rifts revived in the mid sixties, this time based on the economic exploitation of the industrialized regions to develop the poorer ones as well as on tensions arising from liberalization. It is a hard fact of politics that national divisions retain a potential importance and, even after the major political issues involved have long died out, they tend to bedevil and complicate other social problems; thus, although Scottish nationalism is not a serious problem in the United Kingdom, since the Scots generally consider themselves as a separate nation, regional underdevelopment of their country raises much more acute conflicts than comparable problems arising, say, in north-east England. Even apparently well-integrated units can weaken, witness the rifts between the Flemish and the Walloons in Belgium or between the English- and the French-speaking Canadians. It is even conceivable that the existence of the Swiss nation, with origins going back to the thirteenth century, could be threatened by the integration of Europe since the French- and the Italian-speaking portions are subject to the cultural pulls of the respective two nations along the Swiss borders.

The most obvious nationalist problem is that of the divided nations – China, Germany, Korea, Vietnam. Each of the eight governments concerned proclaims that it seeks national unification and represents the true elements of the nation; each of them pursues a communist or anti-communist ideology under the protection of one of the Superpowers and is opposed by an ideologically hostile rival under the protection of the other Superpower.

If the nationalist situation is fluid and conflicts are possible in relatively well-established and stabilized political and national structures, it is even more confused in new states which have come into being since the last war as the result of decolonization. Although in most cases these states were preceded by what we loosely call 'nationalist movements', in fact these movements did not represent stabilized, integrated nations. Unity among their members generally prevailed as long as they were engaged in the struggle for independence but it did not survive independence. Colonial boundaries which cut right across tribal units and economic regions have been retained; regional, tribal, religious, linguistic, cultural, racial and all other differences, submerged during the struggle for independence, have come to the surface since its victorious ending. Strong fissiparous forces are clearly in existence in such different states as India, Ethiopia, Libera, the Sudan, Uganda, Ghana or Sierra Leone; in 1967 Nigeria and in 1971 Pakistan practically broke up; conflicts over *terrae irredentae* and national minorities endanger all regions: the claims of Somalia in East Africa, the boundaries between Thailand and Laos and between Cambodia and South Vietnam, Tunisian claims to Mauretania, are some of the outstanding examples. In the Third World, nationalism clearly does not coincide with state boundaries and this gives rise to grave instability. It is doubtful whether 'administrative' nationalist sentiments designed to fill the vacuum will ever take firm root and prevail against separatist forces, despite the great political efforts put into the task of national integration. If they ever do, this will take a long time which is bound to be marked by political instability.

Since nationalism is the overriding ideology, 'national interest' is the key concept in foreign policy. In essence, it amounts to the sum total of all the national values – national in both meanings of the word, both pertaining to the nation and to the state. This concept is rather vague. One common-sense definition describes it as the general and continuing ends for which the nation acts. It is thus characterized by its non-specific nature, by a degree of continuity, and by its connection with political action. If it is difficult to explain what national interest means in the abstract, it is quite impossible to find general agreement on what it implies in any specific issue. The recurrent major controversies on foreign policy centre around different ideas about what national interest indicates.

National interest need not be so narrowly defined as to exclude moral, religious and other altruistic considerations, but, to be effective, these must have been accepted as part of it. In actual practice it may not always make much difference whether a decision is made by a statesman who subscribes to the Hegelian theory that the state is the supreme good (which is the foundation of totalitarianism) or by another who believes that the state is merely an instrument to satisfy the needs of the citizens. As long as the state remains responsible for the welfare of its citizens in most avenues of life and the purveyor of many social needs, both may interpret national interest in a similar way. They may, however, greatly disagree if, in the future, more human needs have to be satisfied outside the confines of the state. On a narrow interpretation of national interest, all attempts at internationalization are bound to be treated with suspicion and, on the whole, resisted. On a liberal interpretation, no objections in principle need to be raised against reasonable transfers of powers and functions by the state.

All statesmen are governed by their respective national interests, but this does not mean that they can never agree on anything. On the contrary, they often do, but only on the basis of their respective conceptions of these national interests. If a statesman agrees to concessions, he does so only when he is convinced that this brings some advantage to his state, directly or indirectly. For instance, the favourable treatment of the trade of another country may secure not only trade openings but also friendship; support for a partly obnoxious international institution may be worth while in order to secure the continuation of its useful activities or to ensure international goodwill. Co-operation is conditional upon the existence of a suitable framework, of a reasonably stable international order within which the actions of other states are predictable and therefore rational foreign policy is possible. From here stems the interest of all states in this international order, again according to their national advantage. If they find this order congenial, they support it and if necessary defend it; if uncongenial, they endeavour to alter it accordingly.

At least for the time being, no alternative to one's own national interest is conceivable as a general guide to state activities. If a statesman were to give his allegiance to the national interest of another country this would be treason, and treason is extremely rare at the very top level of authority. If his first loyalty were to an international organization rather than to his own state, he would be unlikely to rise to a position in which foreign policy decisions are made. On a liberal interpretation of national interest, clashes between national and international loyalties can usually be avoided but, if one does occur, the statesman's first duty is clearly to his state.

## LIBERALISM, FASCISM, COMMUNISM AND SOCIALISM

Liberalism, fascism, communism and socialism are now the outstanding internationally significant ideologies. In a way all these cut across the boundaries of national states since they can be upheld by several states or by groups within several states. Indeed, being cross-national, these ideologies occasionally come into conflict with nationalism and lead to subversion, e.g. whenever an ideology opposed by the government is employed to appeal to the people as a whole or to a minority. Since we are dealing only with the international aspects of ideologies, we must skip over their impact upon domestic politics except in so far as these affect foreign relations. Two general points can be made about all ideologies; first, they all started about and within domestic politics and became relevant for international politics after some delay. The major agency through which they affect the latter are nation-states which have accepted these ideologies. Discussion of the international impact of ideologies must therefore stress their inter-relationship with nationalism. Second, various meanings are assigned to all of them and there is no agreement on definitions.

*Liberalism* or *liberal democracy* is the ideology characteristic of Western states. Its major feature is its primary concern with the individual rather than the community and with his freedom and welfare. In domestic politics the liberals are divided into two opposed schools: one conservative, *laissez faire*, non-interventionist, and the other progressive, concerned with social welfare, interventionist. In international politics, the liberal ideology can lead to withdrawal and/or concentration upon generalities, but it does also readily lead to interventionism. Liberals like to see all other states liberal; this led in the past to colonialism and exploitation under the guise of some form of *mission civilisatrice* or 'the white man's burden'; it has also led to the two World Wars 'fought for democracy' and to the Cold War waged against communism since 1945. The major dilemma of a liberal is how to come to terms with his nation-state if the latter infringes upon the individual, upon libertarianism. He can become reconciled with his state and support national expansion which leads to international conflicts but this is not inherent in his beliefs. Individualism and libertarianism are not readily acceptable to the Third World since their historical connexion with imperialism is obnoxious.

*Fascism* starts with the opposite assumption – that the collective is the main thing and the individual only serves its purposes. In spite of its international appeal to all anti-liberals (and anti-socialists), fascism invariably becomes strongly enmeshed in nationalism and encourages the ambitions of the nation-state towards expansionism and hence international conflict. Interwar Germany, Italy and Japan are the classical examples but the name 'fascist' has been applied to many interwar and post-war régimes in a rather loose sense. Its stress on the nation-state holds some appeal for the Third World.

*Communism* is an ideology which claims exact, scientific foundations but nevertheless it is not immune to great differences of interpretation among its adherents. It is perhaps inevitable in the dialectical nature of communism, in its insistence on the study of the two opposite aspects of every phenomenon, that conflict and harmony should get confused in the minds of its supporters. In the short run, communism leads to domestic conflicts aiming at the removal of existing régimes through fostering class struggle and, after victory, at the elimination of all opponents. By accepting as an 'inevitable' goal of history a fully communized world, and by striving to subvert and eliminate non-communist régimes it leads also to international conflicts. In the longer run, however, communist theory posits harmony – at home, within a communist society in which class exploitation and class conflict have been eliminated, internationally, in an all-communist world where imperialism and hence conflict among states have disappeared.

The striking historical phenomenon has been the merger between communist and nationalistic ideologies, first in the Soviet Union, then in Yugoslavia and China, and lately in other communist states. Whereas to an opponent of communism this appears to present the dangerous combination of the conflict propensities of both nationalism and communism, it is possible to consider the phenomenon as potentially advantageous. International harmony is less likely to be disturbed by communism harnessed with nationalism which, we know, can mellow, than by communism preserved in its purity.

Through an accident of history, against Marx's prognosis, communism developed first in Russia, a country industrially undeveloped. It became through this enmeshed with large-scale economic planning which, despite its shortcomings, has made Russia the second greatest industrial Power. Although this connection of communism with development through planning is accidental and its success is due to the exceptional resources of the Soviet Union, the developmental aspect of communism makes it particularly attractive to the Third World. The appeals of communism are further enhanced by the lack of historical connection between Russia and imperialism except in the little known regions of Central Asia.

*Socialism* covers a broad spectrum of beliefs in equality, in promotion of human welfare through governmental action. At the one end it merges with liberalism. Socialist or social democratic parties of various persuasions not only exist in all liberal states, but often they form governments or participate in governmental coalitions. Even in the United States, which is doctrinally opposed to socialism, clearly socialist welfare measures are gradually being accepted despite the fear of 'creeping socialism'. At the other end, socialism merges with communism. Both stem from the same doctrinal, Marxist origin although communism went much further away from its humanist, liberal elements.

It is one of the outstanding features of the contemporary world that socialism has become married to nationalism.* This

* cf. David Thomson, *World History, 1914-63*, Oxford University Press, 2nd ed., 1967, or Geoffrey Barraclough, *An Introduction to Contemporary History*, Watts, 1964.

has happened in all political contexts. The nationalist penetration of the communist variety of socialism has already been touched upon. The interpenetration of liberalism and socialism was accompanied by fusion with nationalism since both are firmly anchored to the nationalist ideologies of the individual states. It is true that in the West nationalism is mature, less fanatical and more open to ideas of supra-national integration. It is also a fact that the socialist parties of the European Economic Community cooperate within the European Parliament on ideological lines rather than with their national parties of different ideological persuasion. This cooperation does not, however, extend to politics outside the relatively unimportant European Parliament and Marx's anticipation that horizontal class alignments will overcome vertical state alignments has not been fulfilled.

The most interesting interaction between nationalism and socialism takes place in the Third World where it is largely determined by the stage of political evolution.* In the early pre-independence phase nationalism tends to be 'radical' mainly, often exclusively, in relation to colonialism but it often absorbs a socialist developmental ideology in the last phase of the struggle. After the achievement of independence which is the apogee of nationalism, socialism serves a useful role in deflecting from the government popular dissatisfaction which is bound to arise owing to the inability of the rulers to satisfy 'the revolution of rising expectations'; foreign firms and wealthy members of other races serve as convenient scapegoats while manipulation of taxes and exchange rates can provide a temporary relief from economic troubles. The policy can be pursued also internationally, together with other 'have-not' states, by exercising pressures upon the 'haves' for more aid and better terms of trade. In the longer run, however, radical socialism proves unsuccessful in providing the goods; expertise and administrative skills rather than its profession become the required qualification of civil servants, at least at lower levels of authority. Of course rulers can revert to socialist priorities, as Julius Nyerere did in Tanzania in the later sixties.

*cf. David E. Apter, *The Politics of Modernization*, Chicago University Press, 1966, pp. 335–43.

In sum, socialism and its variant, communism, have penetrated nationalist ideologies all over the world. Despite the considerable degree of both domestic and international conflict involved in the process, once accomplished this penetration may form a reasonable basis for an international ideology, no longer bound to one or a few national states but common to all mankind.

## IDEOLOGIES COMMON TO MANKIND

For mankind as a whole, nationalism is divisive and often, though not necessarily, it gives rise to conflicts. The other ideologies mentioned have become closely allied to nationalism. There are, however, less articulated systems of values which have not undergone this process of nationalization and, being common to mankind, seem to offer a basis for world-wide harmony. 'Seem to offer' rather than 'offer', since their interpretation differs according to the particularist and nationalized ideologies held by those who interpret them. Instead of making for harmony, they occasionally cause conflict.

One such distinct cluster or system of values is called '*Human Rights*'. There exists a world-wide agreement on generalities. The United Nations Charter and the Declaration of Human Rights, which has been accepted by nearly all states, can be adequately summed up by the fundamental catalogue of 'life, liberty and pursuit of happiness'. Agreement dwindles and even disappears when we are faced with particulars, when we get involved in the analysis of what social restraints on liberty are unavoidable and what is the best way of enabling the individual to pursue his happiness. Years have been spent on hammering out the details of United Nations Covenants of Human Rights which, in distinction from the Declaration, will have legal and not merely moral implications. It is possible to claim rather cynically that all Human Rights discussions have been fruitless and have merely bared ideological disagreements between East and West; but it is also possible to regard them as an inevitably slow and laborious process of overcoming national and ideological boundaries towards a world-wide value system. In one respect at least, in the field of racial discrimination, the discussions have led to near-general condemnation of its major manifestations.

The other allied and to some extent overlapping clusters of world-wide values are rationalism, 'scientism', and the belief in the value of development.

*Rationalism* is rarely mentioned perhaps because it is readily taken for granted. Not only liberal but also communist societies pursue ideologies which have grown in the matrix of Western European rationalism in the nineteenth century; the Third World wants to follow suit at least in its scientific and economic development. However much some nations and other groups press for the recognition of moral and religious values as a basis of harmonious international relations, they do not dispute the idea that these relations should be conducted rationally, on the basis of intellectual processes rather than emotions. Unfortunately, it is only the *idea* of rationalism that is universal. Reason no less than God is understood in many differing and sometimes conflicting ways and does not help international harmony any more than the common idea of God helps inter-religious harmony. As a common belief in a Higher Being did not prevent Christians and Moslems, or even Christians among themselves, from engaging in violent conflicts, so common belief in the supremacy of reason does not prevent conflict over the meaning of its application. It scarcely makes much difference in international conflicts whether you call your opponents heretics or infidels or, as we do today, irrational. It will take a lot of mental effort to fathom the implications behind the different systems of logic employed – the dialectical one in communist régimes, the formal Aristotelian one in the liberal West, let alone those of Oriental cultures.

'*Scientism*' gives fewer grounds for disagreement. We must make here a reservation only regarding the peculiar notions of 'Marxist science' which influences the appreciation of scientific investigations not only in social sciences but even in a field ostensibly as remote from politics as genetics. On the whole there exists not only a world-wide agreement that the development of science is a high-ranking value but also a fair agreement about what this development means within each field. Notwithstanding all their ideological differences, scientists from all over the world can meet and evaluate their activities by the same criteria. Rationalism, 'scientism' and the allied belief in the fundamental importance of education have been the foundation of the United Nations Educational, Scientific and Cultural Organization.

The *belief in development* deceptively resembles 'scientism'. If we accept the value of scientific progress and agree on the whole about its meaning, it should be likewise easy to accept the extension of this value from pure to applied science, to the management of human affairs to secure greater material satisfactions. Whatever the present economic level may be, over the whole spectrum between abject poverty and considerable affluence, there exists a substantial agreement about the desirability of economic growth. Unfortunately, economic growth produces many unwelcome social repercussions. To the substantial criticism of 'development' voiced hitherto only by Western intellectuals and by the romantic, in our eyes 'luddite' opposition of some traditionalists in the Third World, we must now add the grave doubts expressed in 1967 by Julius Nyerere, the President of Tanzania. He questioned the wisdom of pursuing development by the present means which include massive industrialization, largely aided from abroad, and also the value of its results. Perhaps some form of much slower, evolutionary change based on the ideas of Gandhi rather than Western patterns, may eventually emerge. And yet, with all the differences of interpretation and all the competing and conflicting methods of supplying and acquiring foreign aid, one harmonious element arises from the value of 'development' – the feeling of world-wide solidarity, of the interconnection between all the states, the responsibility of the rich to assist the poor.

## Objectives

One of the conclusions of the preceding sections was that values and ideologies do not fully determine foreign policy objectives although they influence their direction. While long-range objectives can be reasonably well deduced from an ideology, the shorter the time-scale, the less the necessary correlation between the aspirations and the actual policies. When it comes to day-to-day conduct of state affairs, to the tactics of foreign policy, expediency usually takes precedence over ideological guidance and the behaviour of states may not be influenced much by the latter. Thus, when we assert that communism demands the communization of other countries, we may safely assume that the long-range objectives of the Soviet government are directed towards this end. We are not, however, justified in assuming that its immediate international behaviour, that its short-range objectives are invariably determined by its endeavour to reach the communization of the world as soon as possible. If nothing else, Soviet experiences with China have shown that the blessings of dealing with other communist states are mixed. It requires investigation whether the régime may not be fairly genuine in its avowed and credible desire to settle to some form of 'peaceful coexistence', leaving further spread of the ideology mainly to the 'inevitable process of history'.

The treatment of the subsequent elements will be shorter than that of ideologies. They are generally more familiar and better understood and the literature on international relations caters for them very well* whereas the direct impact of ideologies on political behaviour is often neglected.

The first important limitation upon the significance of the ideology, of the values pursued, lies in the counterposition of values and environment in the minds of the decision-makers. The two extremes in one's attitudes to the relevance of environmental restraints are determinism and voluntarism, belief in free will. Actually nobody can be an out-and-out determinist, believing that environmental constraints fully determine foreign policy objectives and that all that the statesman can do is to learn as much as possible about them and to adjust his objectives accordingly. Likewise nobody can be a total voluntarist since in the international society the free wills of all the constituent units come up against one another, precluding complete freedom of action, as the wills of the individuals confront one another in

* cf. K. J. Holsti, *International Relations*, New York, Prentice-Hall, 1967.

domestic societies. The common-sense middle position between the two extremes is some form of 'possibilism', of recognition that the environment is malleable to some extent, but not to the full extent desired by us, that it both offers a scope for action and incorporates obstacles beyond which action cannot proceed, or can do so only at an exorbitant cost.

By itself, a bias towards determinism or voluntarism does not necessarily influence the conflict-harmony dimension of the policies pursued. Both can be employed to rationalize behaviour and to mobilize the people to endure hardship and danger. These can be demanded when personal fate is considered as pre-ordained, as by the Moslems during their religious wars against the Christians, or when the victory of one's side is 'inevitable', as claimed by the fanatical communists; they can, however, be justified also by the voluntarist liberal democracies who believe that the outcome of the great issues is open and that even the gravest dangers can be warded off, although often only at the cost of the greatest sacrifices and efforts.

If we consider the making of foreign policy, the choice of its objectives, as a rational activity, we can usefully analyse it as the exploration of the environment in order to find out the restraints upon our actions as well as the opportunities to secure our values, and estimate the likely cost to be incurred. Undoubtedly the Soviet rulers engage in this activity when determining policy objectives which arise from their ideologically prescribed expansion of communism. Since United States foreign policy constitutes the major restraint existing in the Soviet environment, the policies actually pursued by the Americans can be usefully interpreted in the suggested terms. Thus, 'negotiating from strength' meant adding substance to the constraints encountered by the Russians; 'containment' meant drawing a reasonably clear boundary and indicating that expansion beyond this would provoke a major war; the policy of publicizing instead of keeping secret, as in the past, the strength of American armaments, served the purpose of making Soviet rulers appreciate the magnitude of the existing restraints; 'nuclear deterrence', particularly in its phase of 'massive retaliation' aimed at reducing the Soviet inclination to risk-taking by making risks uncertain and also overwhelming. If all these policies are interpreted in the terms suggested, on the assumption of Soviet expansionism, it is arguable that the Americans had achieved their major objective of strengthening the restraints, making the potential adversary aware of them, and making him less prone to risk-taking.

The value, the ideological component, is by its nature predominantly volitional, it expresses what we desire to achieve. Recognizing the nature of the environment, determining how much freedom of action it permits, is largely a cognitive element. Before explaining their inter-relationship we must consider the link between them formed in the mind of the decision-makers. In every given situation, the latter are forced to define all the relevant conditions, whether they are domestic or international, whether they pertain to the past, to the present or to the future. The crucial element in this 'definition of the situation' is what we usually call the '*image*'.

Although policy objectives have naturally to be pursued in the real world which is our 'operational environment', our information about this world, upon which we base these decisions, can never be complete and is always at some variance with it. 'Image', a concept first developed in the context of international relations by Kenneth E. Boulding,* does not amount to objective 'knowledge'. It is an internal, psychological concept, the sum total of what penetrates our cognition and is organized into a rather complex structure of subjective knowledge. The image is only an incomplete reflection of reality, peculiar to the individual or the group or the nation holding it. It is therefore a logical exaggeration to call it a 'lie', as Boulding does. The image determines 'the psychological environment' within which decisions are made and hence the deviations from reality, 'the distortions' it involves, can be highly significant for harmony-conflict analysis.

It is therefore useful to investigate how images are organized and how they are frequently manipulated to justify human excesses, cruelty, and outright violence. If major distortions of international images were avoided or at least greatly reduced, if national images were less at loggerheads with the operational environment within which national activities take place, as well

* Kenneth E. Boulding, *The Image*, Oxford University Press, 1957.

as with one another, we might eliminate quite a substantial potential source of conflicts arising from misunderstandings about the environment. Thus the argument is often advanced that had the Germans fully realized that Great Britain would enter the war on the side of the French, the war in 1914 might have been prevented.

At the same time, however, we must not make an assumption that the operational environment is harmonious, that realization of its real nature would eliminate conflict. On the contrary, the operational environment harbours many potential conflicts and fuller understanding of their nature as well as of the restraints operating may increase rather than decrease conflict. The images held about reality by the various states are themselves an important element of reality. The image one state holds of the capabilities and intentions of another state largely determines its policy in relation to its own capabilities and intentions, this in turn affects the image held by the first state, and so on and so forth. The 'mirror-effect' of the mutually held images magnifies their impact and perpetuates them in time. To a large extent images become 'self-fulfilling prophesies'; if they grossly deviate from reality in the present, they may easily affect future reality by being reflected in the images and behaviour of other states. Hence the crucial importance of images for the issue of conflict-harmony. Images can multiply and exacerbate the existing conflicts; they can also reduce them both in number and in gravity.

Images are shaped by our past experiences which provide us with clues for the selection of the elements of perception which we deem sufficiently important to register, and for their organization into a reasonably coherent whole. Once adopted, these images have a strong staying power for the simple reason that they are, to a large extent, self-justifying and therefore self-perpetuating. Information from our environment is taken in only if it corresponds with the image we hold and hence all information adverse to it can be easily ignored, even if our image shows some gross, dangerous deviation from reality. As long as we get sufficient 'evidence' from the area of reality to which our image sensitizes us, we find it easy to leave out of account the remainder, even if the messages that come from it contradict our image. Images cannot be easily adapted; it normally requires a real jolt to make us realize how far astray our image may have taken us. In a way, our conservatism with regard to images is even more fundamental and inescapable than our conservatism with regard to values: values and ideologies can be scaled down to less far-reaching objectives; images affect action directly as there is no mechanism for adapting them.

Having confronted in his mind his relevant values and the image of the relevant sector of the environment, the decision-maker determines his objectives. He endeavours to implement his values as far as the environment, as filtered through its image in his mind, will permit it. Here he performs, usually subconciously, two operations: he counts the cost and he estimates the risks. The *costing* cannot, of course, be done with anything approaching the precision of costing in economics which reduces all values to money. Costs in international politics can be of all kinds, in terms of all other possible values; hence their estimate varies greatly from period to period, from country to country, and from individual to individual. In terms of the subjective value-calculus, it is quite feasible that the cost involved in a policy decision is quite reasonable for the decision-maker, however unreasonable it may appear to others. For instance, refusal of foreign aid owing to relatively mild conditions attaching to its dispensation, or even when it is offered unconditionally but by a suspect or disliked donor, may be absurd to an economically minded Western critic of a developing country. From the point of view of the leaders of that country, however, this may be well worth while; the cost of forfeiting the economic benefits may seem to them slight compared with that of jeopardizing, however little, their political independence.

*Risk-taking* is even more subjective than cost-counting. The statesman or the political scientist investigating a policy decision may calculate, in the subjective terms explained, the costs of the options available and the approximate probabilities of success of these options. It may sometimes be possible even to quantify by multiplying the estimated values of the outcomes by their respective probability coefficients. But what to do when outcomes are similar, when for instance the 25 per cent probability of gaining a million pounds has to be matched with a 50 per cent probability of gaining half a million?

An analogy between statesmen and roulette-players does not take us very far. Admittedly some statesmen are more cautious, less prone to take risks than others, and tend to choose the safer though possibly less profitable course. When, however, we reach the area of really serious risks, gambling by statesmen becomes much less likely. Few of them feel entitled, when playing their political roles, to risk the equivalent of a total loss sometimes sustained by the individual roulette-player. When matters of life and death are at stake, in the upper reaches of the range of risk-taking, the great cultural and individual differences in the propensity to take risks are bound to diminish. About risk-taking below this danger zone, two opposed hypotheses can be advanced. The first one is that a real 'have-not' state has little to lose and hence a lot to gain; therefore it will be prone to risk-taking; the more a state has to lose, the more conservative and averse to risk will it become. This is a possible interpretation of the mellowing of Soviet foreign policy. On the other hand, greater resources spell greater power and ability to win as well as greater capacity to replace serious losses; they may encourage rather than discourage the taking of grave risks. The choice thus seems to depend more upon cultural and personal variables than upon resources.

Analysis of risk-taking is applicable to nuclear strategy, especially to massive retaliation. Here, as in other circumstances, the inclination to take risks rapidly declines with the gravity of the risk involved.

From the angle of the harmony-conflict issue, it could be argued that careful costing and a conservative attitude to risk-taking would tend to diminish the range and scale of conflicts; hence scientific investigation of these directly contributes to the fostering of harmony.

## CHAPTER 6

# POWER, INFLUENCE AND CAPABILITIES

## Power and Influence

BEING central to politics, the concept of 'power' gives rise to a surge of conflicting feelings and interests which obscures both its understanding and its actual use; no wonder that no definition of power can gain general currency. Most modern definitions are concerned with the relational nature of power and agree that it denotes the capacity to produce intended results. Specifically, political power is not over nature, a material, or oneself, but over the minds and actions of other people. One speaks about power when its possession or exercise makes a difference to the behaviour of others, whether of individuals or states. Talking about the exercise of power would scarcely make sense if they would anyway, of their own volition, behave in the desired fashion; this would be a case of cooperation based upon community of interests.

So defined, 'power' means something similar to the cognate notion of 'influence'. The distinction between the two is usually made by reference to the coercive qualities of power although there is no clear boundary between the two. A whole gamut of possible permutations arises in every situation: coercion may exist in the background as an ultimate stimulus or constraint, although no reference is made to it, or a threat of its use may be made in a variety of veiled or open ways, or ultimately power may be actually used, again, in all kinds of ways, ranging from a demonstration or mild application of force to unrestrained violence.

On this definition of power as a relational concept rather than an essence, we cannot go very far in the analysis of the power of any unit in the abstract; we must specify in relation to whom and for what purpose. We do, of course, distinguish between some very general categories based upon the usual attributes of power and say that some individuals or states are strong and others weak but this, too, is of limited use in explaining any concrete relationship. For instance, a slightly built minister of the Church would be classified as 'weak' in terms of physical strength and it is clear that he would not be able to match in a physical struggle a heavy-weight boxer. His spiritual endurance, however, may be so much greater that if the two were confined together under conditions of great stress, e.g. in a political prison, the minister may be able to influence and even coerce the boxer to do as he is bid.

Discrepancies in power affect relations between states in conflicting ways. Sometimes they make little difference; often brawn prevails, the state which has more men, more guns and more money has its way; there are also cases of David challenging Goliath and winning in a contest of wills despite much smaller capabilities. The imbalance in resources can be redressed by the added resources of other states, by the constraints arising from the international system, and also by the greater determination of the less powerful state which, in extreme cases, can take the form of a 'suicidal alternative', the determination to perish rather than give in. Whichever the method by which the imbalance of resources is redressed in any given relationship, power analysis must realistically take it into account.

Although power relationships in real life are diffuse and defy clear-cut classifications, these classifications can be usefully made in theory for the purpose of conceptual clarification; in a real-life situation the various aspects and elements can then be more readily arranged into coherent groups. One fundamental distinction can be made between powers of defence which are to a larger extent self-regarding, and powers used to induce other states to act. Some social objectives can be achieved by suitable domestic politics without involving other states and, in a state which is self-sufficient, independent of other states for the achievement of its objectives, the power required in international politics would be limited to the purposes of defence. Historically, in modern Europe the concept of power developed this way; in the days of relative self-sufficiency and limited international interchanges, it was defined by the capacity to defend the state's territory against possible attackers; if a state was expansionist, its power was defined in a similar way – by the capacity to take over the territory of another state. No wonder that power came to be defined predominantly although, as will be explained later, not exclusively in terms of its military elements.

An increasing proportion of social objectives cannot be satisfied by domestic policies alone; they require some cooperation by other states. In situations where other states are supposed to do something, to act, instead of merely being deterred from attacking, a much more intricate power relationship evolves. Predominant military force may suffice to overrun the territory of another state but not to ensure occupation and performance of the act required. People resist with real determination when they fight in defence of their independent existence; they seem to draw strength from two fundamental attachments – to their nation, which many regard as an enlarged family, and to their territory.* From the concept of a predominantly military coercive power we move in the direction of less coercive influence. This change differs greatly from relationship to relationship; while military power is still playing a predominant, arguably even an exclusive role in Arab–Israeli or Indian–Pakistani relations, its role has been very much reduced in the relations between the United States and Canada or Great Britain, in Scandinavia, or in Western Europe.

Although power is undoubtedly central in international politics, many people seem to be excessively preoccupied, occasionally positively obsessed, with it. This may be partly explained by the crucial importance of the issues involved since miscalculation may spell disaster. Partly, however, this preoccupation may be due to persisting historical patterns of thinking based upon power-relations of the past; the contemporary patterns are too confused and of too recent origin to be fully grasped.

*R. Ardrey in *The Territorial Imperative*, Collins, 1967, seeks a general principle of international politics in the defence of biologically needed territory. However exaggerated, his argument strikingly describes an important aspect of some international conflicts, e.g. of the North Vietnamese resistance to the United States.

The predominant role of power both in political reality and in political thought has resulted in power-relationships being considered the determining factor in all classifications of international systems. This seems to be justified and we shall now try to analyse the concept further and classify its major types or categories. In accordance with the previously suggested tripartite division of political situations, we shall distinguish 'coercive', e.g. military power, largely corresponding with 'fights'; 'utilitarian', e.g. economic or technological power, largely employed in 'games'; and psychological or 'identitive' power, used mainly in 'debates'.*

Even during the balance-of-power system centred upon territorial defence and military power, the utilitarian and the identitive types of power were exercised, although they remained subsidiary. Thus utilitarian, economic power describes the system of subsidies and loans to allies employed by Britain and France during the nineteenth century which was made possible by the rapid economic development of these states and the urgent economic needs of the recipients. Identitive power before the birth of modern psychology could only be adumbrated. Sir Eyre Crowe in his famous memorandum on British relations with France and Germany written in 1907 spoke about 'the general desires and ideals common to all mankind' with which British national policy should be identified in order to avoid the 'universal jealousy and fear' which a dominant power could expect. He discussed in greater detail the specific adjustments which should be made in relations with the allies and with Germany. Mutual adjustments of interests and policies had, of course, been the traditional give and take of diplomacy, but Sir Eyre seems to consider the matter in broader, identitive, cooperative terms. If Britain and the others looked at international politics as a common enterprise serving common purposes, Britain's powers would be much greater than otherwise.

One can describe the utter lack of the identitive power of Germany as one of the major reasons for the failure of her challenge to Britain's naval supremacy early in this century. According to

* A similar scheme is proposed by A. Etzioni, in *Political Unification*, New York, Holt, Rinehart & Winston, 1965, p. 37.

Ludwig Dehio's brilliant analysis,* the German naval challenge aimed at the establishment of a sufficiently strong naval force to form a nucleus of a counterpart to the dominant British force. It was based upon the expectation that other naval Powers would embrace the opportunity to end Britain's naval domination and to extend the principle of the balance of power to the Seven Seas. Following this principle, the other naval Powers were supposed to join the weaker, German side; since they refused to do so, we can say that Britain prevailed over Germany in identitive powers. We must, of course, bear in mind that modern propaganda had not yet developed at that time and therefore neither the policies nor their contemporary analysis could be expected to be articulate and explicit.

The meaning of power in the contemporary international system differs in several important respects from its meaning in the last century. First, the meaning of military security has completely changed. With the development of modern missiles and of nuclear weapons, no state can ensure that its territory will remain immune to attack, however great its military forces may be. The policy of mutual deterrence is employed by the two Superpowers but cannot be regarded as anything but precarious; it makes sense only marginally for the weaker Nuclear Powers. In fact, no state today can ensure the security of its territory by its own military power, even if it can add that of numerous allies. The only form of security which seems logically feasible, although it may be politically unattainable, is through the stability of the international system itself.

The second important feature of our international system can be identified in the multiplication of units as well as of international transactions. Power means something different in every set of relations; power suitable for one purpose or for a set of similar purposes, adequate for dealing with one state, may not serve another purpose or relationship at all; in fact it may have a negative value, it may become 'counterproductive'. The greater the international involvement of a state, the greater the difficulties arising, as shown by the contrast between the perfect

* *Germany and World Politics in the Twentieth Century*, Chatto & Windus, 1959.

matching of power to the needs of small countries like Israel or North Vietnam when contrasted with the obvious incapacity of the United States to prevail over North Vietnam.

The third change has arisen from the growing importance of the people as distinct from their governments. This new, twentieth-century phenomenon has given rise to a whole range of complications. When a government is unpopular and faces a discontented population, it becomes dependent on outside support; this vests power in the major supporting state, e.g. the Soviet Union in her relations with Eastern Germany. A divorce between the people and their government enhances the power also of states unfriendly to the régime by opening the path for direct address to the people, for support of opposition, and for subversion. Advantages to other states are not, however, quite clear-cut since, when government and people are at loggerheads, power over the one weakens power over the other. Moreover, an outside attempt to drive a wedge between the rulers and the ruled can lead to the opposite result by cementing national solidarity; for instance the misguided Suez action in 1956 raised Arab patriotism and restored Nasser's waning popularity. Similarly, destructive power exercised over the people, as in North Vietnam, in the hope of breaking the determination of either the government or the people, if not both, seems to produce the opposite psychological effect and to strengthen unity.

Since power can serve so many, sometimes dichotomous purposes, it obviously cannot serve them all. The idea of flexible multi-purpose power is attractive but unfortunately unattainable. Failing better ideas, states usually pursue the customary methods of securing power even though they are not necessarily convinced that these are the most reasonable ones to serve their purposes. It is hard to test these methods conclusively but it is even harder to test possible innovations; the only existing guides are tradition and imitation of the powerful and successful states. Occasionally, really important breakthroughs such as propaganda through radio, or nuclear weapons, appear upon the scene; very soon it becomes fashionable to imitate these.

Often the question is quite reasonably asked whether money spent for foreign policy purposes is really economically spent.

What about all the costly weapons that are obsolescent by the time they reach production and anyway appear unsuited for the emergencies then arising, particularly nuclear weapons which are never supposed to be used and, in the case of the lesser Nuclear Powers, could scarcely deter? What about the expenditure for propaganda which often antagonizes, and for aid which secures no friendship? And yet in one real sense all such expenditure makes sound sense if we think about the various methods of exercising power not in terms of the direct application of the instruments available but in terms of the prestige attaching to their possession. Possession of modern weapons systems may not be useful for winning a specific fight, the propaganda apparatus may be highly ineffective in a specific relationship, aid may be resented rather than applauded. Yet, if we consider them from the angle of being the accepted appurtenances of powerful states, the prestige accruing from them may be a sufficient justification for the expenditure of the resources involved.

If this seems unreasonable and wasteful, is there a better alternative? If we look at the way the much more easily measurable economic power is expressed, we find that all societies evolve some form of its demonstration which is socially accepted although it cannot be considered as rational *per se*. It makes little difference whether this takes the place of financing a public feast, or of buying the latest machine, gadget or article of clothing, or any other form of 'conspicuous consumption'. In most connotations political power is a potential which cannot be measured since it has not been actually used; what other yardsticks are available but the currently held views about the often untested potentialities which constitute prestige? On such a reasoning there is a rational justification for the nuclear weapons expenditure by France or Britain even if the strategic uses of these weapons seem to be dubious. Ultimately it does not matter so much what the actual capabilities of the state are; what is important is what other states estimate them to be. These estimates may have as little bearing upon actuality as the fluctuating exchange prices of shares sometimes have upon the assets and prospects of earnings of industrial companies. On the whole, the two coincide but sometimes they do not. A high value put upon shares is of paramount immediate importance; if it is very exaggerated, it may involve long-term risks but these, however serious, may never materialize. Likewise an exaggerated notion of the state's power is always welcome and, in the short run, profitable. Discrepancies between the actual power and the prestige enjoyed carry grave long-run risks since, as history proves, eventually somebody will challenge the state and prick the bubble of its power. Nevertheless, the temptation to enjoy happily the prestige and to neglect the actual underlying capabilities is repeated in all times and places. States are vigilant only in situations of danger; when they enjoy a secure and high prestige, their vigilance tends to slacken.

In a relatively stable international system, power is measured by the traditionally accepted basic capabilities. Thus, when towards the end of the nineteenth century Germany decided to challenge the British naval preponderance which was then based largely upon prestige backed by obsolete capabilities, she clearly had to express her challenge in the form of rival naval construction. Today the yardsticks of power are more numerous and less clear. It is arguable that all the traditional attributes of power have lost their customary significance through nuclear saturation. In the words of General Pierre M. Gallois, 'the atom neutralizes the armed multitudes, equalizes the size of populations, shrivels geographical distances, levels mountains, reduces the advantage which the "Giants" derived only yesterday from the vast dimensions of their territories (retreat in space), and disregards atmospheric conditions ("General Winter").'* Since the validity of the traditional standards is dubious, it has become easier to reverse power roles. As stated by the foreign minister of France, a country which itself manages to exercise some power notwithstanding the lack of its major attributes, 'the weak who know how to play on their weakness are strong. This is the secret of women and of the developing countries.'†

* *Pour ou contre la force de frappe*, p. 44, quoted by W. W. Kulski, *De Gaulle and the World*, Syracuse, N.Y., Syracuse University Press, 1966, p. 98.

† M. Couve de Murville, *Observer*, 24 January 1965.

Power relations are usually asymmetrical, one party being dominant and the other one subject, but the asymmetry is never complete or constant and, indeed, can sometimes be completely reversed. The traditional element of power, instead of continuing to serve the purposes of the dominant party, begins to play the opposite role, leading to its dependence upon the subject party. Thus donors of aid cannot let down their more prominent protégés without losing prestige and also accentuating the basic insolvency of all other countries receiving aid; British oil investments and financial interests in the Middle East make her vulnerable to Arab threats. The power relationship could, of course, be reversed again in the original direction if the donors decided to ignore the political and financial risks and to abandon aid, or if Britain made up her mind to scrap her investments in the Middle East and used her position as the major market for the region's oil to ensure adequate compensation and regular supplies.

Perhaps the most promising broad view of the fluctuating power relationships can be gained by using an analogy to the five basic human relationships discerned by Confucius: ruler and subject, father and son, elder and younger brother, husband and wife, friend and friend. Most of these relationships are hierarchical but the power of the dominant party, however great, is never absolute; it is always subject to rules of propriety and law and the inferior party is expected, when necessary, not only to remonstrate but even to refuse obedience and rebel. In the stage of dissolution, when the 'mandate from heaven' seems to be receding, the emperor's powers wane while those of the subjects wax.

Relative weakness gives an opportunity not only for such reversal of roles but also for advantageous non-involvement. The power of the United States or the Soviet Union is bound to be circumscribed by the fact that they are forced to take sides in every single major issue in the world – in all conflict situations taking sides increases power over one side but automatically decreases it over the other. Much more advantageous is the position of a Middle Power, like France, which, lacking the power for intervention, can sometimes retain equally friendly relations with both sides, e.g. India and Pakistan, and can at least attempt to do so with the Soviet Union and China. Where France is sufficiently powerful to intervene, as in the Middle East, she faces the general dilemma of being unable to avoid antagonizing at least one side. In fact she got herself caught up in the contradictions of de Gaulle's policy. Trying to make amends to the Arabs for her large-scale deliveries of arms to Israel, she condemned, without reservation, the Israeli action in 1967; nevertheless, by 1971 she got into a serious controversy with Algeria.

Weakness, like power, is, of course, a relative concept; a ruler or a régime sometimes prevails as the only escape from chaos, simply because there is no more powerful alternative. Thus, for many years President Sukarno used to solve domestic political crises by going for prolonged world tours which managed to convince all his opponents that the only alternative to him would be complete anarchy. Similar was the admittedly uncertain and precarious source of strength of King Hussein of Jordan in the aftermath of his catastrophic defeat and losses in June 1967. The same is true about the survival of such states as Jordan or the Congo.

In the light of all these uncertainties it should scarcely surprise us that although states must obviously take note of their power in determining their foreign policy objectives, they are rarely, if ever, fully governed by it. History is full of cases of both over-commitment, i.e. a foreign policy with commitments greater than the power available, as well as under-commitment, i.e. policy which does not use actual or potential power to the full. The post-war predicament of Britain, burdened with the remaining post-imperial responsibilities, or of the United States, faced with commitments all over the world, are examples of the former; the United States in the period of isolationism or France and Britain in the thirties, are examples of the latter. International stratification, referred to above, is based upon attempts at leadership which, by definition, through their very success, show that they had been adequately backed by power. Many more attempts have failed, again by definition, owing to the lack of adequate power. The fact that we cannot judge whether power is adequate till after the event does not preclude its central importance. Clearly, however, although the states are generally so obsessed with power, they can never be sure whether their power calculations will stand the test of reality, and their behaviour is not primarily governed by such calculations.

## Capabilities

The measurement and comparison of capabilities is obviously important and necessary otherwise states would not, as they habitually do, spend colossal amounts of money on espionage and intelligence. There is, however, no hard and fast rule by which capabilities could be added up to a composite notion of power and, furthermore, as has been argued, power is not the measure of foreign policy; policy objectives are decided upon through the counterposition of values and of environmental restraints. Power is the important means to secure the objectives and overcome the restraints but is by no means the decisive factor. A calculation and comparison of 'the great essentials', the resources relevant for international power between 1925 and 1930, resulted in the ranking of the leading Powers in the following order: 1. The United States; 2. Germany; 3. Great Britain; 4. France; 5. The Soviet Union; 6. Italy; 7. Japan. When we try to rank these states according to the actual influence exercised by them in the period, we arrive at a completely different ranking. We have no clear indices for it, but the United States would be certainly relegated well to the end of the list while France would be elevated to the top.*

When analysing capabilities in order to elucidate the power relationship between any two states, it is important to start with the consideration of the way in which these capabilities can be used. In conformity with the tripartite division of political activities into debates, games and fights (the order has been reversed in order to avoid overstressing fights), state A in its desire to influence state B can either persuade it, or offer it inducements and rewards, or threaten it or inflict punishment (coerce it). A bare

* cf. F. H. Simonds and B. Emeny, *The Great Powers in World Politics*, 1939, quoted by K. J. Holsti, *International Politics*, New York, Prentice-Hall, 1967, p. 199.

analysis of capabilities will not suffice. We must also inquire whether state A has the will to use them and, even more importantly, whether state B believes this to be so; this is described as 'credibility' in nuclear strategy but applies also to non-nuclear capabilities. The reciprocal needs of the two sides must be assessed. If state A wants more from state B than state B wants from A, obviously A requires more capabilities; likewise it will require a larger balance of capabilities for a far-reaching objective than for a relatively trivial one. Finally, state B may be more or less responsive to supply A's wants and needs; the amount of capabilities necessary is bound to increase when the friendship and receptiveness of B diminishes.

Several general rules should govern the analysis of capabilities. First, we must beware of concentrating upon what is measurable to the neglect of the non-measurable elements. No hard and fast rule can be devised as to the proportion in which they should be taken into account. For their power significance, quantities must be qualified by quality. The fact that the Arabs command a population many times more numerous than Israel must be modified by the Israeli levels of education and of technological skills which proved decisive in their repeated confrontations. Second, the single capabilities must be compared within their general 'mix'. When a state has a surplus of one capability over its likely needs, this surplus has little significance. If, on the other hand, it is deficient in one capability, this may destroy the value of other capabilities which depend upon it. Thus the United States would not be weaker if it possessed a much lower steel-producing capacity for the simple reason that this capacity is well above her military and civil needs. Large populations are an element of weakness rather than strength when states lack land and other resources for feeding them adequately; shortages of supplies and weapons likewise reverse the value of large armed forces.

Thirdly, it cannot be taken for granted that the use to which capabilities are put is invariably equally relevant for power purposes. It would be, for instance, highly misleading to compare Soviet and American steel output on a ton for ton or on a per capita basis, merely allowing for the likely differences in quality.

Whereas practically all the Soviet steel is used for essential military or civilian purposes, much of the American output merely serves to replace machinery and gadgets which are going out of fashion although they are still perfectly serviceable. Weapons of similar characteristics have quite different values according to the mechanical skill with which they are maintained and used and the strategic doctrine in whose name they are employed. In 1940 a German tank used in large tank-formations was much more valuable than its mechanical counterpart attached to a French infantry regiment, owing to the superior German strategy. In 1967 even an obsolete Israeli aeroplane or tank was more than a match for its technologically more advanced counterparts used by the Egyptians who were highly deficient both in mechanical skills and in adequate strategy.

Fourthly, the destruction of the Egyptian aeroplanes on the ground during the 1967 war, or of the American fleet at Pearl Harbor in 1940, prove how vital it is to be ready: a time-lag in mobilization procedures or in the alert time required for planes and missiles can make a crucial difference.

Finally, we must bear in mind the incessant changes in the relative importance of the various capabilities. A 'mix' which is sound today may become extremely precarious if a capability in which the state is deficient suddenly rises in importance. By all standards the Soviet Union was an extremely powerful country at the end of the war; nevertheless the invention of nuclear weapons and their temporary monopoly by the United States destroyed overnight the Soviet military preponderance.

The major capabilities relevant for power relations are usually discussed in five major groups: demographic, geographical, economic, organizational and psychological-social, and international strategic. A detailed analysis seems unnecessary. This is an aspect of international relations with which most readers are likely to be quite familiar and on which all writings on the subject furnish much direct and indirect information.* We are concerned here only with the relevance of the single categories for the conflict-harmony issue and this is covered in the preceding

*e.g. J. Frankel, *International Relations*, Oxford University Press, 2nd ed., 1969, Chapter 4.

general remarks, and, indirectly, also in the next and the concluding chapters.

The bearing of power upon the issue of conflict and harmony has not been so far directly discussed because it was necessary first to clarify its relations with the choice of policy objectives. To sum up the argument, although in view of the general preoccupation with power this may sound paradoxical, power seems to be only a means which does not fully determine the ends. The hypothesis about its relation to conflict and harmony which logically emerges is that, similarly, power is not generally decisive in choices between conflict and harmony. A certain circularity may be expected: conflict relations lead to the choice of the appropriate capabilities and the possession of such capabilities may serve as an incentive to conflict relations. In view, however, of the great uncertainties about power, it never becomes the sole determinant of policy although it determines the outcomes of confrontations, of power clashes which frequently occur between states. It is obvious that some capabilities, especially in the military category, are much more closely connected with conflict than others. Nevertheless, despite arguments to the contrary raised by some supporters of disarmament, it seems scarcely reasonable to assume that the link is so powerful that the reduction or abolition of armaments would necessarily lead to an abatement of international conflict or to a substantial reduction in the violence employed for its resolution. In fact it seems much more likely that disarmament would follow the diminution of conflict rather than lead to it.

## Case-study: the Arab–Israeli Conflict

Since power has been of paramount importance in the Arab–Israeli conflict, a brief case-study will serve to test whether the relationship between capabilities and conflict is in fact so loose and erratic.

The Arab–Israeli conflict is particularly acute; it involved the two sides in three major fights, in 1948, 1956 and 1967, and has effectively prevented any cooperative relations. We shall concentrate upon the 1967 struggle and look retrospectively upon the preceding period and then briefly upon the subsequent developments and the likely future. The conflict relationship being so acute, we may legitimately start by asking why no major outbreaks of violence took place between 1956 and 1967? Was this due to some form of a balance of power or only to the international constraints exercised by the United Nations and its Emergency Force?

Israel had come into being by force of arms, in spite of strong opposition from the Arabs who did not become reconciled to her existence and refused to maintain any direct contacts with her. Hence the psychological, identitive type of power was irrelevant for their relationship – the Arabs could not persuade the Israelis to scrap their state any more than the Israelis could persuade them to recognize its existence. Israel possesses considerable utilitarian powers in the form of agricultural and industrial expertise adapted to Middle Eastern conditions which could be of great assistance in the economic development of the Arab world; these could be augmented by the substantial economic benefits which would accrue to the Arabs from American finance offered for such regional plans as the development of the waters of the River Jordan. To balance Israel's utilitarian powers, the Arabs control communications around her, especially the Suez Canal, produce oil which Israel needs, and could offer vast markets for her industry. It is difficult to estimate which side has the advantage of utilitarian power since these powers are only potential as long as the Arabs refuse to have any truck with Israel; one can surmise that the balance does not clearly lie with either side and that therefore there would be considerable scope for bargaining and for the application of the theory of games.

In the stark conflict relationship, only coercive powers were directly relevant and hence the major capabilities of the two sides must be considered from this angle. Quantitatively, the disparity between the Israelis and the Arabs is enormous, just over two million Israelis of Jewish origin confronting some forty-five million Arabs. This disparity in numbers is, however, counteracted by a reverse disparity in quality: the Israeli population has reached a very much higher educational and technological level than even the most advanced Arab countries. Even the large numbers of poorly educated Oriental immigrants have been successfully integrated into Israel's Western type industrial society. This qualitative difference cannot be quantified but its significance is clear; the 1967 war was won not only by the Israeli fighting services but as much, if not more, by the Israeli mechanics who maintained the frequently antiquated battle equipment at a high pitch of efficiency, much superior to that maintained by their Arab counterparts.

A similar disparity obtained between the sizes of the Israeli and Arab territories; here the imbalance was not redressed by any special qualities since the Israeli soil is not as fertile as the better parts of the Nile Valley or of Mesopotamia. It was, in fact, greatly worsened by an exceptionally poor strategic configuration. Israel was long and narrow, as little as ten miles in its narrowest part, its long boundaries were open to infiltrators and all its major cities were within reach of gunfire from across the border. All these strategic disadvantages for the Israelis meant strategic advantages for the Arabs. With respect to wealth and income, Israel was nowhere near the oil riches and the royalties flowing into the Arab world, although on the per capita basis her national income was much higher than that of most Arabs. At the same time, although fully dependent on continuous outside assistance, Israel managed to develop a modern industrial society, greatly superior in its organization to that of even the most advanced Arab countries.

It is in the organizational and the psychological-social group of capabilities that the Israelis readily scored. They commanded a well organized governmental apparatus with a well trained and disciplined military force as opposed to a loose grouping of several independent Arab states, badly organized in themselves and, moreover, poorly coordinated owing to their many feuds and rifts. Although all the Arabs seem to be united in intense anti-Israeli sentiments, their unity is not nearly as strong as that of the Israelis who fight for survival. Thus the Arabs fall short both of the efficient governmental institutions and of the basic psychological drives which give power to their opponents.

The international strategic capabilities were less unevenly distributed, but again in Israel's favour. The Arabs secured full support from the Soviet Union and the communist countries and also received partial support from Western countries. Israel secured a much more reliable and more intensive support (although smaller in volume) from the United States. She obtained also support and military equipment from France and Britain, her allies in the 1956 Suez expedition against Egypt, particularly from the former. In the West, concern with Israeli survival which was openly threatened by the Arabs generally prevailed against widespread sympathy with the Arabs for having been ousted from Israel, particularly with the million refugees still in their camps, twenty years after having lost their homes. However, an additional weighty consideration in favour of the Arabs was their control over major oil supplies and over the Suez Canal as well as the fear that, if thwarted, they might fall under complete communist influence. The two parties were strongly competing for international support in the Third World, especially in Africa, although this was a power contest not so much of immediate as of potential importance. Here the Israelis scored a success in offering effective technical and educational aid to African countries; they managed to counteract, and in some cases to prevail over, the pro-Arab forces based upon Egyptian participation in the Organization for African Unity and the dominant anti-imperialist sentiments which the Arabs endeavoured to direct against Israel.

The two camps thus presented strengths and weaknesses in different capabilities and types of power; the temporary balance of power achieved after the 1956 fighting was precariously kept by the United Nations Emergency Force and both sides were uncertain about their relative strengths. It stands to reason that they tried to bring to bear outside assistance and pressures to adjust the situation to their respective advantage, seeking advanced weapons supplies and greater diplomatic support.

The immediate causes of the 1967 war need not concern us here and we can turn at once to the way in which the various capabilities affected the issue. When, for a while, the chronic conflict turned violent, it became imperative for the combatants to be ready for immediate action, to bring all their power to bear upon the adversary. While, in the long run, the Arabs can score

by their great numerical superiority, the extent of their territories, and their greater wealth, in the short run they could not
mobilize all these. The Israelis managed to surprise and destroy
Arab planes on the ground which, in turn, enabled them to over-
whelm Egyptian land forces and armour. Organization allied
with superior technical skill was sufficient to gain them a re-
markably swift and resounding victory over the somewhat larger
opposing military forces.

The 1967 campaign was fought in two instalments and upon
two battlefields; one in the Sinai desert, the other in the Special
Session of the General Assembly. The Sinai encounter completely altered the balance of military power; instead of being
in a position of rough equality, the Israelis were fully victorious
and had destroyed or captured most of the main adversary's advanced equipment, had routed his armies and captured large
numbers of military personnel, and had occupied territories three
times the size of their country. The complete military victory
put Israel into a very advantageous position since it was difficult
to envisage an outside military intervention which would dislodge her forces of occupation. Nevertheless, the Arabs were not
in a position of complete weakness since they could count upon
United Nations support in their opposition to the drastic altera-
tion of boundaries by the use of force in an area in which the
Organization had taken special interest. In fact, despite their
complete military victory, for some time at least the Israeli
Government did not envisage keeping the occupied territories,
except Jerusalem, but merely intended to use them as a diplomatic bargaining counter.

The diplomatic battle took the form of a tug-of-war about the
recommendation to be adopted by a Special Session of the
General Assembly; the capabilities here involved were primarily
the respective international strategic positions consisting of the
degree of support that the two sides could muster from other
members of the United Nations. All the members agreed that
Israel should give up the territory occupied but the Arabs demanded unconditional withdrawal whereas the Israelis insisted
that they would withdraw only if the Arabs would end the state
of war, recognize the state of Israel, and negotiate with it directly.

Although the Israelis were in occupation and it was unthinkable that a United Nations force could be agreed upon to dislodge them by force, it would have been diplomatically very awkward for them to remain in occupation in defiance of the expressed wishes of the General Assembly.

With the end of fighting, the capabilities which had won the war even with all the substantial fruits of victory added were no longer decisive. In the United Nations the main problem is how to secure diplomatic support. Whereas the Arabs obtained unqualified support from the Soviet Union and the communist bloc, with the sole exception of Rumania, Israel was supported by the United States but no longer by her erstwhile allies against Egypt: Britain adopted a neutral attitude in order not to jeopardize her extensive oil and financial interests in the region; France went even further and gave full support to the Arabs, apparently pursuing de Gaulle's consistent anti-American policies and endeavouring to make use of the discomfiture of others to secure influence in the region. The final outcome was decided by the alignment of the African states. Israel had secured sufficient goodwill with some of them to prevent them from supporting a pro-Arab recommendation and ultimately the Special Session ended without being able to muster the required two-thirds majority to condemn Israel outright and to demand the withdrawal of her troops. Thus we can justifiably say that the decisive capability which Israel commanded in the diplomatic battle was the support of the few African states.

The United Nations round ended inconclusively with a compromise between the contending forces embedded in the British sponsored Security Council Resolution 242 of 22 November 1967, which ambiguously combined an injunction upon Israel to withdraw and upon the Arab States to agree to a permanent peace settlement. Not unnaturally, both sides interpreted the Resolution to suit their ends: the Arabs insisted on a complete Israeli withdrawal before the start of direct negotiations for peace, the Israelis demanded direct negotiations before making concrete proposals about withdrawal. The Resolution was ambiguous concerning the extent of the Israeli withdrawal required: the Arabs claimed that it must be complete, but the Israelis never accepted this claim in full. The Resolution called for the withdrawal of her armed forces, but not necessarily of *all* of them; from territories occupied but not from 'the' or 'all' the territories. As the Resolution stated the right of every state to live within 'secure and recognized boundaries' there was room for claiming adjustments for strategic purposes.

From the United Nations forum the efforts of the contending sides shifted to two major capabilities – military strength and Superpower support. Both of these were, of course, closely connected as the Superpowers which were the only possible major sources of arms. The Russians massively supplied the Egyptians, presumably to preserve their endangered footing in the region, and also to recoup from the loss of face after the defeat of their *protégés*. Not only did they quickly replace the losses but they supplied the Egyptians with increasingly advanced weapons. The military clash rapidly escalated as, from the Spring of 1969, President Nasser became engaged in massive artillery attacks on the Israeli positions across the Canal and began to prepare for an offensive, whereas the Israelis intensified their bombing of the Canal zone, and then penetrated deep into Egyptian territory. The Americans somewhat reluctantly supplied them with advanced planes, especially Phantoms, to restore the endangered military balance; the Russians retaliated with increasing numbers of air-to-ground missiles, finally including a number of the advanced Sam-3 type; they also sent in growing numbers of military personnel. The conflict interaction was rapidly increasing in momentum, threatening the contenders with another round of all-out fighting and the Superpowers with a direct confrontation on their behalf.

Subsequent developments can be interpreted as a growing realization that conflict interaction is wasteful and dangerous and that cooperation, however difficult it may be to achieve, is the only way out. They took place at two distinct levels: of the Superpowers and of Israeli–Arab relations. It was the Superpowers which acted first, fearful in their slowly developing general *détente* that the Middle Eastern crisis may engulf them. At first they seemed to act on the basis of reciprocated unilateral moves rather than in concert; later possibly they went beyond that and actually concerted their behaviour. The beginnings were slow and inauspicious. Despite the Israeli dismay at his initiative of a cease-fire, moved on 25 June 1970, the American Secretary of State, Rogers, managed to prevail on Israel to accept the cease-fire as from 7 August 1970. The first immediate Russian–Egyptian action was in violation of this agreement – they moved into the stand-still zone a large number of additional ground-to-air missiles. The Americans were at first unwilling even to investigate the transgression so as not to jeopardize the cease-fire and the Israelis eventually accepted the violation.

The negotiations between the local parties could not, however, even start to get going, despite assiduous diplomatic efforts of the United Nations special mission of Gunnar Jarring. Both sides were slow in giving up their originally adamant starting positions – the Israelis insisted on direct negotiations with the Arabs before they made a concrete offer and the Arabs demanded a full Israeli withdrawal before they entered negotiations. In fact, despite the absence of any tangible results, both sides gradually moved some way from their original positions, and fighting has not been resumed.

The case-study can be usefully concluded by a brief examination of the major factors conducive to conflict or cooperation in the future. To start with, the internal divisions of the two sides into 'hawks' and 'doves' are gradually hardening. The uneasy Israeli governing coalition is immobilized in any major political initiatives. On the Arab side the situation is dramatically changing. In the last period before his death in September 1970, Nasser seemed to be moving towards a more conciliatory line, and so has his successor, President Sadat; the Syrian regime has become more conciliatory and, in 1971, King Hussein of Jordan finally destroyed the intractable Palestine guerrillas stationed on his territory and constantly challenging his rule. A strong anti-Israeli policy is, however, a traditional mainstay of pan-Arab leadership, which is now aspired to by the ambitious and wealthy leader of Libya, Colonel Gaddafi, who could be decisive in blocking any settlement which may be favoured both by President Sadat and by King Hussein.

Five years after the Six Days War the situation in the Middle

East remains ambiguous. The territorial division seems to be hardening. Israel, having for the first time enjoyed strategically sensible boundaries stretching from the Syrian Hills along the Jordan right down to the Gulf of Akaba and to the east bank of the Canal, is unwilling to bargain her strategic security against anything but fairly hard-cast guarantees. As finally officially announced by her Prime Minister in 1970, she is determined to retain the eastern part of Jerusalem (with some international guarantees for the non-Jewish religions), the Syrian heights of Golan, Sheikh el Sharm controlling the Straits of Tiran and access to it, and some straightening of her previous eastern border with Jordan. Her claims to these are being reinforced by vigorous settlement and development policies. The future fate of the larger part of the west bank of Jordan, which is inhabited by some three quarters of a million Arabs, remains uncertain. The administration of this area, which has been economically successful despite the passive resistance of the population, may be the most promising bridge in the Middle Eastern conflict as here, for the first time, Israelis and Arabs have accepted the situation that they must live together and hence they must cooperate. With King Hussein now free from the immediate danger of a guerrilla-led revolution, an arrangement with him about the west bank seems distinctly possible.

Israel is vitally concerned with a settlement. In the long run, with the expected modernization of the Arab world, her position would become impossible especially as she cannot increase her small population except by immigration from the Soviet Union and Eastern Europe, where some three million Jews live in conditions generally unsatisfactory to them. Many of them would be willing to emigrate to Israel and, in the early seventies some were allowed to do so, but, in the face of the present Arab hostility, there is no hope for the Soviet Union agreeing to large-scale transfers of population. On the Arab side, the belated modernization is further delayed and a disproportionate effort is put into futile expenditures upon arms.

We have been discussing in some detail the fluctuating importance of the various capabilities in a continuous conflict relationship which went through three phases: of a 'cold war', a brief 'hot war' and now the post-war. Although decisive during the fight, the military power is of no avail to force an ultimate settlement; although of no impact upon the 'hot war', the demographic element may prove decisive in the long run; international support can be decisive in some phases, but not always, nor can it be fully relied upon. Neither the Arabs nor Israel have capabilities approaching those of the Superpowers and hence neither can prepare for most possible contingencies; so far Israel has won three times but if she loses in a fourth encounter, she could still disappear from the map. As long as the two sides remain locked in their traditional deadly conflict, one cannot envisage any resolution of it, any settlement brought about by the application of power, by the balance of forces. It is only too easy to suggest that they should abandon conflict and switch over to cooperation which would be of great mutual advantage since they could use their potential utilitarian capabilities, enjoy substantial international assistance, and save on military expenditure. The deadlock in conflict will not, however, persuade the antagonists that cooperation is inevitable. The reasons for it as well as the possibilities of advance in this direction, will be discussed in the concluding chapter.

## CHAPTER 7

# INSTRUMENTS AND TECHNIQUES OF FOREIGN POLICY

## Some General Remarks

WE must reiterate the fundamental fact that the state is the supreme unit of social organization and that there is nothing in its nature or in the nature of the international system to encourage social communication or interaction of any kind across state boundaries just for its own sake. Such communication or interaction takes place only when this is required for some policy objectives which cannot be achieved by state activity within its boundaries. The intensity of state relations varies greatly from period to period and, within each period, from state to state, but the historical record shows a propensity to self-sufficiency, to the restriction of international intercourse.

For many purposes the world has now become one area of activity. On the one hand, no state can now completely contract out from the international system because of the new weapons, communications and world trade; on the other, all states have increased the range of their social needs and cannot satisfy them all at home. We seem to have outlived the old pattern of geographical isolation allied with a very limited range of social needs which was characteristic of the Himalayan realms until this century. Whereas this type of isolation was more a description of a geographical fact than of a deliberate policy, we find in history also the pattern of isolationism, of a policy consciously adopted by states likewise favoured by a degree of geographical isolation but also endowed with adequate resources to exist in a more or less self-sufficient manner and also with reasonable capabilities to defend themselves against intrusion. Such isolationism was pursued by China and Japan until they came under the full impact of Western technology in the mid nineteenth century, or by the United States, and to a much lesser degree also by Great Britain, during their periods of 'splendid isolation'. In fact this isolation was never complete or very splendid and it is unthinkable in a world as closely integrated as it is today. Nevertheless, in the United States, where the basic conditions for a degree of self-sufficiency still exist, the tradition of isolationism survives and has revived in the early seventies. The Yale research on political and social indicators has shown the tendency towards a very strong decline of the foreign trade ratio, i.e. the sum of imports and exports as a percentage of the gross national product, for states with larger populations which can be economically more self-supporting. The nuclear stalemate between the two Superpowers encourages the idea of their withdrawal from entangling alliances into a much more easily managed and hence stabler balance of deterrence maintained by 'second-strike' missiles based upon submarines and their own territories. Notwithstanding the growing integration of the world, for the two Superpowers isolationism is feasible and has obvious attractions both in economics and in defence. Even within the smaller units which cannot aspire to self-sufficiency, intra-national social communications seem to be growing at a faster rate than trans-national social communications. Possibly we are moving not towards world integration but rather towards a further consolidation of the national units.

Perhaps it is a lingering effect of the attractions of isolationism, of the preference for pursuing the national objectives at home rather than internationally, that foreign policies tend to concentrate on one salient issue-area at a time, leaving the other areas largely out of account; repercussions upon these others, less salient or temporarily unimportant areas, are ignored or neglected, in the expectation that the domestic system will be able to cope with them. Thus we find cases of states completely bent on improving their power position and securing allies while neglecting economic and ideological repercussions, e.g. that of the United States since 1945. In the eyes of some Americans, in the late sixties, Britain showed the opposite obsession with her exports, exporting even strategically important materials, at the risk of strengthening enemies and potential attackers. In the same period, the United States objective of containing communist China or the French objective in opposing the United States appeared to outsiders to be similarly dominant over other issues of their respective foreign policies.

Despite all the tendencies to isolationism or to the restriction of foreign policy to one salient field, an increasing number of issues has to be settled with an increasing number of states. To add to the complexity, although links with other states are maintained through their governments which are in charge of their foreign policies, the peoples as distinct from their governments can be ignored only at great peril. Instruments and techniques of foreign policy suitable for approaching the people are, of course, by necessity, quite different, and their employment gives rise to awkward problems of their coordination with the traditional instruments used in relations with governments. Moreover, international organization has become an important agent in its own right. Most important here is the United Nations where foreign policy is subjected to the scrutiny of all the members. Other international organizations make an impact, too; even if they have no supra-national powers over their members, often members have to take them fully into account before acting. Thus an Arab or an African state wishing, after a period of disruption, to restore its diplomatic relations with a Western country, must heed the objections of the Arab League or the Organization for African Unity. Even if the majorities in these organizations favour moderate policies, they find it hard to free themselves from the influence of the prevalent radical tone.

Notwithstanding all this variety, man's political ingenuity has not been spent upon the invention of new instruments and techniques of foreign policy but merely upon their adaptation. These instruments and techniques remain few and most of them are traditional but the changes and adaptations are bewildering. It is obvious that the reasonably well understood rules of operation within the homogeneous and fairly static international system in the last century cannot fully apply to ours, but the changes adopted by the various states differ greatly according to their cultural backgrounds and their attitudes to international order. The general rules of conduct which no longer command universal acceptance persist in an ambiguous way, theoretically still binding, but constantly flouted by the states which refuse to accept them. While international politics become more integrated, the variety of national styles is becoming greater and more perplexing. The reasons for choosing one instrument or technique instead of another, which has never been clear, have become additionally blurred. Therefore, when analysing and comparing the use of instruments and techniques, it has become more important than ever not to lose sight of the wood while observing the trees. Many a well-meaning proposal for the abatement of conflict and for securing peace foundered owing to its excessive preoccupation with one instrument or technique, without regard for their limited roles.

Just as no set of relationships between two states is of a pure conflict or harmony type, so no instrument or technique of foreign policy is limited to only one mode of relationship. All of them are used in relations both with friends and with foes, although not to the same extent; all of them are used both for the purposes of conflict and of cooperation, although not in the same way. They are not, however, completely neutral for issues of conflict and harmony; some of them are much more suitable for the one mode of interaction and others for the other.

The difficulties of choosing values and objectives\* are further accentuated when it comes to the choice of instruments for their pursuit. There is no close, linear relationship between means and ends. In fact the nature of this relationship may become suddenly reversed, e.g. a threat pushed too far may miss its purpose of coercing the other party and may provoke its opposition; a trusted ally may decide to take advantage of a state's increased reliance by raising unexpectedly high demands, etc. etc.

The uses to which instruments and techniques are put are determined by the objectives of the state but we find here a certain amount of circularity which is usual in social matters. States, as all other social groups and individuals, are limited to the means available to them; they naturally prefer to employ those which they think most suitable for their purposes, to act in a way in which they feel they possess most skill. Thus, in a roundabout way, the capabilities possessed by the state influence

\*See above, Chapter 5.

its choices of objectives; if the strength of the state lies in instruments and techniques more usefully employed in conflict, this may create quite a strong propensity to conflict.

Allowing for the dual use to which all these can be put and the resulting lack of clear indices, there would be little disagreement about ranking the major instruments and techniques between the two extremes of harmony and conflict according to the major use to which they are usually put and to the degree of coercion involved: diplomacy and negotiations; economic instruments; propaganda; subversion; weapons, military intervention and war. In policies aiming at the curtailment of conflict and violence, a shift of emphasis away from the extreme of conflict and violence is obviously desirable and hence the advocacy of disarmament or of arms control is justified. This advocacy, however, is generally pushed too far. Restrictions on the instruments and techniques closer to the pole of conflict and violence would remove those temptations of states to use them which stem from the conviction that they allow a more advantageous employment of power and hence give a greater promise of success. On its own, however, disarmament or extensive arms control would go no further than to remove this temptation and this, by itself, would not reduce the incidence of conflict. It would reduce the scale of feasible violence but would also introduce new uncertainties which could serve as another source of temptation to resort to violence.

## *Diplomacy and Negotiations*

The growth of international interaction was closely connected with the growth of communications among states; one may argue that it was based upon it. All sorts of media are used to convey messages: public statements, direct contacts between heads of governments and foreign ministers, the services of third parties. Most of the messages, however, flow through the diplomats, the permanent representatives resident abroad and accredited to foreign governments. Diplomacy is so much a part and parcel of international life that we take it for granted, although it is an instrument of foreign policy of fairly recent origin. Some sporadic exchanges were inherent in any form of coexistence of independent political units but permanent missions were not established until international interaction had become sufficiently intense to necessitate it. This first happened in Renaissance Italy but the network of permanent missions grew at first haltingly; it became a general rule in Western Europe only in the eighteenth century, when the balance-of-power system required constant vigilance in mutual interaction. It is important to note that although diplomacy arose from the needs of the individual states, it gradually transcended a purely national role. While pursuing primarily national interest, the diplomats were also concerned with the maintenance of the international order and were assisted in it by their common cultural and social background.

From its inception, diplomacy was more closely connected with cooperation than with conflict. It is true that before modern times the heralds and envoys were employed also for hostile purposes, to spy and to declare war, but usually their purpose was friendly. The first permanent missions were established between potential allies; once they were general, severance of diplomatic relations became associated with war or acute conflict. This is the historical origin of the continuing Western preoccupation with the maintenance of diplomatic ties even in the face of great difficulties. In their preference for keeping the channels of diplomatic communication open even if nothing cooperative or positive flows through them, Western governments follow the popular belief that a dichotomy exists between diplomatic negotiation and war, that it is better to negotiate than to fight.

The relation between diplomatic negotiation and war is not quite as simple and the dichotomy assumed is not absolute, but undoubtedly maintenance of diplomatic relations has been regarded as a symbolic expression of a minimum goodwill required for constant contact and for any necessary negotiation. The high symbolic value is manifested in the importance attaching to the organization of diplomatic missions. If a state is hostile to another one or to its government, it may refuse it recognition, as the United States did in her relations with the Soviet Union between 1919 and 1933 and with communist China after 1949. Recognition need not immediately lead to an exchange of missions. Sometimes the delay is due to lack of business or of economic resources or of qualified diplomatic personnel, but often it is caused by suspicion, as in the case of Sukarno of Indonesia who continuously postponed exchanges with the Soviet Union and China, and eventually engaged in them only because of great domestic pressures. If relations are lukewarm, missions are established but left in the care of chargés d'affaires, as in the case of the relations between communist China and Britain, seventeen years after their establishment. Finally, the rank of the envoys used to be carefully differentiated into ambassadors and lower ranking envoys, the former rank being accorded only to envoys of Great Powers and to close friends. Today the rank of ambassador has become usual for all. Other symbolic diplomatic actions are used to show displeasure, namely the recall of the ambassador without appointing a successor, and, to express an even stronger protest, the severance of diplomatic relations; the latter is the rule in war-time.

This intrusion of symbolic values runs counter to the constant needs of international intercourse. On the one hand, relations are not entered into or are broken off as the result of international tensions, on the other, new and recondite methods for facilitating contacts are devised. The United States and the Soviet Union have been successfully supplementing diplomacy by carefully thought-out unilateral declarations and activities which are reciprocated; such procedure in matters as tricky as partial disarmament is easier and leaves both sides less vulnerable to criticism at home and by allies. They have opened the 'hot line' for direct communication in crises. The United States refuses to recognize communist China but has been maintaining direct diplomatic contacts since 1955, first through consuls of the two countries in Berne and then through envoys in Warsaw; as a rule the two meet every month in complete secrecy. Despite continuing non-recognition, in 1968 the United States representatives engaged in continuous peace talks with the representatives of North Vietnam and, in 1971, the President's Special Envoy visited Peking, paving the way for the President's own visit in February 1972.

Following the so-called 'Hallstein Doctrine', until 1967 the Federal Republic of Germany was refusing to enter into or maintain diplomatic relations with any country maintaining them with the People's Republic of Germany. She waived this rule only with the Soviet Union but resorted to such palliatives as trade missions with Eastern European countries. Arab states broke off diplomatic relations with France and Britain over Suez, and with the United States and Britain after the June 1967 war, but maintained indirect contacts. Nine African countries broke off diplomatic relations with Britain over Southern Rhodesia, but business between the countries continued, sometimes in a rather paradoxical manner, through British personnel being seconded to the local Canadian High Commissioner; the break in diplomatic relations does not automatically involve cessation of aid.

Since diplomacy is so necessary for the conduct of day-to-day business, it is thus most inconvenient that it serves as a symbolic outlet for protests, especially the walk-out which is effective only in parliamentary practice or in the United Nations.

Much embarrassment arises from the changed nature of contemporary diplomacy which often clashes with the traditional organization of diplomatic machinery. The break between the new and the old diplomacy came in the inter-war period and has become increasingly pronounced since 1945. The following distinctive characteristics of the old diplomacy were listed by the great authority on it, Sir Harold Nicolson:

1. the concept of Europe as the centre of international gravity;
2. the idea of the greater importance and responsibility of the Great Powers, constituting the concert, than of the small ones;
3. diplomatic service in all countries sharing the common standards of professional conduct;
4. the assumption that negotiation must always be a process rather than an episode, and that at every stage it must remain confidential.*

Thus diplomatic activities were essentially cooperative, aiming at the maintenance of the system and at the solution of conflicts. They were also the exclusive and central mode of communication. The new diplomacy reflects much greater complexity and increased elements of conflict in international life:

1. the simultaneous development of communications and

*H. Nicolson, *Diplomacy*, Oxford University Press, 3rd ed., 1963.

increase in the impact of public opinion have brought to bear conflicting and heterogeneous pressures;

2. the composition of international society has drastically changed; numbers of states have increased and the centre of gravity has gradually but decisively shifted away from Europe;

3. traditions are disturbed both by cultural heterogeneity and by ideological differences;

4. alternative methods of inter-state contact have arisen through direct communication between heads of states and foreign ministers and in multilateral arrangements, international conferences and meetings of international organizations.

The traditional diplomatic methods developed in Western Europe and still assiduously cultivated by Western countries, were based upon tolerance, restraint and good manners, upon the idea that the diplomatic channels must be kept open and unimpeded. The great totalitarian Powers in the inter-war period introduced quite a new conception of diplomacy; instead of using it mainly for communication and negotiation, they employed it for propaganda, revolutionary agitation and even intimidation. Breaches of good manners, preference for propaganda, arbitrary interpretation of agreements, blatant use of deception, were the result of the twin influences of the ending of the professional as well as of the ideological unity of diplomacy.

The situation became further aggravated with the rising of all the new states since 1945 which share only marginally in the European cultural heritage and often wish to reject it. All these states had no experience in the old-style diplomacy and started their international activities with a large emphasis on conducting business in the United Nations where they are easily tempted to prefer propaganda to negotiation. Diplomatic protocol and immunities were increasingly ignored and diplomats and their outposts were exposed to increasing violence. A particularly disruptive influence came from communist China, integrated and restored to power under her communist government since 1949. China lacks any traditions of international relations in the

Western sense. For over 2,000 years she considered herself as 'the Kingdom of the Middle', with the whole world being barbarian and subordinate to her. Her first contacts with the West were marked by hostility and humiliation and now, having regained her power, she brought to bear upon her diplomacy the disruptive influences of great national pride and of a virulent ideology. The vicious physical maltreatment of foreign diplomats in Peking in 1967 in addition to the futile record of maintaining diplomatic missions there in previous years, raised the question of the future of traditional diplomacy as the major instrument of foreign policy conducted with China. Diplomacy started as an instrument of cooperation; where disagreements are acute to the point of blocking substantial cooperation and where the common cultural basis is lacking, diplomacy may have no role to play. For a while the idea that maintaining contacts is worth while, in the hope that China will become less violent and antagonistic, did not carry much conviction; it seemed that the basic trouble with communist China was that she was not seated in the United Nations and was therefore self-centred and immune to any external restraints except the ultimate fear of violence. By 1971, however, the situation changed. Having completed the Cultural Revolution, the Chinese régime opened a new, more cooperative phase in its external relations, and was finally seated in the United Nations.

## Economic Instruments

That economics is of fundamental importance is not only a basic tenet of the communist ideology but also a firm belief widely spread in Western countries; although some of the new states occasionally act in a way which appears to us to ignore economic realities, they are all greatly concerned with development. One would expect the instruments of foreign policy in this field to be extremely important. Moreover, in Western thought, the harmonious, cooperative aspects of economics have been traditionally stressed, so that we tend to think about international economic exchanges as an essentially cooperative enterprise in which an international division of labour and maximum size markets secure benefits for all. It is easy to conclude that a dichotomy exists between economics and violence and to seek the substitution of economic cooperation for military conflict. This reasoning is not completely pointless but does, unfortunately, lack a solid foundation.

One source of confusion can be found in the nature of international economic exchanges which, unlike diplomatic exchanges, are not the monopoly of governments. Important private and public interests deal with them, at times appearing to be completely free from political control by governments. In the nineteenth century the apparently complete autonomy of the City of London inspired the illusion that economics is completely divorced from politics although, in reality, the operations of the City were possible only on the foundation of the dominance of the British Navy. The illusion still persists; it is characteristic that in one of the fullest analytical treatments of international relations, *Politics Among Nations*, Professor Hans J. Morgenthau* does not discuss at all the economic instruments used by states. His only fairly brief mention of economics relates to the theories of the economic foundations of imperialism.

Economic interests were in the nineteenth century and still are among the most important influences upon Western governments. This was the foundation of the economic theories of imperialism, propounded by English radicals and by Lenin, which were based upon the conviction that the governments are ruled or, at least, are readily persuaded by powerful financial and commercial interests. The historical record is somewhat ambiguous but seems to point more to the opposite conclusion that, in the classical cases of imperialism in the latter part of the nineteenth century and early in the twentieth, economic interests were more used for political purposes by the governments than the other way around.

There is no doubt about the influence exercised by economic interests upon Western governments also in the latter part of this century. The impact of the 'military-industrial' complex upon the government and the foreign policy of the United States

*Hans J. Morgenthau, *Politics Among Nations*, New York, Knopf, 4th ed., 1967.

cannot be matched by that of its counterparts in other Western countries; nevertheless, all industrialized countries must be concerned with the prosperity of their major industries and of their major commercial and financial interests. For instance it would be just as unthinkable for the British or the French governments as for that of the United States, to remain indifferent to the fate of their national oil interests in the Middle East. Indeed, governments become politically involved on behalf of the major national companies; ultimately, however, they are governed by broader political considerations and they accept nationalization and expropriation, wherever these occur. The British–French expedition to the United Arab Republic in 1956 was to a large extent due to the nationalization of the International Suez Canal Company; the reasons were thus mixed, not merely economic but strategic. It is very unlikely that an intervention would follow any future act of nationalization.

Business firms not only endeavour to influence governmental policies but occasionally act independently and defy governmental direction, e.g. in trading with enemy states in wartime or breaking the sanctions against Southern Rhodesia. Usually, however, they eventually toe the line. Thus United States oil firms obeyed President Truman's bidding to deny transport facilities and markets to Persian oil after its nationalization. They did so despite their great eagerness to break into the Persian market and their long record of hostility to the expropriated British oil interests which, until then, had managed to exclude them from Persia. Economic interests can influence foreign policy only when they are very powerful; middle-sized and small concerns simply do not count.

The autonomy of the powerful economic interests is limited to the West and, even here, it has been recently circumscribed by increasing governmental direction. In communist countries, governments directly conduct their economies. This is true in varying degrees about new states in which private interests, if tolerated, are under close political control. As soon, however, as the governments had assumed their present economic powers, they also began to surrender them to international institutions. The General Agreement on Tariffs and Trade (GATT) strongly limits governmental regulation of trade; the International Monetary Fund prohibits manipulation of exchange rates; members of the European Economic Community have surrendered some important economic powers to the community and, to a lesser extent, this is true about its Eastern European counterpart, the COMECON. Thus the governments are in command of the field, but not without constraints.

Additional uncertainty arises from the dual nature of objectives pursued by economic instruments. International exchanges can be useful for the economic benefits accrued, such as obtaining supplies of needed goods and markets for those available for export, but they also serve political purposes, for offering rewards or meting out punishments. The two sets of objectives sometimes coincide but sometimes also clash, as shown by the Western dilemma over trade with the Soviet Union and communist China in which the political-strategic disadvantages of strengthening an adversary have to be weighed against the economic advantages of developing trade. The dilemma is particularly acute with goods of strategic significance; the United States is more concerned with the political-strategic considerations whereas Great Britain gives higher priority to economic considerations; hence they disagree about the list of strategic goods the export of which should be prohibited.

The generalizations one can readily advance about the incidence of the economic and the political-strategic considerations in economics are rather limited. It seems plausible to hypothesize that attention to the political aspects increases with the power and the world involvement of the state as well as with the degree of governmental control over its economy. Thus we can expect that purely or predominantly economic considerations will prevail in a much wider range of international economic interaction in Switzerland than in the United States, and in the United States than in the Soviet Union. It is possible and useful to calculate and compare the economic and the political-strategic considerations involved in any particular transaction but the result of the calculation is bound to be determined by the ranking of the relevant economic and political values involved and therefore defies a precise evaluation and prediction.

As stated at the beginning of this section, the harmonious, cooperative aspects of economics are rather conspicuous. It is therefore worth being reminded that economic instruments are not exclusively connected with cooperation. They are used between friends and foes, in peace and in war; occasionally they serve purely harmonious purposes but occasionally also purely conflict purposes; normally they combine the two.

Trade is the oldest and still the outstanding economic instrument. International division of labour enabled Britain in the nineteenth century to pursue her industrial revolution through securing supplies of food and raw materials from overseas, and markets for her industries. Free Trade which was Britain's policy between 1846 and 1932, was a most important instrument in her economic development. According to the classical economic theory, it was a fully harmonious one. The division of labour was, indeed, advantageous to both sides, although much more advantageous to Britain than to the primary producers supplying her and to the industrial competitors who arose in the last quarter of the century. Other trading nations considered trade as a 'game' situation in which both sides endeavour to secure the maximum advantage possible; solutions were determined by power considerations, trade was increasingly used for political rather than purely economic purposes: to offer rewards or threaten or impose punishments, to increase the state's capabilities or deprive enemies of crucial supplies, to secure political control. All sorts of restrictive techniques were evolved for the purpose: tariffs, quotas, currency manipulations, boycotts and embargoes.

To the extent that trade is reciprocal and cooperative, its use for punitive purposes deprives both sides of its benefits. If one side, however, is much more powerful, it can more easily endure the loss involved. Thus the Soviet Union severed trade relations with Yugoslavia in 1947, with Finland in 1958, and reduced them with China in 1960, without suffering in the process, but putting considerable pressures on the other parties. The United States has been trying to enforce an embargo on the sale of the most crucial strategic materials to the Soviet Union and, even more so, to China and to Cuba. When dependence is mutual, an embargo may be more damaging to the punishers than to the punished – therefore the Arab oil producers decided to remove the embargo on oil sales to the United States and Britain three months after its imposition in 1967. Complete dependence upon trade, be it for markets or for supplies of important commodities, provides an instrument for complete domination. Thus the control over the main market for Eastern European grain helped Hitler to exercise his influence in the region in the late thirties, since no alternative markets could be found; the Superpowers add to their facilities for political control when they supply others with technologically advanced manufactures, especially weapons, which are unavailable elsewhere. Occasionally the degree of mutual dependence is blurred. Thus in 1967 the Arabs used an oil embargo as an instrument of pressure upon Britain who is greatly dependent on Middle Eastern supplies. In a buyer's market, however, the Arabs likewise depended on their customary market; in the ensuing tug-of-war it was easier for Britain to find alternative markets – the embargo had to be called off. In wartime, trade between the belligerents comes to an end and they have at their disposal a variety of instruments of economic warfare aiming also at the disruption of the trade between the opponent and the rest of the world.

The analysis and the understanding of international trade are highly advanced. Less frequent and also much less well analysed is the use of international finance as an instrument of foreign policy. However, the dual nature of the instrument is quite clear from the record of the run against the pound and the dollar in 1967; the central bankers, who can be assumed to be under firm governmental controls, were all used as an instrument for co-operative purposes, to support the two international currencies, whereas the French not only refused to cooperate but used the instrument for conflict purposes, to exacerbate the crisis.

Assistance to poorer states seems to offer a useful instrument for ensuring their cooperation. Already in the previous two centuries Britain and France used subsidies as an instrument of their foreign policies but only since 1945 has foreign aid become a major instrument. Obviously only a wealthy state can use this instrument extensively and, indeed, the United States has supplied more foreign aid than all the other donors together. The Soviet Union, the ex-imperial Powers – France, Great Britain and Western Germany are the other major donors; for a while at least, aid was extensively used also by communist China.

Aid is a cooperative, harmonious instrument but the relationship is asymmetrical since the economic advantage of the recipient is not matched by an equivalent economic advantage of the donor, although the latter may derive some benefits, e.g. he may be able to get rid of an unsaleable surplus of goods. The *quid pro quo* is mainly political: the donor may secure an ally, buttress a friendly régime and save it from subversion, secure a change in the recipient's domestic or foreign policies in the direction desired, or help the recipient to secure an objective which he finds congenial. Although some 65 per cent of the United States economic aid purports to promote the purposes of development, clearly in most cases the aid has one of these political uses.*

Despite its magnitude, foreign aid has proved highly ineffective in making friends and securing allies, independently of the identity of the donor. Supply of aid offers the immediate advantage of facilitating diplomatic access and, in many cases, helping to deny it to the adversary. In the longer run, however, the recipients refuse to accept political direction. To them politics is more important than economics; moreover, they can seek and find aid from rival sources. Thus aid has not proved to be a reliable instrument of foreign policy. Nevertheless, despite the economic stringencies of the later sixties, it is being continued, although in decreasing magnitudes. Often its political purpose seems to be rather negative – to avoid the disappointment and the subsequent resentment of the expectant recipients. There are some serious doubts also about the economic effectiveness of foreign aid and only its humanitarian purpose remains fairly intact.

*The role of aid in economic development is discussed below, pp. 218–20. For the evaluation of United States aid as an instrument of foreign policy see J. M. Nelson, *Aid, Influence and Foreign Policy*, New York, Collier-Macmillan, 1968.

## *Propaganda*

By propaganda we generally understand any systematic, deliberate attempt to affect the minds, emotions and actions of a given group for public purposes. International propaganda differs from diplomacy in two essential respects: first, it is directed to the people of other states, its effect on governments is only incidental. Second, propaganda serves the selfish national purpose of the propagandist and is generally employed in conflict relations. There are, however, cases to the contrary, e.g. when the United States Government conducts propaganda on behalf of the local governments in South Korea and in South Vietnam.

International propaganda is a form of verbal intervention in the affairs of other states which was impossible on an extensive scale until the evolution of the modern means of communications, especially the radio. It was evolved by and it received its name from the activities of a special sacred congregation of the Catholic Church (*de propaganda fide*), it was used by the British Government during the First World War, but it came into its own as a significant instrument of foreign policy only through its use by the totalitarian states in the inter-war period. Since then propaganda has become the stock-in-trade instrument of all states wishing to exercise any sizeable influence in world affairs. All Great Powers and states aspiring to influence have special departments or agencies which spend large sums of money upon propaganda activities. Moreover, whenever feasible, they appeal to and endeavour to employ foreign groups sympathetic to the propagandist, e.g. the Soviet Union and China use communist parties, Egypt addresses Nasser's sympathizers in other Arab countries.

Although propaganda does not involve any means of coercion, it serves the purposes of conflict both by trying to persuade and subvert the people of other states and by keeping the state's own citizens hostile to others. Cooperation is, however, not excluded. It is possible by mutual agreement and to mutual advantage to limit the scale and the viciousness of propaganda, to restrict censorship, to develop standards of truthful reporting, and even to use the machinery for propagating friendship instead of hostility. A notably successful conversion of propaganda in this harmonious direction has taken place since 1945 in France and in Germany. Whereas their pre-war and wartime propaganda campaigns were hostile to each other, at present both sides endeavour to foster friendship and cooperation within the European communities. A similar transition could take place in the United States–Soviet relations if both sides will it, although it is at the moment difficult to envisage them doing so and, even less so, spending large sums of money for the purpose.

Whereas international propaganda can be considered as a verbal intervention in the domestic affairs of other states, as we pass on to other types of intervention we proceed towards an increased use of weapons and of violence and an increased incidence of more serious conflicts.

## Intervention

States can never remain entirely indifferent to the domestic affairs of other states. Occasionally they find it necessary or convenient to intervene to pursue their objectives or defend their interests, particularly when they wish to promote social values and ideologies which increase their own zeal and also enable them to secure some sympathizers. Interventions in the domestic affairs of other states occur in all periods of history, although usually on a fairly limited scale. After interventions on behalf of coreligionists during the religious wars, dynastic intrigues provided the relatively rare occasions for them during the eighteenth century. The ideological rifts following the French Revolution increased interventions, first by the revolutionaries in their endeavours to replace traditional régimes, then by the conservative victors to scotch any attempts at renewed revolution. With the abatement of revolutionary memories, a controversy began between lawyers and statesmen regarding the legal validity of intervention. The majority deemed it illegal although exceptions occurred, e.g. during the Spring of Nations in 1848, or in Latin America where the United States repeatedly landed marines later in the century.

In the twentieth century interventions abounded, following in the wake of revolutions: out of some 200 revolutions identified up to 1950, some half resulted in an intervention, and about a half of these interventions by more than one state. In the inter-war period the totalitarian countries intervened very frequently and the most notable case of multiple intervention was the Civil War in Spain.

After 1945 interventions not only continued but the con-troversy about their legal validity swayed in their favour; they were now deemed permissible provided vague legal forms were adhered to, as long as the intervening state was invited either by the government in force or by a 'liberation' movement. New states had strong views on the subject: they considered only the latter type as legitimate, being in conformity with the 'national self-determination' principle, while they utterly condemned any intervention by an 'imperialist' Power. Their growing numbers in the United Nations gradually moved the Organization to adopt this distinction; moreover, the United Nations was called upon to establish and deploy its own military forces consisting of contingents provided mainly by new states, in order to replace 'imperialist' intervention or to deal with the aftermath of colonialism.

'Intervention' is an extremely broad and loose concept which describes all sorts of interference in the domestic affairs of other states. No precise political definition can be suggested; inter-national lawyers have been concerned mainly with the types of cases in which intervention is directed against the government of the country and involves the use of force; they have been divided and indecisive also about these. Interventions will be classified here according to the amount of force employed and the serious-ness of the action, and also according to whether they are under-taken by the Superpowers or by other states.

At the outset it must be stressed that intervention is an even more unfriendly instrument of foreign policy than propaganda. Even in its milder forms it is pointedly directed against the government of another state and it serves predominantly conflict relations. It is possible to conceive some clandestine operations, such as bribing of the press or of personalities, or subsidizing within another state political groups or activities acceptable to or even desired by the state within which the intervention takes place. Generally, however, these activities express and serve a conflict relationship – they are undertaken in order to force the government to change its policies or to enforce its downfall. Well-known examples are the Nazi support for the activities of their sympathizers in the United States, or the communist and CIA subsidies to sympathetic publications. Contacts with opposition parties and groups can be quite undisguised but in most cases they are secret, e.g. the communist parties tend to stress their national character and independence and Soviet or Chinese support for them cannot be frequently documented.

Diplomatic interference does not share the odium of secrecy with the previously mentioned types of intervention but can be even more serious. The French parliament was subjected to and withstood the threat of an 'agonizing reappraisal' made by John Foster Dulles to induce it to ratify the European Defence Community Treaty in 1954; repeated American diplomatic intervention aimed at affecting the composition of the governments in South East Asia and in Latin America was often fully effective. The Soviet Union likewise frequently endeavoured to interfere diplomatically in the policies and in the composition of the governments of other states, encouraging anti-American and pro-Soviet alignment, or neutrality. For instance she interfered in the Scandinavian debate whether to join NATO in 1948 and 1949, in Finnish governmental crises and elections, and, even more frequently and forcibly, in Eastern European countries. The Superpowers resorted to diplomatic intervention more frequently than other states but the use of this instrument is not limited to them. In all regions occasions arise when a state, aiming at leadership, resorts to diplomatic interference in the domestic affairs of others; outstanding examples are the records of Nasser of Egypt and of Castro of Cuba.

Subversion is more serious, since it involves the use of force, although only by proxy, through others. We understand by it the support for any rebellious, revolutionary activity aiming at replacing the local government or breaking up the unity of the state. The classical inter-war example was Hitler's support for the Sudeten Germans who served as his major instrument in the destruction of Czechoslovakia as an independent state. Unhappily Czechoslovakia was the theatre of another subversion in 1948, when Soviet pressure was instrumental in helping the Czech communists in a *coup d'état*; a blatant case of United States subversion in Latin America was its support for the Guatemalan revolution in 1954. Both Superpowers have been heavily intervening in South East Asia but since the Americans usually supported the régime in power, it was the Russians who engaged in subversion. The roles were reversed at least once, in Laos, when the CIA supported a *coup d'état* in 1961 to replace a neutralist government by one which was pro-American and anti-communist.

Domestic disturbances on a larger scale, leading to guerrilla warfare, can arise for purely domestic reasons and be conducted by local forces alone. Generally, however, they attract intervention and counter-intervention from abroad and sometimes they even originate from this intervention rather than from internal conflicts. An intervening state usually supplies diplomatic and moral encouragement, economic and military aid, training facilities, and sometimes sends military personnel approximating full-scale military intervention, although the fighting is still done by proxy, by the guerrillas. Examples can be found in Soviet and lately even more so in Chinese and North Vietnamese support for guerrillas in South East Asia and in Cuban support for those in Latin America. Preparations for the use of guerrillas are often made in the form of training camps on the territory of the intervening state in which the fighters prepare for their activities or are given asylum, as the Cuban exiles in the United States prior to their Bay of Pigs attempt to land in Cuba in 1961, or the various African 'freedom fighters' in Tanzania or the Congo. Superpowers have thus no monopoly of subversion or support for guerrillas. Not only the African states mentioned but also Nasser, Castro, and Sukarno of Indonesia used this instrument quite extensively.

Finally, the intervening state can become involved in a full-scale military intervention, sending troops to be engaged in the actual hostilities. While in the inter-war period this was a rare occurrence, the Spanish Civil War being the only large-scale example, military intervention has been quite frequent since 1945. Much of the acrimonious argument on the subject centres around the question of the legality of the intervention and whether it was a primary move or a reaction, a counter-intervention. Independently of the answers given to these questions and of our legal and moral evaluations, from the political point of view we may consider all military interventions as a category of instruments of foreign policy which aims at the establishment or the maintenance of a desired régime in another state. Some military interventions to buttress existing régimes were very peaceful and brief, e.g. those of Britain in Jordan and of the United States in the Lebanon in 1958. The threat of a military intervention by the Soviet troops stationed in Eastern European states was sufficient to stabilize the local communist régimes although these forces nearly became involved in fighting in Poland in 1956 and in Czechoslovakia in 1968, and actually did so in Hungary in 1956. The country most frequently involved in military intervention was the United States. American troops took a rather half-hearted and indecisive but just the same active part in the Bay of Pigs invasion of Cuba in 1961, in the Dominican Republic in 1965 and also in Asia, in Korea in 1950 and, since 1964, in Vietnam; China, sending her forces not as a regular army but in the slightly less direct form of 'volunteers', intervened in the Korean struggle; Britain intervened at the request of Eastern African states to quell military risings, and in Kuwait to protect her against an Iraqi threat; Egypt intervened on a large scale in the Yemen, and Indonesia in North Borneo.

The identity of the intervening states is an important variable. It is understandable that the Superpowers, being more intensely involved in international politics, tend to resort to intervention more than other states. One type of situation arises in their respective spheres of influence. The United States has repeatedly intervened in various ways in Latin America and, to a somewhat lesser extent, in Western Europe; likewise the Soviet Union has repeatedly intervened in Eastern Europe, notably in 1948 and 1968 in Czechoslovakia and in 1956 in Hungary. The second type of Superpower for Radio Free Europe is a milder parallel to communist subversive activities in Latin America and in Western Europe.

The third type of Superpower intervention takes place in the Third World. Here it is induced by the instability of the newly established régimes which leads to frequent requests for intervention, both by governments and by opposition forces. This lends a cloak of legality or at least semi-legality to tempting activities which could secure advantages at the cost of the rival. Although the two Superpowers, especially the Soviet Union, have been extremely careful to avoid a head-on clash, intervention by the one inevitably tends to provoke a counter-intervention by the other.

International conditions after 1945 were encouraging intervention not only by the Superpowers but also by much less powerful states, especially in independence movements and in post-independence issues in the decolonized states. International restraints were greatly reduced because the nuclear stalemate to some extent neutralized the influence of the Superpowers while the United Nations generally took an encouraging attitude to independence movements and remained lenient to post-independence interventions by other new states. Moreover, these states had generally themselves obtained independence through revolution, hence their rulers had the experience and the skills required to intervene on behalf of other revolutions. Finally, their intervention in a colonial or post-colonial issue did not require vast capabilities. This support usually took the form of harbouring refugees and of offering asylum and sometimes training facilities and weapons to revolutionaries in neighbouring territories.

Nearly all governments in new states claim descent from revolutionary movements which had often enjoyed the sympathy, if not the active support, of an outside state. Hence their post-independence period is characterized by a tug-of-war between the influence of the ex-imperial Power which is generally substantial, even if resented, and the influence of the sympathizer. The latter is either another new state which cannot offer any economic support, or a communist state whose support is somewhat unreliable and, moreover, politically dangerous. The tug-of-war between these two conflicting influences causes post-colonial governments to oscillate rather violently between the one influence and the other, creating conditions of instability which, of course, have international repercussions.

Intervention in Korea and in Vietnam were to some extent mitigated by the pattern of partition and the existence of clear-cut though arbitrary boundaries following geographical lines. These provided not only the starting-points but also potential resting-points and nuclei for permanent settlement. Conflict would have been even more dangerous and confused in countries not so divided in which there was no agreed armistice line to which the two sides could return. The makings of such a situation existed in the Belgian Congo immediately after independence; although the United Nations action there is vulnerable to serious criticisms, at least it saved the Congo, and Africa, from a Vietnam-type war.

An interesting example of the tergiversations of the post-colonial government which led to only temporary and limited intervention and counter-intervention is Nyerere's Tanzania. Nyerere managed to restrict Chinese influence to Zanzibar, hopefully neutralizing the island by uniting it but, when faced with a military rebellion, he called upon the British Government to send in troops to squash it. He dealt with another conspiracy in 1967 on his own and it is interesting to speculate whether he would have called again upon the British Government had this conspiracy reached a dangerous stage. Meanwhile relations between Tanzania and Britain had greatly deteriorated while Chinese influence on the mainland part of Tanzania seems to have increased with the inauguration of the massive Chinese aid project, the construction of the Tanzam railway.

The growing incidence of intervention can be accommodated in the traditional framework of government only as long as another government is concerned; then the foreign ministry and, if military force is involved, also the ministry of defence can play their usual roles. Support for rebels is easier to administer by special organs and hence the Soviet Union developed the Comintern, the Nazis had the Gestapo, and the United States has the

Central Intelligence Agency. Since new states consider 'liberation' movements as illegal, they can deal with them more easily through the traditional government departments.

It is difficult to find valid legal objections to military intervention, especially one at the invitation of the legally established government of the country, but political objections to it have been increasing and military intervention by the Superpowers or an ex-colonial state usually incurs the strong opprobrium of international public opinion expressed in the General Assembly. This is probably based upon two general principles, namely opposition to war and therefore anything approaching it, and opposition to imperial interference of one state in the affairs of another. This general trend of international thinking on military intervention is, however, somewhat uncertain. It is affected by the fact that the majority of recent military interventions have been undertaken by the Americans, notably in their involvement in Vietnam. Consequently condemnation of the principle of military intervention is tantamount to the condemnation of present American foreign policy. Even without adopting the opposed pro-American attitude, when discussing military intervention objectively, as an instrument of state policy, it is possible to argue that the Americans have been resorting to it more than others only because it provided the necessary counterbalance to the more effective subversive forces employed by the communists.

Since domestic instability is bound to remain a potential source of international instability, *international* military intervention has been conceived as a useful substitute for intervention by states. Its first application was rather nominal when the United States intervened in Korea in 1950. In the temporary absence of the Soviet Union, the United States obtained Security Council approval and its authorization to use the United Nations flag for an operation in which a predominantly United States force was used in pursuit of a national policy purpose which, admittedly, was acceptable to and approved by the Security Council. The façade served the Americans very well since it reduced international criticism and it secured a modicum of general support. Further major United Nations military interventions took place in the Middle East in 1956, in the Congo in 1960 and in Cyprus since 1964. All of them were conducted by truly international forces the contingents of which came mainly from new states. Rather characteristically, all the occasions for the interventions arose from the aftermath of imperial rule.

Possibly the United Nations is taking over this traditional instrument of foreign policy and in some future time its use by individual states may become banned. Apart from international opinion, a decisive factor in this transition may be the increasing ineffectiveness of the instrument for the purposes of state foreign policy, a phenomenon closely connected with the even greater crisis of war. Guerrilla fighting has been brought to such a pitch of efficiency in the last prolonged wars of colonial liberation, in Indo-China and in Algeria, that participation in such fighting is bound to become increasingly less effective and attractive. The involvement of Egypt in the Yemen and, even more so, of the United States in Vietnam, are grave warnings to statesmen contemplating military intervention.

Probably we have passed the peak of military interventions by states in this century, which may reflect a certain abatement of the ideological rift and may, in turn, help towards more conciliatory and tolerant attitudes. At the same time, however, the many dissident social, national, racial, and also ideological groups continue opposing the majorities and the governments of their countries. As long as they exist and voice their dissent we can envisage the likelihood of intervention by some state sympathizing with the dissident group or antagonistic to the government which it opposes. Milder, non-military intervention is likely to continue and to increase in proportion to the growing communications and ties among all the countries of the world. Nowadays domestic conflict can scarcely be kept in a tight domestic compartment; unless a solution is found for it, it is certain eventually to have some international repercussions.

## Weapons and War

The lack of effective institutionalized restraints upon the use of force constitutes a major difference between international systems and domestic ones. States are never secure from the dangers of an attack and, failing an effective substitute, they maintain military forces. These are considered not only essential for national security but also for prevailing over other states which, unless militarily weaker, may assert themselves and refuse to submit.

Weapons, the military, and wars undoubtedly have been and still are the most important instruments and techniques of state behaviour. They play a central role in the relations of some non-nuclear Powers engaged in violent conflict, e.g. India and Pakistan, or the Arab states and Israel, or the African states and South Africa and Southern Rhodesia. At the same time, however, their role is becoming rapidly transformed in relations among nuclear Great Powers. First, large-scale modern military forces are now so expensive that even the richest states can maintain them only at the cost of other essential social values. Second, the efficiency of the instrument is increasingly dubious. As best illustrated by the case of Vietnam, a Superpower may be defied by a small state despite an immense military effort.

A large-scale use of nuclear weapons would inflict damage and inexorably lead to retaliatory damage which would be totally unacceptable to any society; losses must be counted in terms of 'mega-deaths', millions of casualties, the outcome could be complete destruction of our civilization. In this section discussion is limited to the instrumental role of force and the techniques of deploying it in the interests of states. Their analysis as a major danger threatening the international community and all its member states will be left to Chapter 9, as one of the problems which require an international solution.

Full reliance upon one's own military forces has been a rare phenomenon in history. Even the most powerful states require allies and supporters, and this is true about the Superpowers today. Smaller and weaker states in suitable geographical situations and diplomatic configurations could sometimes ensure security either through the protection of a Greater Power or through rivalry among a few of the Greater Powers. Today's situation has become even more blurred in Africa where most of the new states feel reasonably safe from territorial infringement and hence do not possess military forces; their ultimate defence is provided by continental politics and by the United Nations. Nevertheless, force was repeatedly resorted to in the post-war period and some struggles were resolved on the battlefield; the demarcation lines in Kashmir, in Korea, or between Israel and her neighbours, were all determined by combat.

Powerful weapons are by and large a governmental monopoly and hence share the characteristics of diplomacy and propaganda. Occasionally dissident groups procure sufficient quantities of weapons to challenge a government, usually together with some form of intervention from abroad, but as soon as this happens, they begin to claim recognition as a 'liberation' movement and, if they occupy and control a sizeable territory, they become a rival government. Military force is not only the prerogative of a government but, whenever it arises outside the government, it inevitably leads to the establishment of governmental structures.

The high expenditure involved is the major reason why the government enjoys a near-monopoly of sizeable and advanced weapons systems. According to *The Military Balance 1967–1968*, published by the Institute of Strategic Studies, only two countries managed to limit their expenditure to under 2 per cent of their Gross National Products: Luxembourg to 1·3 per cent and the Philippines to 1·8 per cent. Both, of course, enjoy exceptional security positions. Where this position is exceptionally bad, as in the Middle East, the defence expenditure of all the Arab countries and of Israel ranged between 10·5 per cent and 12·2 per cent of GNP. The expenditure of the two Superpowers was staggering. The United States spent $67,950m., 9·2 per cent of its GNP, and proposed to raise it in the following year to $73,000m.; the Soviet Union spent $29,800m., 8·9 per cent of her GNP, and proposed to raise it to $32,000m. China spent some $6,500m., 10 per cent of her GNP, and proposed to increase it to $7,000m.; the social effort for a country with a per capita income of some $85 can be imagined. The high defence expenditure of Great Britain, of $6,081m., 6·4 per cent of her GNP, can be justifiably thought to be a major reason why she could not achieve prosperity similar to that of France, with defence expenditure now running at the rate of only 4·4 per cent of GNP, or of Western Germany at 3·6 per cent.

Weapons and the military are primarily instruments of conflict relations but their use is not limited to war. In fact, there is no rigid division between the states of peace and war as could be inferred from the existence of two separate bodies of international law dealing with the two. Legally the Peace Treaty of Westphalia constituted a real revolution in the international system by establishing peace as the normal mode of international relations in Europe. Actually, however, the break was not really so great. Although the state of war was considered normal before 1648, it was mitigated by frequent special agreements establishing peace or truce, or by actually refraining from the use of force, while the post-1648 period was marked by the outbreaks of numerous wars. The post-1945 Cold War, a relationship of neither war nor peace, of acute conflict involving the use of force, but only on a relatively limited scale, is only a new, formally recognized example of the many instances disproving the rigid division between war and peace.

Clausewitz was fully justified in attacking a similarly rigid distinction occasionally made between international politics and military strategy. In conflict relations between two states both diplomacy and war are used for similar purposes, in order to prevail over the opponent. Although diplomacy is the major instrument employed in times of peace while weapons and the military are the major instruments employed in times of war, states freely change over from the one to the other and often use them both simultaneously. There is, however, a great difference between peacetime and wartime use of weapons and the military.

The traditional role in peacetime is to provide the background of strength to diplomacy, enabling it to pursue its objectives with assuredness and without being subject to intimidation. History seems to demonstrate the wisdom of the idea of 'negotiating from strength', e.g. the contrast can be made between the determined Western stand against Soviet pressures on their exceptionally exposed position in Berlin in June 1945 and the abject capitulation of Britain and France to Hitler's demands in the late thirties. Although many other factors were involved, the great contrast in Western military preparedness in the two periods did, undoubtedly, play a large part. States can confidently resist pressures and threats which can be brought to bear upon them only if they are confident of meeting force with force and of defending themselves adequately.

The possession of military strength serves its peacetime purpose only if other states are aware of it. This strength is therefore occasionally demonstrated in a general way: national-day parades or friendly naval visits serve as occasions to show troops and weapons, manoeuvres of armies and navies not only prepare for battle but often serve a similar purpose. Sometimes demonstrations by one state are directed against another specific state; in this case, instead of being merely a general reminder of military power, they serve as a warning that the use of this power is contemplated in the specific relationship. The methods frequently used are the massing of troops along the border, as was done by the Chinese and the Russians in the sixties, or the dispatch of a fleet, frequently resorted to by the Americans since 1945.

'Deterrence' in its traditional meaning describes all these ways of employing the military in peacetime since they all serve the purpose of deterring other states from the use of force by showing one's own power and likely superiority. This serves to ensure that other states will be readier to comply with one's objectives and particularly that they will refrain from attack. Since the war, however, 'deterrence' has assumed another, more technical meaning, restricted to nuclear weapons and the possibility of a nuclear attack. Deterrence is an extremely complex policy based upon subtle psychological and strategic calculations; its contents have been changing with the evolution of increasingly subtler weapons systems and strategies but its fundamental principle is quite simple. In one way it resembles the deterrent role of the pre-nuclear weapons which was to impress a potential attacker with the defender's military power. It is, however, important to stress that this pre-nuclear deterrence was based upon the capacity of the state to defend itself against an attack; the capacity to launch a counter-attack was, of course, important but only subsidiary. At present, the defence of national territory against a nuclear attack is impossible and it is extremely dubious whether even an improved anti-ballistic missile system will achieve more than to limit the damage. The basis of nuclear deterrence lies in the possession of a nuclear force capable of surviving an enemy attack and of inflicting an unacceptable damage on the opponent. This is called 'second-strike capability'.

The policy of deterrence was evolved in the relations between the two Superpowers, and all the other Nuclear Powers, which trail a long way behind these, are developing weapons systems and strategies derived from the primary United States–Soviet relationship. We are, therefore, justified in inquiring into the employment of nuclear weapons as an instrument of deterrence policy primarily in terms of this relationship. Never in history has a strategy been as carefully analysed and discussed both within the governmental machineries and by outside experts. We can, therefore, with a fair degree of confidence define the main premises of deterrence as they have been evolved by the United States and followed by the Soviet Union. The strategy assumes a rational opponent who weighs and calculates costs and risks, finds unacceptable the damage likely to be wrought by a full-scale nuclear war, and is in full control over political and military decisions which may involve or provoke nuclear exchanges.

Nuclear strategies have been shifting between the horns of the dilemma of how to maintain the threat of a nuclear attack at a sufficiently high level to make the resulting destruction unacceptable and, simultaneously, of how to make the opponent regard this threat as 'credible', to keep the opponent convinced that the nuclear strategy would be followed, or at least strongly apprehensive that it may be. The original American strategy of 'massive retaliation' was one of maximizing the threat. It meant that any serious Soviet expansionist move, e.g. in the vulnerable and threatened Berlin area, would meet with the response of a full blast of United States nuclear weapons. Rather ironically, the doctrine was fully articulated only in 1954, a few months after the Soviet Union had exploded its first hydrogen bomb. As the Soviet arsenal increased in size and began to include 'second-strike capability', the credibility of 'massive retaliation' was rapidly reduced. The conviction that the maximum threat involves also a minimum credibility logically led to the strategy of 'graduated deterrence', which endeavoured to resort to the alternative policy of combining a minimum threat with a maximum credibility. This strategy purported to establish a nuclear exchange calculus by the use of which exchanges could be stopped at any level before they had escalated to a full nuclear war and could even be graded so as to 'de-escalate', making the response weaker than the challenge so as not to provoke another move.

In the uneasy situation both Superpowers busied themselves to raise their nuclear capabilities by increasing their stocks of nuclear weapons and by making them as invulnerable as possible for the second-strike role, first through dispersal and then through the 'hardening' of land sites and the building of missile-carrying submarines. Once the Soviet side had become sufficiently powerful to inflict unacceptable damage on the United States in a second-strike attack, the American superiority in the numbers of weapons became less important; both had enough and the surplus capacity which became known as 'overkill' was of only marginal importance. However, even with a reasonable balance of capabilities, the stability of the relationship was still not fully ensured. It was endangered by the possibility of some mistake or lack of communication, of the escalation of a limited conflict between the Superpowers or their involvement in a conflict among others, of an accidental military action or nuclear explosion, of insubordination, or of faulty intelligence and interpretation of intentions. After the experience of reaching the brink of a nuclear war during the Cuban missile crisis in October 1962, the two Superpowers endeavoured to plug all the loopholes for errors or indiscipline in their governmental and military machines and also established the 'hot line', a means of direct communication between the two governments which was effectively used some dozen times during the Middle Eastern crisis in 1967.

In the early sixties the balance appeared to be reasonably stable despite the possession of nuclear weapons by Britain and France, since neither of them possessed either sufficient nuclear capability or the inclination to act irrationally in defiance of the rules of deterrence developed by the Superpowers. The situation changed with the appearance of China as a nuclear power. Notwithstanding her relative poverty, China devoted sufficient means to develop rapidly a nuclear striking force, and also exhibited a frame of mind which cast doubts upon the rationality of her behaviour within the rules of deterrence. By 1967 the stability of the United States–Soviet nuclear deterrence was threatened not only by China and by the possibility of proliferation among other, smaller states, but also by new technological developments. Fairly effective area-defence through nuclear explosions in outer space led to the Soviet deployment of an Anti-Ballistic Missile (ABM) system and to a rather limited similar United States construction, while war-heads became increasingly sophisticated to include several individually targeted bombs as well as decoys. The hitherto clear-cut comparison of destructive nuclear capabilities has to be replaced by a much more complex count of the effectiveness and the cost of further increases either in striking or in defensive power. Several hypotheses have been advanced about the origins of the new developments which have disturbed the relative stability of deterrence; whatever their validity, one major reason seems to lie in the Superpowers being caught up by the advance of technology. One encouraging aspect of the situation is their willingness to discuss it in the Strategic Arms Limitation Talks (SALT).

Undoubtedly, the strategic use of nuclear weapons has been again called into question, not only for Britain and France, but also for the two Superpowers. For China its use appears to be clearer. She may intend to use her nuclear armoury as an instrument of intimidation in an expansionist policy at the cost of her neighbours; perhaps more plausibly, without assuming such expansionism, she may wish to reassert herself as a Great Power and force the Superpowers and the other states to acknowledge her status.

Smaller states rely on the military in their international relations to a varying degree. At the one extreme we find the new African states which are a hitherto unprecedented category of states so secure in their territorial integrity and political independence that they keep very small forces. They show, however, how ineffective foreign policy becomes when it has no military power behind it. Despite strong international support, they are unable to prevail against the racialist régimes in Southern Africa. Somewhat similar is the case of Japan, with armed forces and a foreign policy which are not at all commensurate with her great economic power. At the other extreme are states engaged in acute conflicts which lead to recurrent violence. As long as these conflicts persist, none of these states can neglect the military instrument since this would entail unacceptable risk. The other states fall within a broad spectrum between the two extremes.

CHAPTER 8

# RESTRAINTS UPON STATE
# BEHAVIOUR

THE last three chapters were dealing with state behaviour: its goals and the capabilities, instruments and techniques used in their pursuit. In this analysis the state itself, which constitutes the domestic environment of the decision-makers, was considered as a source of capabilities and its international environment as the object of its activities. Both environments will now be looked at in another, negative role, from the angle of the restraints they impose upon state behaviour.

*Domestic Restraints*

Limitation of capabilities is the most fundamental restraint upon foreign policy. Admittedly the relationship between resources and objectives is not straightforward: decision-makers may be mistaken in their estimate either of the resources available to them or of those necessary for the attainment of an objective, or of both; they may also deliberately take the risk of overstretching their resources or decide to refrain from employing them to the full. Hence history is full of cases both of overcommitment and undercommitment, sometimes of quite a drastic nature. Yet it is important to remember that even the most powerful state cannot regard itself as being sufficiently powerful to pursue *all* its values and hence is restrained in its action.

The exact extent of the discrepancies between declaratory policies and actual state behaviour is generally unclear. The avowed objectives of Soviet and Chinese communists to communize the whole world, of the two parts of divided Germany, of Korea and of Vietnam to unify their respective countries, of the Pakistanis to take the whole of Kashmir, or of the Arabs to eliminate the state of Israel, are all unattainable owing to insufficient capabilities. Are we to infer that the real intentions of all these states diverge from their declaratory policies? If so, would they continue to diverge if these states suddenly obtained power sufficient to achieve what they profess to want?

Public opinion is the major source of domestic restraints. Foreign policy is determined and pursued by governments who in various ways represent and ultimately depend upon the opinion of their people. The nature and the degree of dependence varies greatly between the various types of régimes and also among single states within these types. The relationship is clear in the Western liberal states where public opinion is articulated and structured and governments depend upon being re-elected. It is also obvious in the majority of new states where public opinion is unstructured and where urban mobs can be suddenly swayed and remove the government from power. It is somewhat less clear but is by no means absent in rigidly governed communist countries where it is organized from above and is deprived of ready opportunities of expression against the government; as shown by the events in Czechoslovakia in 1968, even here the rulers could scarcely act with impunity against serious opposition for any length of time.

Of course, in so far as they defer to domestic public opinion in the choice of their objectives, the decision-makers reflect not only the wishes and aspirations of the people but also the restraints the people wish to impose upon the pursuit of these. These restraints are built into the decision-makers and are not readily identifiable. Public opinion acts as a clear restraint only when the decision-makers diverge from it, which happens in all régimes, whenever the government wishes to pursue an important policy objective which is unacceptable to the majority or an influential minority of the people. For instance, the successive Presidents of the United States in the fifties and sixties found it very difficult to recognize the Central People's Government of China and the rulers of Egypt found it equally dangerous to inaugurate a conciliatory policy towards Israel. Perhaps the Soviet rulers would come under a similar restraint of public opinion if they decided to give up their aspiration to world revolutionary leadership in order to achieve an effective *détente* with the United States. Until a potentially unpopular policy is actually tried, the degree of the constraint can only be guessed; in fact it may be deliberately exaggerated in order to convince other states that governmental policies cannot be altered.

Two categories of public opinion restraints recur sufficiently frequently to warrant singling them out. The first one arises from the proverbial dilemma of having to choose between guns and butter. In the pursuit of foreign policy objectives, governments use up some scarce resources and hence these become unavailable for domestic consumption. Even in the exceptionally affluent United States, by 1968 the cost of the fairly limited war in Vietnam was blocking any large-scale social welfare programmes; consumption needs in the Soviet Union are much greater and are also rising much faster. Small states face the dilemma much earlier and in a much starker form. The other category of restraint arises from war-weariness. The French could scarcely be stirred to further fighting towards the end of the Louis XIV and Napoleonic campaigns; the Russians greeted with complete apathy the declaration of war against Japan at the end of their exhausting struggle against the Nazis; the Americans built up increasing opposition to further fighting in the long-drawn Korean and Vietnamese campaigns which gave no promise of reasonable success.

In view of the grave dangers which could arise from serious discrepancies between the rulers and the people, governments habitually endeavour to sway public opinion towards their way of thinking. Propaganda directed to this effect exacerbates international differences since it invariably consists of what the Americans call an 'oversell' of the dangers imminent as well as of the remedies proposed.

Finally, public opinion can act as a restraint through insisting that certain moral rules must be observed. The impact of morality as an internal restraint upon state behaviour is no clearer than its impact upon other types of human behaviour. It is always possible to make out the extreme cases both for the all-pervading importance of morality and for its complete ineffectiveness; the controversy between the 'moralists' and the 'realists' is repeated in every generation. In fact much of allegedly 'moral' behaviour can be explained by utilitarian, expediency considerations. As giving alms to a beggar can be attributed either to charity, or to the selfish desire to avoid unpleasant pestering, or to the wish to enjoy the prestige of being thought charitable or to avoid the opprobrium of being thought mean, so the explanation that international behaviour is governed by ethical considerations is never fully convincing.

The dialogue between the rulers and their peoples is invariably conducted in moral terms: statements of policy objectives are represented as moral and just, if not explicitly then at least by implication; also actual actions have often to be represented and defended in moral terms. Sometimes the moral considerations are 'internalized' by the decision-makers. For instance, Churchill had no hesitation in rejecting Stalin's proposal made in 1944 to eliminate some 50,000 German officers after their capture (if this proposal was ever made seriously), and Roosevelt had no hesitation in rejecting the division of Europe into spheres of interest, proposed by Churchill and Stalin. We can imagine that if something really drastic happened to the British diplomats who were subject to maltreatment in Peking in 1967, e.g. if some of them were executed or killed, the British Government would not execute or condone the lynching of the Chinese diplomats in London.

Moral sentiments are, however, erratic and rather slow in being awakened. With very few exceptions, British and United States public opinion accepted the bombing of German cities and the use of nuclear bombs; opposition based upon moral grounds to the fierce war waged by the United States in Vietnam took some two years to get off the ground. Government actions are explained by the plea of necessity, of *raison d'état* and on the basis of rational calculation, setting off the losses likely to be incurred if the restraints were adopted against the smaller sufferings of the adversaries. Nevertheless, public opinion can become politically significant. For instance, popular support for the United States involvement in Vietnam dwindled in 1967 to the point of making it distinctly possible that a restraint on future actions might here arise. The opposition, however, was based not only upon moral considerations but also, probably more so, upon war-weariness and the fact that no solution was in sight.

Not many moral rules can be identified as serious restraints operating upon actual behaviour. Moreover, although these restraints may arise within the domestic environment, usually they are derived from rules which are internationally accepted. Historically, public morality stems largely from the Christian faith and was partly accepted and partly transformed by the individual states; thus the international context was the original one. Likewise new rules of morality are likely to be evolved internationally, within the context of the United Nations, e.g. concerning human rights, before they are adopted by individual states. We can therefore consider domestic moral restraints not so much as an autonomous force but rather as a reinforcement of international moral restraints which will be considered in the next section.

## External Restraints

In broad analytical terms, external restraints can be equated with domestic restraints in that both circumscribe the freedom of action of the state in pursuit of its national interest and that both are closely linked in their effects. A state may increase its freedom of action by working at either end, through increasing its capabilities and diminishing domestic restraints, or through trying to reduce external restraints; likewise additional limitations can come from both ends. Changes at home and abroad may reinforce one another or counteract or cancel one another, as the case may be. We can conceive the pursuit of national interest both in terms of the energy put into it by the state and in terms of the resistance or inertia with which it meets in the international environment; the limitation of state capabilities is matched and reinforced by the resistance of other states or of the international system, whereas the restraints imposed by domestic opinion are paralleled, and greatly surpassed, by the much more elaborate network of international norms of behaviour for which international public opinion is the major vehicle.

In the course of history, the organization of international restraints has greatly progressed. The moot question how far we have advanced here from conflict towards cooperation can be tackled only after the various restraints have been analysed and classified with this question in view.

It is obvious that when two states begin to interact, before they form or join some form of international system, the only external restraints come from their wills and capabilities. For instance, when the Romans first came up against the Parthians it was the will of the Parthians to resist which prevented the Romans from subjugating them. It is possible to shift the emphasis to the limitation of Roman capabilities and to say that these were insufficient to overcome the logistic difficulties and the Parthian resistance, but it is clear that there were no 'systemic' restraints since the international system embracing the Romans and the Parthians scarcely existed. Similar were all cases of international interaction in its very early stages, before some sort of an international system had been formed; the absence of articulated systemic restraints may be considered as one of the important circumstances differentiating Spanish colonial expansion in the Americas and her rivalry with Portugal, from the 'scramble for Africa' in the nineteenth century.

When a state is blocked in the attainment of an objective by the will and capabilities of others, unless it is ready to forgo its objective it is naturally driven to the expedient of increasing its own capabilities. If this is impossible or very difficult to achieve by the state's own efforts, it can do so by enlisting the support of other states. Such support, of course, is not free. Whatever its nature and form, some *quid pro quo* is required and, moreover, outside support can never be as fully relied upon as the domestic resources which are subject to full governmental control. Although modern states invariably depend on some form of outside support, whatever their own power may be, they are also acutely aware of the danger of excessive dependence upon such support and they endeavour to rely as far as possible upon their own resources, at least to be able to fall back upon them if let down by their allies.

The traditional form of securing support from another state or states is an alliance, i.e. an agreement to help in specified conditions and usually against a specified joint adversary. All alliances involve a certain loss of freedom of action, whether the state joins one based upon relations of fair equality or one which is hierarchical, and whether it is a weak or a powerful partner in the latter. The freedom of action preserved actually seems to depend not so much upon the power of the state as upon the rigidity or flexibility of the international system. When the system is sufficiently flexible to allow changing alignments, when reasonable alternatives are offering, the state is relatively free, however weak it may be. If, by contrast, the system is rigid, if the change of alignment is extremely dangerous or unthinkable, it is much more difficult to modify or reject existing links and even the most powerful state is limited by them.

To take an example from the contemporary system – while the Cold War was at its height, the smaller partners in the Atlantic alliance as well as in the Warsaw Pact had to forfeit their freedom of decision on the most important international issues in order to ensure the continuing protection of the Superpower on which they were dependent. By the beginning of the seventies this dependence had greatly diminished; arguably this is due to the considerable abatement of the dangers felt to exist and the consequent weakening of the basic conflict between the blocs. Another possible complementary explanation is that, with the mutual deterrence system, the two Superpowers no longer offered a credible protection to their associates since it was difficult to imagine them engaging in a nuclear exchange to support any one of them. Thus the defence capabilities of the protected associates had been drastically curtailed but at the same time the limitations upon their independence and freedom of action were similarly reduced. The new freedom was not immediately realized but it clearly formed the logical basis of President de Gaulle's foreign policy aiming at the complete revision of NATO. The Superpowers, however, were similarly limited in their freedom of action through their alliance ties. Admittedly, in the original stages, much of this limitation was merely theoretical since the obligations arising from the treaties were coinciding with the policy objectives of the Superpowers. With the degree of stabilization of the nuclear balance and of the *détente* now reached, many of the commitments undertaken were, in fact, becoming embarrassing ties. No wonder that the post-war alliances are going the way of all previous alliances in the past – as soon as the common enemy becomes less feared, the alliance loosens.

The expedient of extending one's capabilities by adding the capabilities of other states can become institutionalized through the international system in the form of a balance of power. 'Balance of power' describes the international system obtaining in Europe between 1648 and 1914, the tendency towards equilibrium in general, as well as state policies directed towards such an equilibrium. We are considering it here only from one angle, as a form of external restraint upon state behaviour. The states have to accept the infringement of their freedom of action by the system as the price to be paid for the benefits obtained for their defence. In a way, participation in a balance-of-power system resembles that in an alliance – in exchange for being allowed to count upon the support of others, the state has to promise reciprocal support, and tie itself accordingly. In another way, however, there is a difference. The balance-of-power system is a form of international order which both adds more to the state's capabilities and subtracts more from its freedom of action than simple alliances. The international order implies an additional guarantee – its stability being in favour of all its participants, in theory at least, all of them would refrain from policies endangering the stability of the system and the existence of its members; if an ally within the balance-of-power system proves unfaithful, others should be sufficiently interested in the preservation of the international order to intervene and restore the balance. Corresponding restraints are imposed upon the members: regard for its stability and for the perpetuation of its members and the preservation of equilibrium preclude grossly expansionist policies.

While restraints based upon balance of power combine the traditional power-political calculations of the capabilities of individual states with a degree of pressure stemming from the nature of international order, other restraints stem exclusively from the international system. It is no longer the case of extending the state's own capabilities through adding those of another state; the foundation of international as much as of all other social restraints is found in the very act of membership.* No society can operate without some normative control over the

* Subsequent paragraphs are paraphrased from J. Frankel, *International Relations*, Oxford University Press, 2nd ed., 1969, pp. 186–9.

behaviour of its members. If every member were a law unto himself, behaviour would be unpredictable and the resulting anarchy would preclude any social order and would negate the very existence of society. International society differs from national societies in that it consists of states instead of individuals and is only loosely organized. Nevertheless, analogies from a society of individuals are not unwarranted, provided they are not pushed too far and the differences are kept in mind.

A legal system is the most highly evolved form of expressing social order; but human behaviour is governed by many other, non-legal norms, those of morality and of what is often called *mores*, such as custom, etiquette or fashion. Some thinkers prefer to derive the highest of these norms, those of law and of morality, from higher superhuman principles but it is possible to explain them, together with other social norms, as the expression of social needs. Societies differ in the degree to which they permit variety in human behaviour and in the stress they put upon conformity. On the whole, the nature of the rules is governed by their social importance and is expressed in the type of sanction provided in cases of breach. If the social importance of the rules is slight, mild social disapproval suffices. For instance, a woman defying the dictates of fashion may be slightly ridiculed or hampered in her social intercourse with more fashion-conscious individuals. If the dignity of an institution or occasion calls for the wearing of customary attire, anyone not so dressed may be refused admission – thus a woman in a sleeveless dress may not be allowed into an Italian church.

Social sanctions increase with the degree to which human behaviour seriously affects others. Some norms are incorporated in the law of the country and are enforced by a central authority which tries to prevent their infringement and punishes their violation, but law cannot meet the whole range of socially undesirable possibilities. Hence law is supplemented by rules of morality which are not enforced in the same way but are generally considered to be quite important. The sanctions for the violation of moral rules lie not only in individual conscience (which is assiduously trained in the desired direction at home, at school and in all social intercourse) but also in strong social pressures. If cruelty to children is to be avoided, the law can define only a limited number of punishable offences, but a person treating children cruelly, although not committing any of these specified offences, is likely, if discovered, to be condemned by his friends and neighbours. This too is a strong form of sanction.

These well-known and rather simple distinctions are mentioned here because they illuminate the more abstruse nature of the norms regulating the behaviour of states. As in domestic societies, the scope and nature of international norms are determined by those of social needs, but there is an important difference in the degree of social agreement which can be reached about them. By definition, domestic societies embody a good measure of fundamental social consent, without which they would not have come into being or would disintegrate. If such social consensus existed internationally, it would lead directly to world government. International order is based not so much on the consensus of its participants as on the physical fact that states exist and cannot escape from interaction. It is a world characterized largely by the stark necessities of a Hobbesian society which has not yet evolved a fully articulated social contract.

Interaction among states is much less varied than interaction among individuals, and therefore the customs and conventions, the *mores*, of international society are not quite as complex and voluminous as those among individuals. As in a domestic society, the sanction for their infringement is social disapproval of suitable severity. In stable periods, such as that of the fairly homogeneous balance-of-power system, *mores* were generally observed, but in revolutionary periods they are deliberately and flagrantly violated. A good illustration may be found in the determination shown by the bolshevik rulers of Russia, after they had come to power, to substitute direct relations with the peoples of other countries, and later with their communist parties, for traditional diplomatic relations. In a few years, when the dust had somewhat settled, the Russians reverted to the traditional forms of diplomacy, including ceremonial dress and titles, although they did not abandon their attempts at subversion. The world is now rent by an ideological conflict and crowded by numerous new states with divergent cultural backgrounds; hence the traditions of the small homogeneous world of European diplomacy in the last century require substantial adaptation. Here the General Assembly of the United Nations plays a crucial role. Being a 'town meeting' of nearly all the peoples of the world, it compels them to make mutual adjustments in their behaviour and to accept a common code. Although much less homogeneous than its nineteenth-century predecessor, the international society of today can operate because states have become much more aware of the repercussions of their behaviour on others. To use a sociological term, from being predominantly self-centred they have now become 'other-oriented'. Needless to say, this does not mean that they are always willing to take the desires and susceptibilities of others into account.

## *International Morality*

'Morality' is perhaps the most blatant example of the ambiguities engendered by transplanting concepts based upon the behaviour of individuals into the analysis of the behaviour of states. Whether acting as individuals or as statesmen, men profess to follow moral rules and rarely, if ever, make a distinction *in principle* about the nature of rules binding them in these two capacities. In practice, however, they do draw distinctions when acting as statesmen; on many occasions they claim exemptions based upon *raison d'état* or necessity which would be completely unacceptable as excuses for similar actions in their private capacity.

An obvious tension is inherent in a situation in which the notions of public and private morality are not clearly distinguished. It is possible to insist, as Kant does, upon an unqualified equation of international and private morality, but this is a statement of the 'ought' rather than a description of the 'is'. It is also possible to go to the opposite extreme of denying the existence of international morality altogether, as Machiavelli does. The majority of writers do neither. They accept that some form of international morality exists, attributing to it varying degrees of importance, and they differentiate between it and private morality.

We must, of course, distinguish between international morality and moral rules operating within individual national societies which constitute a restraint within the domestic environment.* Owing to the great cultural and ideological differences between single states, their national moral codes undoubtedly differ. It is, however, a moot question whether any domestic rules ever constitute a really serious restraint upon behaviour unless they are also internationally accepted and generally reciprocated.

Since moral rules are obeyed for a variety of reasons, the dictates of conscience being only one of them, it is impossible to evaluate their impact upon behaviour with any degree of clarity. Thus did the Americans refrain from using the nuclear bomb or from threatening to do so when they were in the position of nuclear monopoly because they were acting under moral restraints, although many of them suspected that the Russians may not have done so in a similar situation. Undoubtedly the cultural moral constraint existed but it was reinforced by additional constraints stemming from the international environment and from sheer expediency. On the whole, when it comes to matters of real substance, Machiavelli was probably right in claiming that no prince can subject himself to moral restraints greater than those accepted by others, although he was wrong in claiming that consequently no international moral constraints exist at all.

The incessant invocation of ethics and moral rules under a variety of names (e.g. justice, fairness, peace, stability, security, equality, etc. etc.) can be regarded as hypocrisy, as a convenient but generally unconvincing justification of state behaviour. While these principles are invoked in statements of general policy objectives and are professed to govern the rules of behaviour, in actual practice they are conveniently forgotten. Hitler's claim that the military reoccupation of the Rhineland was undertaken in the interests of peace is only a more obvious case of the recurrent discrepancy. This convenient hypocrisy apart, rules of international morality, if universally accepted, can serve not only as a nationally convenient, but also internationally useful agency for peaceful change, as an instrumentality for the revision of the rules of law which could not be otherwise achieved except through

* See above, pp. 176–8.

violence. The moral justification of the political pressures for colonial self-determination since 1945 has greatly contributed to the revision of the legal rights of the colonial Powers; had it not been for the Great Depression and Hitler, German protests against the Peace Treaty of Versailles as an immoral dictate might have achieved its peaceful revision.

Moral rules are not, however, restricted to these roles of rationalization of national policy and of agencies of peaceful change. They act as restraints for two distinct reasons: the first is found in the sanctions imposed for persistent deviation from the internationally accepted moral standards of conduct which, as in domestic societies, lies in social disapproval. All countries, however powerful, are sensitive to the dangers of losing the reputation and prestige of acting morally. All countries are expected to abide by the generally accepted standards of conduct, and are fully aware of the opprobrium arising if they are breached. Since all political behaviour comes under public scrutiny and is nearly always morally evaluated, the moral principles frequently professed as a cover-up for purely selfish national policy assume a momentum of their own; in order to avoid the unwelcome reputation of hypocrisy and duplicity, however insincere they may have been in their protestations, statesmen generally find it more expedient to follow the professed principles than to violate them.

A good example of the relevance of this restraint is shown by the complete disregard of moral considerations by many experts who are relatively free from direct scrutiny by public opinion. This is particularly pronounced in the thought of the contemporary nuclear strategists who analyse deterrence in terms of the theory of games or of bargaining, and view the mass destruction and the 'mega-deaths' of a nuclear war in terms scarcely thinkable for a statesman. The fact that the substance of nuclear policy may be finally decided on the basis of their morally neutral analysis presents a problem of great gravity.*

The other root of restraint is found in the moral sentiments and consciences of the statesmen themselves. This was particu-

* For a critique of the leading nuclear strategists, see: A. Rapoport, *Strategy and Conscience*, New York, Harper Row, 1964.

larly true about the practice of Great Britain and the United States in the nineteenth century. Both countries enjoyed then an unequalled 'moral opportunity' by being exceptionally secure; moreover, international moral rules closely approximated their domestic moral codes internalized by their statesmen. It is safe to assume that these statesmen preferred to act morally rather than otherwise, unless, of course, a really vital national interest appeared to be at stake. Perhaps a similar assumption, although with lesser force, can be made about statesmen in other times and places. These, however, are often governed by national moral codes differing from the international one and, even more importantly, they have to operate in conditions of lesser security so that their vital national interests are likely to prevail much more frequently. It is interesting to note the divergence in the evaluation of nuclear strategy by some United States nuclear scientists governed predominantly by considerations of conscience, and by the United States statesmen governed mainly by considerations of national security.

Exceptions occur and are of first importance. In many periods and in many international systems a 'rogue' state arises which challenges the international order. It may glibly invoke morality as a justification for the changes in law demanded, but it is not particularly heedful of the internationally accepted moral rules; its domestic moral code usually diverges from them and hence its statesmen are not subject to the restraints of their individual conscience.

The only external restraint they accept is opposition by the will of other states, backed by adequate power. Nazi Germany is a fairly clear-cut example but the Soviet Union in the inter-war period or contemporary China may well fall within the same category. The hypothesis can be advanced that powerful revisionist states are scarcely subject to any international moral constraints.

Even an extreme idealist would not assert that moral restraints actually prevail over what states consider to be their vital interests. For instance, nobody could realistically assume that, if faced with mortal danger, the two Superpowers or either one of them would refrain through moral qualms from inflicting devastating nuclear damage upon the opponent. This is the very basis of the strategy of deterrence. The question that is sometimes asked, whether the Americans would employ to the full their available second-strike capacity if subject to a full-scale Soviet nuclear attack, is generally raised more upon the level of expediency than morality. In actual state practice it is impossible to single out one instance in which moral restraints prevailed over what the statesmen considered a vital national interest. Any cases quoted can be explained either by the fact that expediency governed them as much if not more than morality, or that they refused to consider the particular interest as vital. Anyway, statesmen usually act in response to immediate contingencies and conceive the issues in their own terms rather than in terms of the moral issues concerned. The study of such cases as appeasement in the thirties, the area-bombing of Germany, or the use of nuclear bombs over Japan, clearly show that full moral evaluation came only *ex post facto*.

Finally, moral restraints clearly operate much more effectively in the relations among friends and allies than among adversaries. This is readily explained by the principle of reciprocity – good behaviour which is expected to be reciprocated is not only good in moral terms but is also advantageous. Machiavelli was right in noting that, failing an expectation of reciprocity, statesmen tend to behave as badly as they expect to be treated, an important instance of the vicious circularity of images to which we shall return in the concluding chapter.

## International Law

However much the interpreters of international morality disagree about its nature, they are at least in general agreement about its impotence and its lack of significant influence upon actual state behaviour. Interpretations of international law are even more fundamentally confused – not only is the realm of the 'is' confused with that of the 'ought', but the existing international law, now in a state of transition, is excessively equated either with the law which was prevailing in the past or with that expected to evolve in the future.

A major difficulty arises, as in the case of the notion of 'morality', when a concept evolved in inter-personal relations is applied to relations among states. Within the state, individuals are bound by law and the state wields sanctions against law-breakers. International law operates within a fundamentally different social context – instead of being *above* the individuals and potentially enforced by the overwhelming might of the state, it is merely *among* the single states, and it is not backed by any overwhelming sanctions against potential law-breakers. The situation in the international system which is dominated by its units is so anomalous that some lawyers deny the legal character of international law altogether. The very concepts of sovereign individual states and of an international legal system are fundamentally opposed: if the states are truly sovereign, the legal rules cannot be binding; if the legal rules are binding, the states cannot be truly sovereign. In legal theory this is resolved by the theory of consent which bases the binding character of international legal norms upon their acceptance by the states. This theory is a somewhat far-fetched legal fiction, especially since consent is not always explicit and has to be implied. It takes some straining of imagination to accept that the state is exercising its sovereignty by the very fact of agreeing to limit it, a difficulty resembling that of explaining the 'social contract' as the exercise of the individual's freedom expressed in the accepted limitation. The strain becomes scarcely bearable when we are asked to believe that a state may be exercising its sovereignty even when it surrenders it under duress and accepts incorporation into another state; this is as convincing as the contention that a free man would exercise his freedom by formally agreeing to accept the status of a slave into which he is forced.

In practice, this inherent contradiction between state sovereignty and the binding nature of international law results in the limitation of international rules to relatively unimportant matters. As with respect to sanctions and to its relationship with the units, here again international law fundamentally differs from 'municipal law'. Normally within the state law regulates only the more important forms of human relationships, leaving their minor aspects to regulation by other moral and customary rules which do not enjoy state-administered sanctions. The contrary is true about international law. It is limited in its application to the relatively less important aspects of inter-state relations which do not affect their vital interests, while really important matters have stubbornly evaded legal regulation. The best example is the crucial question of the right preserved by the states to decide issues of peace and war; the legal limitations hitherto devised have circumscribed this right but have not affected its essence. Only in areas pertaining to vital interests and to power are the rules of international law to no avail. This does not affect the rapid growth of rules governing the increasing range of other international transactions, or detract from their importance.

Bearing in mind the limited scope of international law, it is important to stress that international transactions are generally conducted with strict observance of its rules. With the great expansion of interaction among states, some kind of legal order is essential and the states on the whole endeavour to maintain it. This is true notwithstanding the occasional spectacular breaches of law. Although generally states go to considerable lengths to maintain the reputation of being law-abiding and hence trustworthy partners in international transactions, whenever their leaders feel that some 'vital' interest is being affected they break the inconvenient rule. We have now moved away from the rather pious contention of the inter-war generation that being law-abiding is a virtue while being a law-breaker is a vice inherent in the régimes and ideologies of the various states. The reasons for the varying attitudes are found not so much in virtue or vice but rather in the satisfaction or dissatisfaction with the existing state of affairs. Law is an essentially conservative institution which preserves the *status quo* and it is to be expected that 'have' states, satisfied with the *status quo*, would uphold it, the law, as it is, being in their interests. It is likewise to be expected that the 'have not' states, dissatisfied with the *status quo* and wishing to revise it, would be more prone to ignore law which buttresses the unacceptable existing order; their obedience to law will often be more the result of their weakness than their scrupulousness. In fact both the law-abiding upholders of the *status quo* and the law-breaking revisionists do no more than pursue their respective interests: although the law-breakers are more dangerous to the international system, their disregard for law is due merely to the nature of their interests.

Throughout history, states have disregarded some legal obligations. Instances are not limited to the utter disregard of treaty obligations by Nazi Germany or the freely avowed use of international law rules as policy instruments and propaganda weapons by early Soviet rulers against class enemies. The Americans persistently violated the air-space of other countries by high-altitude intelligence flights and supported the Bay of Pigs invasion of Cuba in 1961; Britain attacked the French ships at Oran in 1940 and, more recently, violated a number of treaty obligations when she imposed a temporary 15 per cent surcharge on import duties in order to restore her balance of payments; India in Kashmir and Goa, and the majority of other states have acted similarly with disregard, or only scant regard for international law.

All these breaches notwithstanding, international law is generally observed and even these spectacular exceptions in a way confirm this rule. No state freely admits its disregard for a rule of law; on the contrary, even when breaking it, it often exerts great efforts to persuade the world that no breach is being committed; if this is impossible, it stresses the element of necessity involved and the exceptional character of the breach. There is a moral basis for maintaining the rules of international law since they constitute the foundation of the international system which would otherwise sink into chaos. For being law-abiding, every state obtains also individual advantages in the form of prestige as being trustworthy and of an increased expectation that partners to transactions will likewise abide by the law; if the state breaks the law, it loses prestige and risks reprisals.

Although one source of the rules of international law can be found in natural law, the practice of states, whether expressed in treaties or in customary law, has been the more important source, at least over the last two centuries. At present the development and adaptation of law through state practice has, however, become increasingly difficult. A nucleus of the international system, as the Western European states were in the nineteenth century, no longer exists, and the swollen numbers of states are unwilling to take the cue from the Superpowers or from any other grouping.

Often the distinction is made between the 'old' or 'classical' international law and the 'new' one. The former, as evolved in the eighteenth and nineteenth centuries, recognized states alone as its subjects, was based upon the pr: ctice of the major Western Powers, was essentially conservative, and could be clearly distinguished from other norms of behaviour. The 'new law' differs in all these essential characteristics. Although states remain the major subjects of international law, international organizations have joined their ranks. Moreover, international law is becoming increasingly concerned also with individuals, to the point that some lawyers accord them the position of full subjects of this law. This 'new international law' is shaped mainly in the General Assembly of the United Nations where political considerations often prevail over pure legal logic, and is becoming increasingly reformist. The formulation of norms of international behaviour by the General Assembly is not limited to legal rules, and the traditional distinctions between legal and other norms are becoming blurred. In fact, so central and complicated has become the role of the United Nations that no analysis of international restraints would be complete without discussing it in some detail.

## *The General Assembly as a Source of External Restraints*

The record of the General Assembly during the first twenty years of its existence clearly demonstrates the blurring of the traditional boundaries between legal and other norms of international behaviour; it reflects the social necessity of having some norm-making authority in the international systems, although it deviates from traditional legal distinctions which were incorporated in the Charter.

The Charter provided for a relatively modest role of the General Assembly in the field of law by asking it to 'initiate studies and make recommendations for the purpose of . . . encouraging the progressive development of international law and its codification' (Article 13 [1]). The Assembly set up in 1948 an

International Law Commission to undertake studies and prepare draft codes and declarations for submission to the Assembly; sometimes it acted directly, preparing such conventions and declarations, e.g. the 'Declaration of Human Rights' in 1947, or the 'Convention on Genocide' in 1948 or on the 'Elimination of All Forms of Racial Discrimination' in 1965. It would be difficult to expect a great degree of consensus in a period of history marked by sharp antagonism among the major states, and the record of the General Assembly has not been very impressive. Nevertheless, some useful codification and legislation was completed under its auspices, e.g. the Law of the Sea was extensively codified, although no agreement could be reached upon the vital problem of the extent of territorial waters; likewise conventions were adopted on the régimes of Antarctica and of outer and planetary space.

At the same time, the Charter provided for the Security Council to act as a guardian of international peace and security and hence endowed it with the power to make decisions in this field binding on all the members (Chapter VII and Article 25). The distinction frequently made between legal and political norms of behaviour should not obscure the fact that this meant that the Security Council was established as a source of legally binding rules. The Cold War prevented the Council from operating effectively: since passing the rules was contingent upon the concurrent votes of all the permanent members of the Council who enjoy the 'power of veto', the Council could operate effectively only in the extremely rare cases of such agreement.

Whereas neither the Security Council nor the General Assembly in their 'quasi-legislative' capacities functioned as envisaged in the Charter, the General Assembly developed its powers under the provisos of Articles 10–14 'to discuss any questions or any matters' within the scope of the Charter and to make recommendations upon them. These fairly vague powers, insisted upon by the middle and small states represented at the San Francisco Conference, served as a foundation for activities the full extent of which nobody could anticipate in 1945. 'Recommendations' are, as their name indicates, not legally binding decisions. No state is legally bound to accept a General Assembly recommendation and some of them have, indeed, persistently refused to do so, e.g. South Africa. At the same time, these recommendations have been increasingly influential in controlling state behaviour to the point of approximating binding rules of international behaviour and becoming their important source. The growing tradition of compliance makes disobedience increasingly difficult.

The debate about the extent of the legal powers of the General Assembly frequently centred around the so-called 'domestic jurisdiction clause' (Article 2 [7]) which states that the United Nations is not authorized to intervene in matters that are essentially within the domestic jurisdiction of a state, except when taking enforcement measures envisaged for threats to and breaches of international peace and security. Some states took the view that the clause could always be overridden by considerations of international peace and security; others insisted that whereas discussion and recommendations of a general nature regarding the domestic jurisdiction of all states do not amount to intervention, the Assembly has no power to make specific recommendations regarding the domestic matters of a particular state.

Theories about this issue diverge. As put in a fairly legal form by Dag Hammarskjöld who was influential in extending and consolidating the powers of the Assembly, in so far as the recommendations express a majority consensus and involve the application of the binding principles of the Charter, they may be expected 'to come more and more close to being recognized as decisions having a binding effect on all those concerned'. Although strictly speaking devoid of legal status, recommendations in fact assume it on the basis of the authority of the Charter. This is, of course, a far-reaching doctrine which is, understandably, more acceptable to the Afro-Asian countries which utilize their majority position in the Assembly than to others.

Equally vulnerable is the theory attributing the binding nature of General Assembly recommendations to the fact that they are representative of the international opinion of mankind. The voting system of the Organization scarcely warrants such an assertion; on the basis of the 'one state one vote' principle, the smallest states enjoy equality of vote with the most populous, hence recommendations based upon a majority of votes may have, in fact, the support of only a small minority of mankind. In 1947 Mr Dulles went so far as to assert that the Assembly had the right to pass 'moral judgements of the conscience of the world' but his opinion was clearly influenced by the fact that the United States could then confidently count upon full majority support on all major Cold War issues.

The third view leaves aside the contentious legal and moral issues and considers the General Assembly as a standing diplomatic conference. Members are not legally bound by any majority rules which they refuse to accept but, for reasons of sheer expediency, consider them according to the weight of opinion and power behind them. This is why all states prefer to avoid the censure of the General Assembly which, however unrepresentative it may be, is still the broadest international forum in existence. In a way this view may appear to be unorthodox, positively revolutionary; in another way it is essentially conservative. State practice has been the main source of the norms of international behaviour, and state practice remains the main source. The only difference between the situation today and that in the last century lies in the definition of this 'practice'. Instead of looking into the practice of the major Western Powers which provided the decisive paradigm in the past, we are now on the way to accepting the General Assembly as the paradigm for the present. Non-compliance is inexpedient and occurs only when a state is concerned with what it deems to constitute its 'vital interests'.

In some cases the 'quasi-legislative' powers of the Assembly are fairly clear. In 1948 the Council of Foreign Ministers referred to it on the issue of the future of the Italian colonies which were still under British military occupation, and the Assembly resolution determined the issue. The issue of Palestine is only slightly less clear. In 1947 the United Kingdom referred the determination of the future of the Palestine mandate to the General Assembly which decided in favour of a partition plan. Had the Arabs accepted this resolution, it would have determined the legal status of Palestine. As it was, the Arabs rejected it and Britain consequently refused to implement it. The division of

Palestine was effected on the battlefield between the Israelis and the Arabs and the boundaries deviated from the 1947 partition proposals.

Decolonization is the major field in which the Assembly's powers have been successfully exercised. The colonial Powers were sufficiently influential in 1944 and 1945 to preserve their dominant position in their empires. The new institution of 'trusteeship' accorded to the United Nations somewhat further-reaching powers of supervision than the mandates system had accorded to the League of Nations, but the system was limited to the relatively small and unimportant group of ex-mandates and territories taken away from ex-enemy states as the result of the Second World War. No colonies were voluntarily submitted to the régime, as was envisaged in the Charter. In their imperial possessions, the administering Powers accepted the principles of a 'declaration regarding non-self-governing territories' (Chapter XI of the Charter) which provided for the evolution of self-government but did not even mention full independence. They were under no obligation to accept any form of United Nations supervision in the performance of their tasks, except to transmit regularly to the Secretary General, for information purposes, reports regarding the conditions in their territories, significantly omitting the political ones.

These innocuous provisions served as a basis for continuous and increasing pressures by the General Assembly for complete decolonization. Ignoring the provisions of the Charter and the opposition by the colonial Powers, the General Assembly gradually ensured the inclusion of political conditions in the reports, and discussion by a succession of special committees. The process culminated in the famous Declaration of 14 December 1960 on the Granting of Independence to Colonial Countries and People (Resolution 1514). Despite all their opposition, the colonial Powers, except Portugal, eventually accepted the resolutions as binding upon them.

# PART THREE

# INTERNATIONAL ISSUES
# AND PROSPECTS

CHAPTER 9

# MAJOR INTERNATIONAL ISSUES

### World, International and Domestic Politics

NOWADAYS we are often reminded that we live in one world or that the whole world is one area of activity. In a sense this is no more than a truism but in another sense it is an exaggeration. It is rather futile to argue whether the outstanding feature of the contemporary international system is to be found in its traditional domination by its subsystems, the states, or in the recent growth of a network of modes of behaviour and institutions transcending the state; it is possible to make a reasoned case for either. If the distinction is expressed by counterposing the activities of states and those of the international organizations, as is sometimes done, the old pattern appears to be dominant. It is, however, possible to conceive world politics more broadly. Although the international system commands only few specialized instrumentalities in the form of international institutions, the states, too, act on its behalf. In the past the Great Powers used to be the main upholders of the balance-of-power system and today all the members of the United Nations act not only for their respective national interests but, occasionally at least, also on behalf of the organization as a whole.

Thus we can distinguish between the state-regarding international politics and the system-regarding world politics not according to the identity of the actors but according to the nature of their activity. Unfortunately this distinction, however convenient theoretically, does not allow clear differentiation in practice, owing to the circularity of all arguments. If we approach the problem from the angle of states, as is usually done, we can postulate that all state actions are, by definition, undertaken to foster some national interests; if these actions are on behalf of or for the international system, we must postulate that the state considers the maintenance of this system to be in its national interest. Likewise an international organization to which the state belongs must act for the state's national interests, otherwise it would withdraw from membership; however, in order to secure the general benefits accruing from membership, the state is willing to accept a certain amount of organizational activity not concerned with its national interest or sometimes even opposed to it, e.g. when Britain accepted some unwarranted anti-colonial strictures from the United Nations on Gibraltar or South Arabia.

From the angle of the international system, the picture stands upside-down. All national activities by state interaction form part of the international system but whereas some of these are conducted mainly with regard to the individual states, others are conducted more with regard to the system as a whole. It is obviously difficult to identify the proportions of the state- and the system-regarding characteristics of any single action, especially since it is convenient for states to present predominantly national interests as systemic (cf. the case of the United States action in Korea which was conducted as a United Nations collective security action) and likewise to brand any undesirable international activities as merely serving as a cover for the selfish interests of another state (cf. Soviet criticism not only of the Korean action but of many quite innocuous United Nations activities as being in the interests of the United States).

It is unnecessary to dwell upon the confused argument. We need not agree about either the method of analysis or the contents of the international and national elements in any given action. All we need to do is to postulate that some actions, both by states and by international organizations, deal with issues of interest to the whole international system or a large number of its members, and that some of these are undertaken in full awareness of this inter-relationship. Part Two was devoted to the self-regarding behaviour of states; this chapter discusses the system-regarding behaviour both of states and of international organizations. Often the same action requires analysis under both headings.

The broadest possible explanation of the gradual shift from international politics to world politics can be sought in the rapid recent growth in social communications on a global scale. This growth accounts also for the concurrent internationalization of hitherto domestic issues. Legal theory in this respect no longer corresponds with reality. According to this theory the state is sovereign, which means that it has full legal control of everything that takes place upon its territory; this constitutes the domain of its 'domestic jurisdiction' which cannot be infringed except on the basis of some rule of international law which, by legal definition, must have been at least impliedly accepted by the state concerned. The theory of sovereignty approximated the actual practice in the eighteenth or nineteenth centuries when the territories of states, at least of the Great Powers, were reasonably impenetrable to intrusion from the outside and when international transactions did not cover more than a small proportion of social life.

Today the situation has fundamentally changed. Territories of all states, even the Superpowers, are vulnerable to modern weapons and propaganda, economic needs go far beyond the possibilities of satisfaction from domestic resources and require a much larger range of international transactions. With the growing global interdependence, other states and the international system as a whole are becoming increasingly involved in many issues hitherto, as the Charter of the United Nations puts it, 'essentially within the domestic jurisdiction' of the individual states. A domestic decision to develop a new weapons system may upset the international strategic balance; political instability and revolution or infringement of minority rights may lead to intervention; economic instability and decisions about international trade may affect the vital economic interests of the producers of the imports or the consumers of the exports of the country affected; alterations in the exchange rate or in the central bank rate can have similar repercussions. The problem is not, of course, new, but its magnitude definitely is.

Since many problems have greater international repercussions, the extent of the exclusive concern of single states has shrunk accordingly. International concern has been rapidly growing in all such matters and some of them are at the point of becoming essentially international or have already become so. This can happen in a variety of ways. The least revolutionary one is the mitigation of unilateral state behaviour by an increased awareness of its likely international repercussions. In the past such awareness did not prevent occasional unilateral moves very much to the detriment of other states, especially on the part of the Great Powers. Nowadays such moves are generally preceded by explanation and discussion and are often subsequently modified. The unilateral and sudden temporary surcharge on tariffs decided upon by the British Government in 1964 was internationally so unpopular and politically so costly that it may be legitimately regarded as an exception which proves the rule. A good illustration of the new interdependence is the contrast between the violent fluctuations in the exchange rates in the past, and the careful negotiations preceding similar moves in the nineteen-sixties. The British devaluation of the pound in 1967, which had been fully discussed internationally, strongly contrasts with the previous two devoluations in 1949 and 1931. When the United States resorted to traditional unilateral action in August 1971, this was followed by strong international pressures and, ultimately, agreements.

Often internationalization goes much beyond the state modifying its behaviour owing to the expected international repercussions. The state decides unilaterally on its behaviour but this amounts to a direct invitation to another state to reciprocate and offer a *quid pro quo*.

Clear examples can be found in reciprocated Soviet and United States reductions in armed forces, de-escalation of propaganda warfare, maintenance of certain restrictions upon hostile behaviour within the context of the Cold War, and finally, avoidance of a major confrontation. These may be preceded by semi-official or official negotiations, or by unilateral announcements, or by neither. Finally, states may go so far as to accept formal agreements limiting their freedom of action in important matters. In the economic and financial domains such restrictions are effected by the acceptance of the GATT agreement, or the membership of the European Economic Community, the European Free Trade Association, or the International Monetary Fund; in the field of military strategy by the limited Test Ban Treaty of 1963 and the Convention regarding Outer Space of 1964.

Legal limitations, however, are not fully dependable. When its vital interests are concerned, a state cannot be relied upon to observe the legal restraints. Britain, for example, recently imposed the above-mentioned temporary tariff surcharge in breach of several international agreements.

It may be added that some of the encroachments upon domestic jurisdiction arise from relations with other states on an inter-governmental basis, while others arise from joint membership in international institutions. Whereas in the majority of cases these institutions cater for matters in which international cooperation has already advanced relatively far, the General Assembly of the United Nations has been instrumental in reducing 'essentially domestic jurisdiction' in many important issues by interpreting the Charter as permitting debate upon such matters. Although such a debate is rarely conclusive and cannot lead to legally binding recommendations,* it has decisively shifted into the international domain the issue of colonialism and, somewhat less decisively, also that of human rights.

Finally, internationalization restricts occasions for conflict and opens new possibilities for cooperation. The behaviour of one state can be, of course, positively damaging or hurtful or unpleasant to another state, both when it is unilateral and when it is partly internationalized but, in the latter case, the offending state is at least under some form of international restraint. Internationalization is much more helpful when no hurt or offence is involved. The state intending to act can explain its intentions and hear comments in advance and thus avoid misunderstandings both on its own part, about the repercussions likely to take place, and on the part of other states, about its intentions. Moreover, only internationalization offers full scope for cooperation. This seems to be the only way open to the states to escape from their traditional inclination to pursue mutually damaging behaviour due to distrust and the risks involved in cooperation. It would often help them if they could shift the emphasis from competing for a larger slice of the existing cake to a cooperative task of increasing the size of the cake: the game theorists would talk here about escaping from 'the prisoners' dilemma' or about

*cf. Chapter 8, pp. 193 ff.

transforming 'zero-sum' to 'non-zero-sum' games through increasing the 'pay-off'.*

The rapid shrinking of the exclusively domestic sphere of jurisdiction and the recent spurt in the transition from international to world politics require not only a major institutional adjustment by redefining the place of the national state. Also its citizens would have to give up the exclusive loyalty given to each state. Allied to this problem is that of curbing violence and of avoiding a major war.

## Violence and War

Violence and war are traditional methods of settling international disputes and hence have been considered among the instruments and methods employed in the conduct of policy in Chapter 7. They have always been a very crude and uncertain method and in the twentieth century they have become increasingly costly. After 1918 the popular saying was 'wars do not pay'; the question who won the last war has been likened to that asked about who won an earthquake.

Violence possible on the contemporary scale is often considered an affliction, the roots of which must be sought in order to eliminate it, rather than as an unwieldy but just the same useful means for conducting foreign policy. And yet it is certainly not true about past wars, even the two world wars, that they did not pay anybody. The Slav nations liberated from the Austro–Hungarian Empire or the colonial people liberated from imperial rule would not agree that the world wars did not pay. Moreover, despite its scale of destruction, even the Second World War did not leave lasting traces and, within one generation, the world not only has recovered from the human and economic losses but has surged in its population and its economic development. Finally, when vital interests are thwarted, violence still seems to remain the only ultimate arbiter, as shown recently in the Arab–Israeli or the Cypriot conflicts.

Until a few years ago it was fashionable to refer to the 1914–

*cf. Chapter 2, pp. 50-51.

18 and 1939–45 wars as being of a new 'total' variety, i.e. involving much higher level of technology, larger numbers of men, greater civilian involvement, and higher cost. However, the real division-line in the history of violence and war lies not in one of the two world wars but rather in the post-1945 period. Violence has now suddenly escalated so much that it has become fairly pointless to think about it in the traditional way. Natural barriers such as the Channel or the Great Russian Plain which had proved significant in stemming the Nazi advances in the forties, have lost their strategic importance in the age of intercontinental ballistic missiles. The destructive power of the existing nuclear weapons would probably suffice to wipe out most of mankind; a full-scale nuclear exchange between the Americans and the Russians is estimated to result in some ten 'mega-deaths' on each side; this means that some hundred million on each side are vulnerable to a pre-emptive strike by the opponent.

The anti-ballistic missile systems now being established by both Superpowers may greatly reduce the damage but in all probability to nothing less than two or three or four 'mega-deaths' on each side; would such damage be, as the nuclear strategists say, 'acceptable'? We are not very remote from what Herman Kahn has termed 'the doomsday machine', which will be capable of terminating all life upon earth. The instruments of biological and chemical warfare are being assiduously developed and although their military utility may remain dubious, they could easily be used in a 'spasm' reaction if a full-scale war broke out.

Consequently it is logical to look upon violence and war as no longer a method of settling inter-state disputes but as a mortal danger to mankind. Much of human thought had been devoted to their curbing and elimination in the past but not only further thought but also immediate action seem imperative today. The theories of war fall within three broad categories. Some explanations search for the psychological roots of war and blame the wickedness of human nature; others stress the internal structure of states, and others again the anarchic nature of the international system. No single explanation is satisfactory and in order to understand the social role of violence and war it is necessary to use all the three approaches.*

The manner of thinking about war is important because it underlies the various approaches to its prevention adopted in international practice. For instance, Unesco endeavours to improve human nature through education; the 'functional' approach aims mainly at ameliorating conditions so as to reduce the causes of international friction arising from domestic dissatisfactions. The most important approaches, however, tackle the international system and try to establish procedures and institutions which would either facilitate peaceful settlement of inter-state conflicts or deter states from employing violence.

Three general observations can be made about all the approaches. First, through the very fact that they aim at avoiding violence or preventing war all these approaches are cooperative even though they are applied to disputes the substance of which leads to acute conflict. By employing or being impelled to employ any of the ensuing procedures, parties to a dangerous dispute are joined in a cooperative venture. This, unfortunately, does not necessarily lead to the settlement of the conflict between them. On the contrary, the contemporary methods aiming at the prevention of violence and war sometimes achieve the opposite result – by preventing their solution by force, they freeze conflicts for which no solution can be found peacefully. All approaches to peace should therefore be carefully checked and compared – some are fully compatible with one another but others may cancel one another out.

Second, it would be logical to attack the problem of violence both by trying to prevent and curb it, and by striking at all its roots, reforming human nature as well as the nature of the states and of the international systems. Unfortunately the latter are slow, uphill jobs and the United Nations has been concentrating upon war and violence as manifested in the successive post-war crises rather than upon their roots.

Finally, third parties are often asked to participate in the various procedures. Their roles and the amount of constraint

* cf. the striking analysis by Kenneth N. Waltz, *Man, the State, and War*, New York, Columbia University Press, 1959.

they can bring to bear upon the parties are of sufficient significance to serve as a convenient basis for the classification of procedures.

The contemporary efforts to prevent war started with the League of Nations in 1920 and continue to centre upon its successor, the United Nations. Hence, bearing in mind that the parties to a dispute still generally retain their central position in all procedures, subsequent discussion centres upon the United Nations Charter and practice.* The point must be stressed that the United Nations is primarily concerned with the maintenance of international peace and hence it is not particularly concerned whether differences among states are settled fairly or in conformity with some standards of justice, or are, in fact, settled at all. The stress lies upon preventing violence. Hence, under Article 33 of the Charter, members are obliged to seek '*pacific* (meaning peaceful) *settlement*' only for disputes which 'are likely to endanger international peace and security', in other words sufficiently important for at least one of them to be prepared to resort to violence. The parties to such dangerous disputes should, 'first of all, seek a solution by negotiation, enquiry, mediation, conciliation, arbitration, judicial settlement, resort to regional agencies, or other peaceful means of their choice'. The first six methods suggested are neatly arranged in order of third party involvement: negotiations are between the parties to the dispute alone: in mediation (and the omitted related procedure of offering 'good offices') a third party merely brings the antagonists together: in conciliation the third party helps in reaching the actual terms of settlement: in arbitration and judicial settlement the parties to the dispute accept in advance the settlement which will be arrived at by the arbitral body or tribunal. Regional agencies or arrangements can assist in all these procedures.

The basic assumption of the pacific settlement of disputes is that war is a dangerous, old-fashioned and irrational method of settling inter-state quarrels. Hence the procedure stresses the

*I am indebted to Inis L. Claude, Jr, for his analysis of the United Nations in his *Swords into Plowshares*, University of London Press, 3rd ed., 1965, on which the subsequent paragraphs are based.

importance of a 'cooling-off' period in which passions can subside, and of fact-finding and impartial inquiries to eliminate misunderstandings and ignorance of facts. It provides convenient, face-saving formulae and often ingenious ideas beyond the scope of the imagination of the parties themselves; it brings to bear international public opinion as a restraint upon irresponsible behaviour. The Charter merely states the obligation to submit to the procedures; it does not impose an obligation to accept a settlement. In practice, the vicious circularity of international relations appears here again: the procedures which are readily acceptable to the parties of the dispute are those which do not lead to binding terms of settlement, while the procedures which lead to such binding terms (adjudication and judicial settlement) are not readily acceptable and hence, despite great international efforts, have not played a really significant part in world politics.

One fundamental limitation on the pacific settlement of disputes is frequently slurred over. The most acute disputes do not arise from differing interpretations of mutual rights and obligations which can generally be expected to be settled by some peaceful procedure. The real difficulties arise in situations where one party demands a change in mutual rights and obligations and the other one refuses it. 'Peaceful change' is a favourite topic of many analyses of international organization but it has not been and probably cannot be successfully institutionalized. Even in peaceful domestic politics, power, although rarely physical force, must be brought to bear before far-reaching changes are instituted. In the much looser international system, physical force and its threat have traditionally served as the ultimate means of ensuring change and we have not devised a substitute.

Therefore the Charter is realistic in assuming that not all dangerous disputes will be settled and that violence will not always be avoided. In Chapter VII it proceeds to establish a system of *collective security*, concerned with 'action with respect to threats to peace, breaches of peace, and acts of aggression'. This procedure is concerned only with outbreaks of violence, whatever their cause may be, and proceeds on the assumption that members of the international system have accepted that 'peace is indivisible', that violence anywhere endangers the whole system and hence every one of them. 'One for all and all for one' is a neat summary of collective security in the real meaning of the word. In fact, the word has been greatly abused in being used to describe such highly selective security systems as NATO.

'Collective security' is an innovation stemming from the experiences of the First World War. It was launched as the basis of a new international system no longer based upon balance of power; whereas the latter was directed against excessive power, collective security is directed against aggressive policy. The historical record of collective security under the League of Nations was unhappy. Its basic objective assumptions regarding distribution of power, reduction of levels of armaments, and the effectiveness of economic sanctions, all proved invalid, and the elaborate legal and structural apparatus ineffective. The United Nations Charter attempted to avoid these reasons for failure by providing for a collective security force capable of applying military sanctions and supplied primarily by the Great Powers, but this plan was one of the first casualties of the Cold War. Thwarted by the Soviet vote in the Security Council and assured at the time of a comfortable two-thirds majority in the General Assembly, the United States attempted to retain a collective security scheme in a different form and under the control of the latter organ. The successful Korean intervention and the subsequent Uniting for Peace Resolution which was its basis, are extensions of the Charter. The Russians have always denied their legality, claiming that all enforcement actions are reserved to the Security Council, whereas the Americans retort that the General Assembly is legally entitled to operate the scheme in order to maintain international peace and security whenever the Council fails in its primary duty.

In fact, this dispute is of no more than historical significance. Although a temporary euphoria over the success in Korea disguised the position, the very concept of international enforcement had become obsolete in the thermo-nuclear age. When nuclear weapons came within the reach of even Middle Powers, enforcement short of a nuclear force becomes ineffective while the use of enforcement through nuclear force is unthinkable.

211

Although the Uniting for Peace Resolution was to be of universal application, in 1956 the United States could not bring itself to apply it either together with the Soviet Union in the Suez Crisis or against the Soviet Union during the Hungarian rising. Subsequently the rapid influx of new members deprived the United States of its automatic majority, and collective security under the Uniting for Peace Resolution was effectively buried.

The failure of collective security in the Suez Crisis was the occasion for a successful initiative by the Secretary General, Dag Hammarskjöld, for a less ambitious type of United Nations intervention, usually referred to as *preventive diplomacy*. The starting-point was the acceptance of the situation that the United Nations is ineffective in major issues of the Cold War and that, even in other issues, it cannot operate with military contributions drawn from the Superpowers. The new procedure was devised by the Secretary General during the Suez crisis in 1956 when, under the instructions of the General Assembly, he improvised the United Nations Emergency Force (UNEF) which enabled the intervening troops to withdraw and, after their withdrawal, interposed a screen between the hostile Israeli and Egyptian troops. He conceptualized the procedure in the introduction to the Annual Report for 1959–60. The major limitation of such a force lies in its dependence upon the consent of the receiving state and the goodwill of the states supplying the contingents. This basic flaw ended UNEF in 1967 when President Nasser demanded its withdrawal and the Secretary General was forced to comply immediately; not to comply with the Egyptian demand would have contravened the rules of state sovereignty and would also have been impracticable, being contrary to the wishes of the major contributors to the force.

If UNEF at least maintained peace on one troubled frontier for eleven years (although it can justifiably be accused of having merely frozen a situation which was bound to explode, as it did in 1967), ONUC, the other major United Nations force employed in the Congo in 1960, is even more vulnerable to criticism. It was sent in originally to facilitate the withdrawal of Belgian troops and to restore law and order, but it then became unhappily mixed up in Congolese domestic politics and when it withdrew, the country remained in a chaotic state. Minor United Nations forces were sent also to the Lebanon and Iraq in 1958, to Laos in 1959, to Yemen in 1963, and a somewhat larger one to Cyprus in 1964.

The basic objective of preventive diplomacy is to localize the conflict, to exclude the Great Powers, and to prevent an escalation of the minor conflict into a major one. This principle of exclusion of the Great Powers clearly distinguishes it from the previously discussed procedures. It is not incompatible with pacific settlement to prevent the escalation of the local situation, and thus enable settlement procedures to come into their own; this was particularly clear in the Suez and the Cyprus cases. The distinction between preventive diplomacy and collective security is more subtle. The former not only excludes the Superpowers but also has a somewhat different objective from the latter. Preventive diplomacy aims at localizing and abating a dangerous confrontation, whereas collective security is directed against aggressive intent. Hence the disagreements in the case of the Congo: the United States and the majority chose to interpret the action as preventive diplomacy, whereas the Soviet Union considered it as a collective security action against the Belgians; naturally the two sides could not agree.

The close inter-relationship of *disarmament* and the other procedures is succinctly stated by Claude: 'Whereas pacific settlement leaves states with nothing to fight about, and collective security proposes to confront the aggressors with too much to fight against, disarmament proposes to deprive nations of anything to fight with.'* The principle is simple but, despite prolonged negotiations and subtle and sophisticated arguments, disarmament has proved a failure, both in the inter-war and the post-1945 period. It would be a logical complement to any other procedure aiming at peace but could scarcely be expected to precede rather than follow success in other fields. Nothwithstanding arguments to the contrary, armaments can more usefully be considered as the result rather than the cause of international

*Inis L. Claude, Jr, *Swords into Plowshares*, University of London Press, 3rd ed., 1965, p. 262.

tensions, and cannot be expected to be substantially reduced as long as these tensions persist.

The great revulsion against war in the twenties found expression in attempts not only to develop the above-mentioned procedures but also to *abolish war* altogether. The preamble to the Covenant of the League of Nations solemnly declared that the High Contracting Parties accepted obligations not to resort to war but the text of the Covenant clearly left open the so-called 'gaps', situations in which war was still permissible. The early League years were spent in futile attempts to close these gaps. These attempts culminated in the Kellogg–Briand Pact of 1928 which was meant to constitute an unequivocal renunciation of war as an instrument of national policy and to supplement the Covenant in this respect. Alas, even this declaration, signed by nearly all the states, was not unequivocal. It merely demonstrated how unrealistic are such mere declarations and also how gullible is public opinion which temporarily accepted the Pact as a real achievement. In fact, the Pact did not outlaw war altogether; war remained fully legal for self-defence, as explicitly stated in the correspondence among the signatories, for enforcement of international policy such as the League of Nations Covenant or the Locarno Pact, against non-signatories or states waging war in breach of the Pact, and for certain vital national interests specified by the United States and Great Britain, the Monroe Doctrine and the so-called British Monroe Doctrine usually understood to embrace the Middle East. The actual origin of the Pact was by no means idealistic; it arose from the French initiative to the United States to conclude a bilateral agreement which would reinforce the French *vis-à-vis* Germany, and the United States counter-initiative to multilateralize the agreement and thus render it innocuous. Although the Kellogg Pact played a part in the Nuremberg indictment and can be legitimately considered as a statement of human aspirations, it can scarcely be regarded as a practical success.

The members of the United Nations reiterated a slightly reworded undertaking when accepting the obligation stated in Article 2, para. 4 of the Charter: 'All Members shall refrain in their international relations from the threat or the use of force against the territorial integrity or political independence of any state, or in any other manner inconsistent with the Purposes of the United Nations.' However, 'the inherent right of individual and collective self-defence if an armed attack occurs', stated in Article 51, remains a broad escape clause which can be very liberally interpreted by the individual states.

The outlawing declarations, as well as all the procedures devised to maintain peace and curb violence, have thus proved either completely or largely ineffective and have contributed little, if anything, to the curbing of the surge of violence which started with the Manchurian crisis in 1931, culminated in the Second World War, and has continued ever since. Nevertheless, a new development can be discerned from the mid fifties, a determination of the two Superpowers to keep clear of a major confrontation and to prevent minor conflicts from escalating into war. The lessons of 'the balance of terror' were fully considered by them, although they were not institutionalized or based upon formal agreement. The two Superpowers behaved with fair circumspection and restraint, even during the Cuban missile crisis in 1962 and the recent escalation of the war in Vietnam. Their behaviour is based upon expediency and prudence alone and hence has been aptly named by Inis Claude 'prudential pacifism'. The habit of direct communication symbolized by the 'hot line' is important and is by no means limited to it. Other links have been opened, e.g. the semi-official and official dialogue on disarmament is the major hope of preventing a disastrous arms-race. Needless to say, this prudential pacifism is by no means fully reliable but it can be regarded as an important addition to the other procedures to maintain peace. Its limitations merely show how little we have advanced in this crucial field.

## Economic and Social Issues

In the past the solution of economic problems, as much as that of all other international problems, could be pursued along the path of conflict or along the path of cooperation, or simultaneously along both. When in need of raw materials or of some products, a state may try to conquer the territory of another state which has them, or to develop trade and persuade the other state to sell it the goods needed or exchange them for some other commodities it can offer. When incapable of finding economic employment for all its citizens, a state may try to conquer relatively empty territories to settle them, or make arrangements for peaceful migration of its population surplus. The historical pattern is chequered. Mutually advantageous trade appears together with thinly disguised economic exploitation; the great shifts of population in the decades preceding the First World War were governed mainly by economics and did not involve conflicts between the sending states and the receiving states in the Americas and in Australasia, although they were preceded or accompanied by violent conflicts with the indigenous people. The inter-war Japanese Greater Co-Prosperity Sphere was only theoretically based upon cooperation and actually led to acute conflict; Hitler's *Drang nach Osten* did not even pretend to be based upon anything but conflict.

Present-day international economic problems are much greater in scale and gravity. Not only are they insoluble by domestic means within the confines of the majority of individual states, but they seem to be also increasingly intractable to the traditional methods of state-interaction: conflicts do not solve them while cooperation needs new forms of a different nature and intensity. Most economic and social issues thus require that we fundamentally reconsider the nature of the boundaries between domestic and international politics.

Pollution is an example of a recently realized urgent need for international cooperation. Three outstanding examples have been chosen for discussion here: the population explosion and economic development, in which internationalization has proceeded quite far, and the régime of raw materials, in which it has not.

THE POPULATION EXPLOSION

'Over-population' is a highly imprecise term, rightly rejected by the demographers since it is impossible to arrive at an absolute judgement about an optimum or maximum population which can be carried by a given territory. Just the same, in most periods some places are suffering from the feeling of 'over-population' –

e.g. in times of famine, or when the citizens feel sorely deprived of desired economic opportunities.

Until this century it was possible to believe that equilibrium between resources and population could be brought about by automatic social forces. Rapid population growth in Western Europe was accompanied by increased prosperity as a result of industrialization, and by the settlement of territories overseas. Moreover, the demographic prospects changed under the impact of industrialization and urbanization. While improving hygiene and nutrition continued to decrease the death-rate, the birth-rate began to drop too, so that an equilibrium could be expected; in fact in the thirties, during the dark days of the Great Depression, the United Kingdom achieved it while France registered an actual loss of population.

Moreover, outlets for Europe's surplus population were open throughout the world – Britain peopled several colonies of settlement; Ireland, which by 1846 reached the staggering population of eight million inhabitants precariously depending upon potatoes as their staple diet, lost a quarter of her population during the potato famine, but was able to settle overseas another quarter; during the first decade of this century some million and a quarter immigrants from continental Europe entered the United States every year. After the First World War the situation changed. No longer needing a large additional labour force, the United States reduced immigration to a trickle; Italy and Germany, the two European states with the strongest drives to find outlets for their 'surplus' populations, embraced the paths of conquest.

Emigration from non-European countries never reached the same dimensions. Admittedly emigrants from the crowded parts of China and India and also a few Japanese spread over the shores of the Pacific. They were, however, admitted only in small numbers to suit the convenience of the receiving countries; the influx of larger numbers was curbed for political reasons especially when, in the last decades of the nineteenth century, Australia and the United States began to fear 'the yellow peril'. Asian immigration never reached a dimension in which it could serve as a sizeable outlet for population.

Meanwhile the demographic picture in the world conquered by the European Powers was quickly changing. Improved health conditions and reduced violence were rapidly decreasing death-rates while birth-rates were not falling accordingly. The dramatic rises in the populations of such countries as India or Java, which did not at first attract much attention, presented an insoluble problem when the increasing numbers began to place a strain on land resources. While in the nineteen thirties discussion was still in terms of the domestic problems of the individual states which tried to improve their positions and to secure more emigration outlets, since 1945 the previous demographic trends became further accentuated through the eradication of malaria. It is characteristic of the present appreciation of the scope of the world population problem that it is invariably discussed in global terms. Naturally, individual states are primarily concerned with what is happening within their own boundaries but they do not expect, and are not expected by others, to cope with their problems alone.

A few figures will readily show the magnitude of the problem. World population reached its first thousand million in 1830, took a whole century before it reached its second thousand million in 1930, but only a further thirty years before it reached its third thousand million in 1960. Whereas in the second half of the last century the average population growth was about 6 per cent per decade, between 1950 and 1960 it was about 17 per cent; in 1965 no less than sixty-five million were added to our numbers. If present trends continue, by the year 2000 world population will reach some six to seven thousand million. To project our forecasts even further into an increasingly fanciful future, in some three to four hundred years, the whole earth would become one gigantic city and, within seven or eight hundred years, there would be standing room only upon our planet; apparently, multiplying at the present rate, by the year 3000 we would reach the astronomic number of one trillion and by the year 6500 the population would equal the mass of the earth.

Obviously all these projections belong to the realm of science-fiction although they are useful in making us visualize the magnitude of the problem. It is to be expected that some form of social equilibrium will be eventually found in population growth as it is in such intractable social problems as road traffic in cities; we can expect that life will not come to a complete standstill but will crawl on, as the city traffic invariably does. The interesting and encouraging new phenomenon is that the population–food question has become so pronouncedly international.

The short-term problem is how to enable the present numbers to exist; the long-range problem how to stabilize the population increase. Unfortunately any advance in solving the short-term problem does not contribute to a long-term solution; on the contrary, by saving people from starvation now, we may only enable larger numbers to semi-starve in the future. On the food side of the equation, undoubtedly the production of food could be immensely increased by improved cultivation and animal husbandry and probably by development of sea-farming. The snag lies in the cultural obstacles in the most needy countries. The twenty years indicative world plan for agricultural development now being prepared by the Food and Agriculture Organization will be technically feasible but not necessarily attainable. The spectre of hunger is hanging over the world but it is impossible to conclude whether, in the long run, the pictures of doom projected by some writers are more plausible than the optimism of others; in the short run, large-scale famines are likely.

At the other end of the equation, population can undoubtedly be stabilized, although only in the long run. The expedients are many – postponement of the age of marriage, effectively used by the Irish, is now resorted to by the Chinese. To urban pressures which invariably reduce the size of families, the Japanese add facilities for contraception and abortion; the Indians resort to the new cheap and simple methods of contraception but also encourage sterilization. The diffusion of ideas and techniques is world-wide and from 1966 the United States has been including birth-control assistance in her aid programmes. International co-operation transcending state boundaries is encouraging, but cultural obstacles and political difficulties persist. Not the least of them is the widespread suspicion that the white race, especially the capitalist West, tries to preserve its power position in the world. The predominance of the West in the past was based on a rapid population increase in the last century but its proportion of world population has been declining in this century; this relative decline is bound to become accelerated by the differentials in population increases which range between 0·9 per cent per annum in Europe and 2·8 per cent in Latin America. It is difficult to imagine that the power position of the white race will be retained if its share, now some one-quarter of the world's population, is, in time, halved.

ECONOMIC GROWTH

Since population control is inconceivable for some time to come, it becomes imperative to find a way of enlarging the resources available. Not only are there increasingly more mouths to feed but, for the time being, while the additional numbers are predominantly young and under working age, no social product can be expected from them; on the contrary, great additional resources are needed for training them. The proportion of the under-fifteen age group in the Third World is staggering; some 43 per cent in Africa or South East Asia.

Economic growth was introduced to the non-European parts of the world partly under colonial rule and partly through cultural diffusion. With the notable exception of Japan, growth was, on the whole, slow and was governed by the individual circumstances of the country and by the policies pursued by its colonial rulers. The situation has fundamentally changed since 1945. The growth problem has become internationally accepted to be a world problem as much as is the population issue. The motivation of the various states differ – the new states need foreign aid and assistance in growth, the two Superpowers vie with each other to secure influence; the ex-colonial Powers try to establish and consolidate new ties with their previous dependencies. Selfish and power-political elements mingle with altruistic ones, although most people now recognize that it is iniquitous that people in many countries cannot reach minimum subsistence levels whereas in others they are, on the whole, opulent.

In the confused early post-war period most economists were stressing the great need for capital investment common to all the poor countries. Calculations abounded as to how much – or how little – is required from the well-to-do countries to satisfy the needs of the others. While the problem was often analysed in global terms, in practice it was dealt with mainly on the traditional state-to-state basis, where aid was given or refused according to political expediency; truly international aid, through the United Nations, was extremely limited in extent and the bulk of it was forthcoming from the United States, with large contributions also from the Soviet Union, the ex-colonial Powers and China.

It did not take very long to discover that economic development is much too complex a phenomenon to require capital alone. Even where capital was forthcoming, formidable social obstacles had to be overcome in education, technology, public administration and political organization. Certainly the needy societies were not in a position to utilize fully even the capital available, though it was never made available to the full extent claimed as necessary by economic experts. Moreover, the traditional state-to-state arrangements regarding aid led to widespread dissatisfaction on both sides. The recipients were affected by the psychologically understandable resentment of having to ask for charity and of not receiving enough, or as much as others. The donors did not obtain the expected political objectives of securing a degree of control over the recipients owing to the latter's usual suspicions of 'neo-colonialism'; moreover, they resented that much of the aid was uneconomically used, sometimes almost entirely wasted.

In the early sixties the pattern began to change, although at first only slowly. The donors began to restrict the amount of aid and to insist on its better utilization; at least one leader of the recipient countries, Julius Nyerere of Tanzania, proclaimed in 1966 serious doubts about the utility of aid altogether. The socially, and, in the long run, economically more promising pattern of economic growth may lie in the Gandhi-type development based upon native industries rather than reliance upon foreign aid for industries of a modern type. At the same time, international attitudes to the problems of growth were becoming transformed. Pressures, especially in the United Nations, were continuously mounting, development was becoming an increasingly international concern rather than that of each individual country and perhaps its previous colonial ruler. The very change in the terminology employed showed how firmly the claims of the needy countries are now accepted and also how tender has the world become of their feelings; from being simply 'poor' or 'backward' in the past, they became 'underdeveloped' immediately after the war but are invariably now referred to as 'developing'. The 'developing' countries now feel firmly entitled to reasonable support and aid from the well-to-do countries for purposes of development, and they expect it in a form in which it does not in any way infringe upon their complete political independence.

The first United Nations Conference on Trade and Development (UNCTAD) convened in 1964 was the first manifestation of the new trends. 'Trade not aid' was the slogan, a demand to the well-to-do countries to open their markets more fully, to ensure adequate and stable prices for the produce of the developing countries, and to prevent the violent price fluctuations which often cost them more than all the aid received. The remarkable feature of the Conference was the united front of all the developing countries and the vulnerable position in which the well-to-do countries found themselves. The demands were not fully met, but by the time the second UNCTAD Conference was to be convened in 1968, the international climate further advanced towards the recognition of the equity of these demands. Although this Conference failed, international public opinion is in fairly general agreement that the developing countries should be ensured exceptionally favourable terms of trade to enable them to plan their development ahead. The United Nations is likely to play a much greater role in the coordination of the technical assistance and of the capital aid which will be required in smaller quantities if the proceeds from trade are stabilized.

RAW MATERIALS

The spectre of mankind starving itself out of existence is accompanied by a lesser one of it wastefully exhausting essential raw materials. This apprehension was particularly acute in the pre-

1945 period. The greatest fears were raised about sources of energy – at that time almost exclusively found in coal and oil, fossils available in large but finite quantities. Calculations of the rapidly growing demands for energy and of the proven fuel reserves led to many gloomy forecasts that mankind would run out of sources of energy well before the turn of the century.

The energy problem today seems much more readily soluble. Nuclear energy provides an effective alternative source and, if the process of fusion is industrially harnessed, the problem will disappear altogether. Moreover, large new exploitable reserves of fossil fuels have been found to tide us over the immediate decades. Geological surveys have become more sophisticated and have been effectively extended to hitherto relatively unexplored regions, especially in continental shelves and in the Soviet Union and China. Also, improved exploitation techniques permit the mining of many deposits previously considered uneconomic owing to the difficulties of reaching them or to the low concentration of the mineral. Production and the proving of new reserves does not, however, always follow step by step the phenomenally increased consumption, and serious bottlenecks still arise in single materials, especially when consumption suddenly grows as it did during the period of the Korean crisis. Technological advances enable us, however, to develop substitutes for a widely increasing range of uses, e.g. aluminium instead of copper for electricity, aluminium or plastic instead of steel for some structural purposes, or to reduce the quantities required for specific purposes.

The spectre of 'entropy', of irretrievable dissipation of scarce raw materials, seems now more remote. By the time the iron-ore deposits have become depleted and steel products have disintegrated into rust particles, we may not need any steel at all. By the time we have used up all the deposits of potash and phosphorus from the soil, digested them in our food and finally dissipated them in rivers and oceans, we may have devised methods of retrieving these and other minerals from the oceans. It is not beyond man's ingenuity to counteract the tendency towards 'entropy' and to ensure the continuation of our civilization.

It is indicative of the less immediate urgency of the problem of raw materials that, in contrast to those of population and economic growth, notwithstanding specific inter-governmental agreements of the traditional kind, governments have refused to entertain proposals for internationalization; raw materials remain fundamentally the concern of each individual state. The traditional arrangements remain in operation: states endeavour to be as self-supporting in raw materials as possible although only the two Superpowers can approximate self-sufficiency. Failing that, they try to secure the raw materials on as favourable economic terms and on as assured a basis as possible and, for emergency, they stock-pile sufficient quantities to see them through likely crises. The position is not very satisfactory for any state. The producers cannot be assured of reasonably steady prices which greatly affect some developing states, e.g. those dependent upon sales of tin or copper. Likewise the consumers cannot fully depend upon assured supplies and occasionally, as during the Korean crisis, they face shortages and sudden drastic increases in price. Moreover, supplies of strategically important raw materials can be inconveniently withheld for purely political reasons, as shown by the interruption of Middle Eastern oil supplies to Britain and the United States following the Arab–Israeli clash in June 1967; a refusal of customary markets could similarly affect the producers.

Despite occasional serious conflicts over sources of raw materials, the pattern of handling them through international trade has become firmly established. The terms of trade in the past were considerably more favourable to the Western states than to others and it seems inevitable that, in their politically stronger position, the non-Western producers, especially of oil, should now try to improve the terms: it seems also inevitable that this occasionally leads to conflict. On the whole, however, the danger of an acute international shortage of raw materials seems to be remote in the majority of crucial commodities. Hence instead of the feared exacerbation of international conflicts to secure adequate sources of supply, we may envisage a continuation of the existing forms of cooperation and, if the political climate allows it, even forms of internationalization which would stabilize the markets and prove advantageous both to the producers and to the consumers.

## CHAPTER 10

# RETROSPECT AND PROSPECTS

THE preceding analysis leads to the conclusion that conflict and harmony are to be found, generally in a rather confused relationship, in all areas of international relations. It is impossible to determine the exact roles they are playing since political phenomena defy simple explanation and often exhibit considerable circularity.

When we approach the prospects of international politics, analysis becomes by necessity somewhat speculative and we have to engage in political conjecture. Again the attempt will be made to apply both the conflict and the cooperation models but the intrusion of wishful thinking is here both more difficult to avoid and also more excusable than in the treatment of the past. It is surely legitimate to express the wish for less international conflict and violence and more cooperation and harmony, as this sentiment is shared by the overwhelming majority of mankind and professed – although not necessarily pursued – by a similarly overwhelming majority of governments. It is reasonable to structure the discussion of the future around this desire and to look into the prospects for its fulfilment; political judgements and desires influence human behaviour and, to that extent, are self-fulfilling.

The alternatives are fairly clear – the incidence of conflict and violence may stay as it is now, at a somewhat reduced or increased level, for quite a long time; it may also rise even to the point of total war which could destroy our civilization and even life on earth altogether.

Further discussion is therefore focused around the question of how to *improve* international politics. It is arranged in sections dealing with four major levels of analysis: first, the behaviour of the states, based upon the assumption that no fundamental changes take place either in the international system or in the attitudes of man; second, the interaction among these states and the international system; third, the evolution of international organizations which somewhat overlap with the international

225

system; fourth, a fundamental transformation of the nature of man and of political institutions. These sections progress from a mere projection into the future of the dominant patterns of the immediate past and the present to what, at the moment, appears to be only remotely possible if not altogether utopian. They do not purport to outline four alternative 'scenarios'; the world is unlikely to go exclusively in any one of the four directions indicated. Attempts at improving world politics can therefore concentrate upon any one or all of the levels at which crucial decisions are made.

It seems much more probable that future international changes will continue taking place simultaneously at all these levels, although not necessarily on parallel lines. Some of them are likely to move towards greater harmony, and hence reinforce one another; others are likely to lead to exacerbated conflict and violence and thus have the opposite effect. In the short run, the behaviour of states is likely to remain predominant but, in the longer run, the centre of gravity may shift to larger units; perhaps, if global integration takes place in some form, it may shift to the behaviour of the people as individuals. Instead of engaging in the thankless task of speculating about the likely priorities and connections between these levels, subsequent sections will merely sum up very briefly the conclusions arising from the preceding analysis and outline the major possibilities ahead of us.

## The Behaviour of States

History has proved wrong all the grand ideas, such as those of Voltaire or of Kant, about reforming the nature of the states through transforming the nature of their régimes. Some sociologists linked militarism with the feudal system but their expectation that industrialization would lead to peace was disappointed; unfortunately, industry became militaristic instead of society becoming peaceful. Likewise the substitution of democracy for monarchy and of socialism for capitalism proved to no avail; the democratic and the socialist states did not eschew conflict and violence and cannot be considered as less bellicose than their predecessors. The attempts at segregating the sheep from the goats and at limiting international organization to 'peace-loving' countries undertaken in differing ways by the League of Nations and the United Nations, have scarcely contributed to peace.

As far as values and *ideologies* are concerned, the major contemporary division-line lies between the individual-oriented liberal democracy and the community-oriented ideologies, at present mainly of the left-wing communist but also of the right-wing fascist varieties. The question of how relevant this division is likely to remain in the future can be fruitfully tackled on the basis of the distinction made above* between the 'aspirational' and 'operational' levels of analysis. This distinction is based upon the realistic assumption that adherents of all ideologies tend to accept the fact of life that they cannot get all they want, however ardently they desire it. One must, therefore, assume that they are always subject to a degree of tension between their aspirations and their activities and achievements; in each time and place they resolve this tension in their individual ways.

The historical record of the ideological clash between liberal democracy and communism in the period since 1945 does not provide a firm basis for predicting how likely future conflict is. On the operational level, the confrontation between the Soviet Union and the United States, the major representatives of these ideologies, has undergone a substantial transformation from extreme conflict, occasionally coming to the brink of full-scale violence, to a fair degree of cooperation. Although this is often disputed, possibly also on the aspirational level, the two ideologies have moved somewhat towards what is referred to in the West as '*détente*' and in the East as 'peaceful coexistence'.

Until 1971 there was practically no visible advance at either level in the relations between the United States and China but a dramatic breakthrough arose in 1971 with the visit to Peking of the presidential adviser Professor Henry Kissinger which prepared the ground for a visit to Peking of the United States President himself in February 1972.

Are we advancing towards 'an end of ideology'?† This may be

* See Chapter 5, p. 94.

† The title of Daniel Bell's book, New York, Free Press of Glencoe, 1960.

more than mere wishful thinking; there is some sociological substance in the argument about it. It seems plausible to assume that, in industrializing societies, the transition from rural to urban existence involves a complete break with tradition and raises fundamental social dilemmas to which total answers are sought in ideologies.*

When society is firmly settled in urban conditions and starts moving towards a new, 'post-industrial civilization', the reverse seems to happen. Instead of seeking fundamental answers, we try to break down our problems into small, quantifiable and therefore more manageable parts. These can be approached pragmatically with good prospects of resolving them. While the United States has advanced furthest in this direction, a similar transition can be detected not only in Western Europe but also in the Soviet Union. An increasing range of social problems is being subjected to investigation and pragmatic resolution and here Soviet 'working sociologists' do not differ much in their methods or objectives from their Western colleagues. When it comes to such mundane problems as increasing job-satisfaction, or reducing juvenile delinquency, although Soviet and Western sociologists explain the phenomena in fundamentally different ways and although they profess different social goals, their methods of investigation and the practical measures they propose are becoming similar. The idea is quite plausible that the similar problems of large-scale industrialized and urbanized societies have led, or at least are leading, towards the 'convergence' of the American and Soviet systems. This phenomenon is, however, by and large limited to the 'operational' level. Will a similar 'convergence' take place on the 'aspirational' level, or is it perhaps already slowly taking place? Perhaps, as the rapprochement with the United States indicates, the mellowing of the Chinese ideology, at the operational level at least, is merely the function of industrialization and time?

A certain convergence can also be detected regarding national-

*This transition was least acute in the United States in which there were no feudal traditions to forget, which may explain why the Americans have not articulated an ideology as much as have other industrialized nations.

ism. Virulent as it is with new nations, it tends to abate with maturity and with satisfaction of the basic national aspirations of independence. This is allied to a realization that the state, as the political organ of the nation, is proving increasingly less adequate for the growing range of objectives which are included in 'the national interest'. The future of the ideology of nationalism clearly depends upon the future of the national state but a circularity rather than a clear-cut causal nexus is likely to determine their connection. If and when national differences diminish in importance, the so far diffuse clusters of values which can be described as a loose form of socialism, human rights, rationalism, and beliefs in science and in economic development, may gain importance and become fully international in form.

Before they can be translated into action, values and ideologies have to be confronted with the environment; hence the *image* of this environment held by the decision-makers is of crucial importance. Obviously images grossly distorting the environment are dangerous since they block a rational estimate of costs and risks and opportunities. A better understanding of the environment would eliminate these dangers but could not be expected to eliminate conflicts of substance; in fact, it may even exacerbate them by making the decision-makers more clearly aware of their existence. Nevertheless, the clarification of images seems to be not only a means of resolving conflicts based upon ignorance and misunderstanding but also the necessary foundation for the rational tackling of substantive conflicts.

The basic image of international politics is likely to play a fundamental role in the shaping of state behaviour. As a rule this is an image of a threat system in which every single state pursues its individual national interest, on the whole ruthlessly, regardless of the cost to others. An exception is made for states considered as friendly and particularly for close allies whose interests are taken into account, although often only as long as a state's individual vital interest is not affected.

An image based upon fear and distrust has a strong self-fulfilling propensity since the other state, when treated with fear and suspicion, tends to reciprocate. It is less easy to consider behaviour based upon trust as having quite as pronounced 'mirror-image' effect upon others. There is a chance of it but exaggerated trust may be disappointed, and this can lead to fatal results for the state; hence statesmen are justifiably cautious. Perhaps the most important quality to be expected from an image is that it remains flexible and is subjected to frequent empirical tests. Whether this image is gloomy or rosy it remains true, as Chesterton said: 'What really produces trouble between peoples is when one is quite certain it understands the other and in fact doesn't. . .' Although rather grim, this interpretation of state behaviour does not postulate the worst possible world. A world of power politics in which states are bent upon pursuing their individual 'national interests' is preferable to one in which states would aim at the destruction of others, violence and war for their own sakes.

As long as statesmen are faced with the very real risk that the threat system is an actuality, it seems futile to ask them to abandon the image of a power-political world altogether, as is done by some writers.* Progress towards harmony and cooperation can scarcely be achieved by a dramatic decision to replace the image of a threat system by one directly its opposite. It is much more realistic to expect and advocate that parallel with a conflict, power-political model, statesmen should be encouraged and prodded to think also in terms of a harmony model. If this becomes widespread, the chances of progress from conflict and violence towards harmony and cooperation are likely to be enhanced. The progress at first must be expected to be painfully slow and very uneven, but it may gradually gather momentum. One promising way lies in the study of the conduct of day-to-day 'non-crisis' diplomacy, in which we may discover patterns of behaviour and options applicable to crisis situations, whereas, under stress, we have scarcely time for reflection and we tend to react to any threat perceived by a similar counter-threat. By drawing attention to general patterns of state behaviour, such study would also introduce a degree of democratic check upon

* cf. Kenneth Boulding, *The Meaning of the Twentieth Century*, Allen & Unwin, 1965; or John Burton, *International Relations: a General Theory*, Cambridge University Press, 1965.

decisions which are bound ultimately to be taken by small groups of leaders.

All human behaviour is based upon assumptions about the behaviour of others, and the functioning and effectiveness of human institutions depend to a very large extent upon the general acceptance of the conventions underlying them. Confidence is the indispensable basis of economic activities; in its absence financial institutions could not keep solvent and commercial contracts would not be considered dependable. In domestic economics, such confidence has been reasonably well established in the last few generations, although it becomes disturbed during periods of depression. Since confidence in international economics is much more brittle, the need for building it up is widely felt. This explains the close cooperation of international bankers during the run on world currencies in 1967 and 1968. Likewise, when members of the international consortium repeatedly save India from bankruptcy, they do so not only to help India but also to maintain a basic confidence in the solvency of states as international debtors.

If we want to alleviate the politico-strategic insecurity of states, this can be done only through the building up of confidence that other states constitute no real threat or that they would be effectively restrained in any aggressive designs. This can be achieved only through transforming the international system. All that the statesmen can do meanwhile in order to avoid violent conflict and war is to be ready to re-examine their stereotypes, to eschew the symbolic values attached to many issues of little substantive importance and, without any risky and naïve optimism, to consider whether, even in issues of vital importance, a harmony-based approach may not lead to a more rational pursuit of 'national interest' than an approach postulating basic conflict. Even in the Arab–Israeli conflict, analysed in Chapter 7, where the intractable problem is that the two sides claim the same land, it is not impossible that coexistence with its prospect of peace for Israel and of economic development for the Arabs will prevail over their respective desires to retain the territories gained and to attempt to reconquer them by force of arms. While for the time being, on the basis of a threat system, both sides marshal military capabilities and diplomatic support, their policies and prospects would be fundamentally transformed if the threat system basis were removed or even weakened.

One of the gravest dangers inherent in the choice of *capabilities* lies in the traditional reliance upon weapons and means of violence which, even if they may not be directly conducive to violence and war, are at least closely connected with it. This reliance is due to past history when survival depended upon defence. If, however, we view power not as an essence ultimately determined by the military potential and its economic and social supports, but as a relational phenomenon, as the capacity for making others act according to our wishes, the choice of capabilities may be extended. At present it is difficult to compare capabilities; in the area of coercive power we contend with the rating of the destruction potential of untried new weapons and of defence arrangements, as well as with the comparison of these with 'conventional weapons'; we have no yardstick for comparing military power with utilitarian or identitive power.

Three points are, however, fairly clear. Defence of national territory cannot be ensured and its dependence upon a policy of deterrence cannot be thought to be very stable or satisfactory. Second, advanced mass-destruction weapons are of little or no use outside the deterrence relationship. Third, the cost of advanced weapons has been rising so fast that, however crude any cost-effectiveness analysis may be, it is worth trying to compare them with other capabilities which may prove much better value.

The objectives for which capabilities are developed are hard to elucidate. A good illustration can be found in the confused arguments advanced during the controversies about British nuclear arms. Despite their limited scope, these weapons could inflict sufficient second-strike damage upon a nuclear attacker, even as powerful as the Soviet Union, to be legitimately regarded as effective in a deterrence policy; moreover, the diplomatic standing of states has been traditionally, and still is being, largely determined by the amount of resources put into weapons, however little use is envisaged for them. On the other hand, the advocates of unilateral nuclear disarmament claimed that, after having proved her technological prowess in developing the weapons,

Britain could have achieved much more prestige by unilaterally giving up the weapons than by keeping and developing them at a high cost.

It is only too easy to go to extremes. The modern state which persists in spending large sums of money on weapons has been strikingly likened to an individual who persists in buying improved and increasingly costly shot-guns though he does not know against whom he may use these, and who even buys plastic explosive with which he may blow up himself together with others, if he ever does use it. It is clear that military capabilities remain decisive in acute conflict situations, e.g. between the Israelis and the Arabs. In less acute situations, however, reliance on utilitarian or persuasive power may be more effective and less costly. Unfortunately the transition is difficult to conceive unless a lead is given by the successful and, through their very success, influential Superpowers. It is arguable that this has already started to happen although many other states do not seem to have realized it.

A similar argument can be made about the choice of *instruments and techniques* of foreign policy. In the broad spectrum stretching from diplomacy at the one end to war at the other, the utility of war as an instrument of foreign policy has become increasingly circumscribed. A total nuclear war goes far beyond the boundaries of anything which can be thought useful although an argument can be made for the development of nuclear weapons in a policy of deterrence. The incidence of violence has, however, increased in the various forms of intervention and all the other instruments and techniques can be and are being used both in conflict and cooperation. The actual choice of the mode in which they are used ultimately depends upon the individual estimate of the national interest involved but is likely to take into account the general climate of international relations and one of its major elements, i.e. the behaviour of the Superpowers.

## *Interaction among States and the International System*

In the previous section state behaviour was viewed from the angle of the individual state; now it will be considered from the angle of state interaction within the international system. This interaction can be based upon either conflict or harmony, or some mixture of both; the trends and prospects in single areas are too intricate and confused to permit much generalization. At first glance, there seems to be much more conflict and violence at present than in the latter part of the nineteenth century. We must, however, bear in mind that modern communications enable us to learn about many remote events which may have escaped our notice in the past. Moreover, if we allow for the multiplication of men, of states and of weapons, the incidence of violence and conflict may now be proportionately not greater than in the past. The advance of technology has a dual effect; while opportunities for the use of violence have broadened, the increased destructiveness of weapons, especially of the nuclear variety, has had a strong inhibiting effect upon large-scale use of violence. Conquest was rational only as long as its cost was lower than its expected benefits; today the exploitation of nature offers much greater scope than the subjugation and exploitation of other nations. The means of violence are not only costly but involve grave dangers of escalation to unacceptable levels. Moreover, excepting the colonial liberation movements, violence generally incurs the unwelcome opprobrium of the General Assembly.

Unfortunately this picture of the world is not without signal exceptions. In Vietnam, caught in an intervention which cannot be brought to a successful ending and reluctant to admit defeat, for a long time the Americans were increasing violence more and more without being able to break the will of either the Vietcong guerrillas or of the North Vietnamese who support them. The Vietnam political situation is not, however, typical. Even when reluctant to relinquish their dependencies and friends, countries with smaller capabilities were on many occasions simply forced to do so. Large-scale escalation of violence on the Vietnamese pattern is clearly entirely beyond the capacity of any other state. Complete retreat is not necessarily the only option; sometimes de-escalation is possible, as in Hong Kong in the latter part of 1967. Here, throughout repeated outbreaks of violence within the colony and of border incidents, the British invariably responded to hostile moves with the minimum of violence possible, aiming at de-escalation. Once the British forces unilaterally withdrew mortars and machine-guns a hundred yards away from the frontier where they had been placed to ward off attacks; to 'show the flag', the Ghurkas marched up and down the village street playing their bagpipes to which the Chinese on the other side of the border 'retaliated' by giving a concert of revolutionary tunes.\*

The use of violence can no longer secure the traditional objectives of states – security, economic advantage, and glory. Nevertheless, violence remains the traditional ultimate means of resolving acute conflicts and its threat remains an important technique of state behaviour. The distinction between the actual use and the threat of violence provides a partial explanation of the present confusion about its role. Threats continue and require increased military capabilities to make them credible; the nuclear policy of deterrence is the most pronounced example. The use of violence, however, although it quite frequently occurs, is singularly ineffective and does not lead to the resolution of conflicts. It is not an accident that all the major post-war conflagrations have proved inconclusive, e.g. in Korea, in Palestine, in Cyprus, or in Vietnam.

The logical conclusion is obvious – the threats of violence and the supporting capabilities require a searching reappraisal, but what is going to replace them? Here the techniques mentioned in the preceding chapter can be developed – pacific settlement of disputes, disarmament, preventive diplomacy, etc. Transition, however, from the traditional power-political approach to one in which the existing systemic limitations and restraints are increased, must be expected to be slow and gradual. Statesmen cannot abandon traditional defences, even when they are of dubious effectiveness, unless and until reasonable substitutes are offering.

Hence the importance of creating a suitable mental climate to facilitate the transition. To return to a theme already mentioned in the previous section, state interaction is bound to be governed by the 'mirror-effect'. Statesmen reflect in their behaviour the images they hold of other states, their behaviour is

\* *The Times*, 18 July 1967.

reflected in turn in the images and behaviour of these states, and thus each image and action contains a self-fulfilling element. One need not be very pessimistic about the outcome. It is possible to detect in international relations a faint parallel with a tendency to move from competition to cooperation, identified by Professor Galbraith in sophisticated economic systems; this is true about some aspects of international trade and is a distinct possibility in the field of disarmament. If this is so, it is of paramount importance that the behaviour of states should fully reflect this tendency.

Again no dramatic transformation can be expected. Change may come in two directions. First, the statesmen may come to appraise and take into full account the differences between the aspirational and the operational levels of ideologies and values and between immediate and long-range interests and principles. It seems profitable that the states should concentrate upon relationships in which cooperation is most promising and to endeavour to avoid those in which conflict is likely to be most acute. There is no hard and fast rule about the matter. Since Afro-Asian members of the United Nations readily agree among themselves about some principles but clash about many immediate interests, it is logical that they concentrate so much upon these principles. Likewise justified is the way in which the United States and the Soviet Union have been recently concentrating upon immediate interests in which they can cooperate, rather than upon irreconcilable principles.

Second, state interaction is based upon a basic contradiction between the demands of sovereignty and state needs which can be satisfied only by interaction limiting this sovereignty, sometimes to the point of demanding for greatest efficiency some form of supra-national organization which would take decisions binding the state. Traditionally the dilemma, whenever acute, was solved in favour of state sovereignty. This may not be the pattern of the future. Thirdly, interaction is greatly affected by the basic images of friendship or hostility governing the relations between individual states. Statesmen should constantly revise these images and, even if these prove intractably hostile, should nevertheless endeavour to engage in limited cooperation.

The last-mentioned recommendation has served as the basis for the simple and attractive *functional* approach to peace. Since harmony and cooperation thrive in inverse proportion to the intensity of the politico-strategic interest involved, it seems profitable for states to concentrate upon the economic and the social issues within these 'functional' areas. The thin threads of cooperation may eventually be twisted into a mighty rope holding all the states together; we may reach 'peace by pieces' or 'federation by instalments'. The approach appeals both to selfish national interest which can be more efficiently satisfied through international cooperation, and to humanitarian instincts; it does not postulate either liberal or conservative attitudes and it in no way precludes other approaches to peace.

The functional approach underlay the unexpectedly successful social activities of the League of Nations and played an important part in wartime plans for the United Nations Organization which was, in fact, preceded by the establishment of several specialized agencies. The undisputed successes in the field cannot, however, obscure the fundamental limitation of the approach. The scope of the specialized agencies has remained modest. They collect information and endeavour to standardize and harmonize the activities of member-governments but the latter rarely delegate to them an operational role. When they do so, this role is restricted, e.g. to technical arrangements in communications or to dealing, on a temporary basis, with the post-1945 problem of refugees. The transition from functional to political cooperation is by no means as simple as envisaged; instead of serving as a stepping-stone to political cooperation, functional cooperation is often violently affected by politics, e.g. in the more controversial fields of foreign aid and trade. We are up against the usual circularity. It is arguable that an international order is the necessary precondition for effective functional cooperation rather than the other way around. Nevertheless this approach seems to offer a greater promise of breaking or at least denting the vicious circle than any other international endeavour. Developing and cultivating the habit of cooperation is likely to have at least a limited 'overspill effect' into the politically more sensitive areas, e.g. even a restricted amount of trade and joint membership in a few quite unimportant international organizations could be instrumental in smoothing the path towards friendlier United States–Chinese relations. Even the most limited cooperation proves that the other party is a possible partner to transactions and not merely an implacable adversary.

The idea of *international trusteeship* shares with the functional approach the assumption that social welfare is the basis of a good society which, in turn, is conducive to international peace. To this is added the assumption held by the liberals and the communists alike that imperialist rivalries have been a major source of war. Both assumptions are vulnerable to criticism. Moreover, during its brief history, first as the League of Nations mandates system and then as the United Nations trusteeship system, the idea has suffered greatly from its dual motivation: it was advanced both by the anti-imperialists to combat imperialism, and by the imperial powers to disguise it.

International trusteeship has not been successful but is no longer necessary. Post-1945 political pressures, lately channelled mainly through the General Assembly, have resulted in a rapid disintegration of the colonial empires. The remaining few dependencies still give rise to trouble, but the problems of colonialism and imperialism based upon territorial conquest and domination of other peoples are clearly a matter of the past. The solution, however, was not found in international trusteeship. However small and, by traditional tenets, non-viable, the ex-colonies are emancipated from imperial tutelage not through its replacement by some form of international responsibility but by becoming fully-fledged independent states. Many problems facing these new states are clearly far beyond their limited capabilities, especially those of national integration and of economic growth. This logically leads to sporadic interventions by other states and by the international community. Perhaps future historians of international trusteeship will express deep regret about its failure; it could have saved the new states and the world a great deal of conflict and hardship.

Functionalism attempts to transcend the vertical division of mankind into territorial states and to mitigate it by horizontal ties which would cut across national boundaries. *Trans-national* *link*s exist at so many levels that one may go to the length of thinking about a 'trans-national society' characterized by such links as trade, movements of people, and common beliefs, institutions and modes of behaviour. For instance, in pre-1914 Europe such a trans-national society was based upon the common heritage of Christianity and rationalism; there existed 'internationals' of monarchs and diplomats, of traders and financiers, of socialists; movement across national boundaries was easy; several international institutions had been established. In the inter-war period, fundamental ideological rifts and exacerbated nationalism weakened this trans-national society in many vital dimensions but, simultaneously, technological progress and international organizations strengthened it in others.

Since 1945, the trans-national society has been weakened by the Cold War, especially during its acute phase, and by the resulting 'iron curtain', as well as by the estrangement of China, but has been immensely strengthened by the rapid improvement in social communications. The dense network of international organizations is not limited to governments but combines millions of individuals and their groupings, cutting across national boundaries. People sharing most of the professions and occupations, interests, arts, sports, or other pursuits, are rarely content with activities limited to a single state; for full satisfaction they generally demand international links. This applies to all walks of life, as innocuous as butterfly-collecting and as strategically important as nuclear science.

Particularly relevant are the trans-national links among scientists, social scientists, and lawyers. Many members of these professions are concerned with the central issues of international politics, and can bring to bear upon them the habit of cooperation with their counterparts abroad as well as the habit of looking at conflict situations objectively and from a long-term point of view. They enjoy the additional advantage over the politicians in that they can be bolder, that they can envisage greater risks, that they can advocate measures which may not be immediately practicable. The difficult transition from conflict to cooperation may be greatly facilitated by a simple comparison of the 'pay-offs' available when a competitive 'zero-sum' game is converted into a cooperative 'non-zero-sum' one.* Although politicians naturally can and often do ignore advice, with time, increasing numbers of politicians may be analytically trained, which would make them more receptive to expert discussions and arguments. Although rarely noticed, the fact that the majority of the members of the Politburo have had some form of higher technological education may constitute a crucial element in the changing of the foreign policy of the Soviet Union.

Some of these professionals have become greatly interested in the problems of peace and have established special trans-national links in order to cooperate in this field. If, as seems likely at least in the technologically advanced countries, we are advancing from industrial civilization into what has been variously called a 'post-civilized' or 'technotronic' age, it is possible to consider these intellectuals as an 'invisible college' engaged in preparing mankind for the transition.† In the forties such a proposition would have sounded absurd, today it is still utopian but, if sufficient people accept the idea, it may well become an important political reality within our life-time.

Turning back from the realm of uncertain ideas to political reality, although many conflicts seem at the moment insoluble we can point to others which have been settled, or at least reduced to a point where the use of violence is most unlikely or even unthinkable – the ending of the religious wars, of Anglo–American and Anglo–French hostility and, more recently, also of the French–German and Italo–Yugoslav conflicts. Following the medieval tradition of the 'lines of amity' and of areas of friendship, 'security communities' have arisen in which violence is not expected to be used in the resolution of any conflicts, however acute they may become.‡ Violence is unthinkable, for example, in the relations between the United States and Canada, in Scandinavia, in Western Europe, in 'the Atlantic community' on the shores of the North Atlantic. In view of the traditional acute

* cf. pp. 50–51.

† cf. Kenneth Boulding, *The Meaning of the Twentieth Century*, Allen & Unwin, 1965.

‡ Karl W. Deutsch, et al., *Political Community in the North Atlantic*, Princeton, Princeton University Press, 1957.

Interaction among States and the International System

Greek–Turkish and Rumanian–Hungarian conflicts, the NATO and the Warsaw Pact areas belong only marginally to this category. Plans have, nevertheless, been proposed to amalgamate the two into one 'security community' as a possible solution of the German problem, but, so far at least, this seems to be a wishful thought rather than an actual possibility. The most important recent case is the abatement of the Cold War to which the next few paragraphs are devoted.

We may never find full agreement about the ways to define the intensity of conflict with any degree of precision. Nevertheless it is unlikely that anybody would question that the Cold War has become much less virulent since its zenith at the end of the forties and the beginning of the fifties. Not only the professionals dedicated to peace, mentioned above, but many others, including the leaders of communist China, believe not only that the acute conflict relationship between the Superpowers is being attenuated but also that it is now being accompanied, possibly partially replaced, by a form of cooperation. The new interaction has been variously called '*détente*', 'peaceful coexistence' and 'interdependence'. Its actual forms are constantly changing and its evaluation is subject to violent disputes since some writers discern a fundamental change from the Cold War while others vehemently deny this. Another contribution to this debate would be of little value since equally plausible arguments can be advanced for either view. The pessimistic view – that the conflict has changed little and only in form – scarcely requires elaboration but it may be of interest to outline at least two of the opposed opinions.

One of them, espoused by the well-known psychologist Professor Charles E. Osgood,* calls for a policy of 'graduated and reciprocated initiatives in tension-reduction' (or GRIT for short); this policy closely resembles many of the actual moves undertaken by the late President Kennedy. The author outlines the principles of a calculated de-escalation of international tensions based upon interpersonal relations and learning principles. He applies his argument to United States foreign policy and explains how the Americans could extricate themselves from

*Perspective in Foreign Policy*, Palo Alto, Pacific Books, 2nd ed., 1966.

241

Vietnam and change their attitudes to China. The argument is convincing as an analysis of the Cold War and of the subsequent basis of *détente* with communist China.

The other analysis is quite substantial. Vincent P. Rock* advocates the transition from conflict to interdependence between the two Superpowers in three stages: first through a revision of images by replacing 'the traditional by the instrumental stream of experience in the community'; second, through the shift of emphasis from the divisive distinction between capitalism and communism to the distinction between the industrialized and unindustrialized worlds according to which the two Superpowers belong to the same grouping; third, through the evolution of world order not through narrow concentration upon one's own bloc but through cooperation in the world-wide economic development. Rock is quite realistic about the difficulties inherent in the change despite the fact that sophistication of thinking and the appreciation of basic interdependence have increased on both sides. Specifically he mentions, on the Soviet side, the so far unstable society, the communist ideology (despite its abating virulence), and the lingering Soviet view of world unity; on the American side, the military interpretation of the concept of containment and the allied influence of the 'military-industrial complex'; within the 'balance-of-terror' system itself, its precarious dependence upon repeatedly occurring crises. The mutual interests which Rock ably examines should, in his opinion, suffice to persuade the Americans to change their policy and, in turn, also the Russians, although he does not expect that the transition would be easy or speedy. Rock's opinions are strongly America-centred but may nevertheless lack appeal even for the Americans themselves, let alone for the Russians; he does not deal at all with the Chinese. The point must, however, be remembered that both Osgood's and Rock's ideas, far-fetched as they appear on the basis of traditional views of power politics, do no more

* *A Strategy of Interdependence: a Program for the Control of Conflict between the United States and the Soviet Union*, New York, Scribner, 1964. See also review article by T. V. Satyamurthy, 'From Containment to Interdependence', *World Politics*, October 1967.

than extrapolate into the future some of the recent trends in the Cold War and hence should not be dismissed as completely utopian.

The decision to progress from conflict to cooperation must be taken by the states and must be implemented in their inter-action; nevertheless, the international systems as a whole and international organizations will undoubtedly play a major role in any change. As instruments of the member-states and as organs of the international system, international organizations, especially the United Nations, are likely to play a focal role in moderating state interaction. In addition, they may also supersede, partly or fully, the states as the basic units of the international system. They will be considered in this role in the following section.

## *From the Sovereign State to International Organization*

A recurrent theme of the preceding discussion has been the grave crisis of the national territorial state, the supreme form of political organization evolved in the past. As cogently stated by Professor John Herz,* the boundaries of the state, even of a Superpower, are no longer impenetrable: the state is no longer economically self-contained; its citizens are directly accessible to foreign propa-ganda, and, most significantly, it cannot effectively defend its territory. Clearly the state is only a segment of a larger whole, of mankind; for many essential purposes, only the whole world is a significant area of activity.

Some thinkers look ahead and discern clear signs that we have already reached not only a 'post-industrial' but also a 'post-nation-state' era. Barbara Ward,† for example, argues that although the individual still gives his supreme loyalty to the national state, this is scarcely a situation which can continue for long in a world which is one. Not only has the nation-state proved inadequate for the basic physical needs of society but nationalism is increasingly less satisfying spiritually. Neither the capitalist nor the communist ideology fills the void created

* *International Politics in the Atomic Age*, New York, Columbia, 1962.
† *Nationalism and Ideology*, Hamish Hamilton, 1967.

by the decline of both; spiritual rejuvenation, even if man deliberately turns to it, is bound to prove arduous and slow.*

Interaction among states offers little promise for finding more than palliatives or, at the most, partial remedies for the ills of international society. The most promising and more frequently sought way out appears to lie in some form of integration or unification of states, or of international organization. The three terms are used here interchangeably, all describing the strengthening of the bonds among the members of the international system. It is important to stress that sovereign territorial states are the starting-point. However severe a crisis may be facing them, they already exist and they have a near-monopoly of physical power. It is to be expected that it will prove very difficult for the states to coalesce.

In a way we are justified in regarding states and international organizations as two juxtaposed elements of international politics; the former embody and are strengthened by centrifugal forces; the latter embody and are strengthened by centripetal forces; there is an inverse correlation between the intensity of nationalism and that of internationalism or support for international organization. We should, however, beware of pressing the dichotomy too far. In fact international organization serves, in the first instance, not the purposes of larger communities desirous of incorporating the individual states but, on the contrary, the purposes of the member-states. It thus protects and buttresses centrifugal forces; if it were not for the essential strategic-political guarantees and economic support supplied by international organizations, in all likelihood many states would be incapable of continuing in existence. Moreover, international organization is a growing source of political legitimacy for many international activities; the Bandung Conference, the Organization for African Unity, and particularly the United Nations, all have served many times this important purpose.

In the theory of international organization, scholars differentiate between 'inter-governmental' institutions, which more or less correspond with the above description, and 'supra-national' institutions. The latter, instead of or parallel with serving the

* cf. the following section, pp. 247 ff.

interests of the members, serve also some interests of the community of these members and, with respect to these common interests, are empowered to take decisions binding upon the members. On the whole, however, this distinction is only theoretical and legal. On the one hand, every organization must serve some, though sometimes only minimal, needs of the community, over and above the needs of the members; it must, at the very least, maintain the institutions of the community. On the other hand, very few international organizations have supra-national powers of any importance and, even if they have them, the scope of their activities is determined by the realities of the political process rather than by the letter of the constitution. For example, the constitution of the European Coal and Steel Community specifically mentions supra-national powers of the community, while the constitution of the European Economic Community does not; nevertheless their powers are so similar that their organs have now been amalgamated. Moreover, the powers of decision of the Commission are not quite clear; one of their bases, the famous Luxembourg Compromise of 1965, is interpreted quite differently by France and by the other five members.

Not only the method of integration but also its geographical scope varies greatly from case to case and is sometimes blurred. The major division-line here lies between regional integration,* whatever its boundaries, and universalism. Obviously, integration generally gives rise to fewer difficulties on a regional than on a world-wide scale. There are better prospects for a consensus based upon some unitary features; communications and governmental arrangements are easier.

As in the formation of all social groupings, conflict seems to be the necessary starting-point of all integration; merging in a larger unit involves social costs and these are incurred only under stress, in response to a threat.† Two recurrent major patterns of regional organization can be discerned: the hegemonial one, in which a Great Power serves as a nucleus around which the lesser powers

---

* cf. E. Plischke (ed.), *Systems of Integrating the International Community*, Van Nostrand, 1964, or R. J. Yalem, *Regionalism and World Order*, Washington, Public Affairs Press, 1965.

† cf. Chapter 2, pp. 39 ff.

cluster, either to seek protection against another Greater Power which is a common enemy or because they are afraid of the 'protector'. The other, much rarer type is that of political units with less pronounced disparities of power which unite against a common danger; the classical examples are the Swiss cantons which were threatened by the Habsburgs and the thirteen American colonies which rebelled against England. Although serving as a basis for cooperation within themselves, regional organizations thus tend to perpetuate, occasionally even to exacerbate conflict with the external enemy.

Nearly all of the post-war regional organizations have been of the hegemonial type: the Organization of American States (OAS) marks out the Western hemisphere as the exclusive sphere of influence of the United States, although this influence is today much less imperious than in the past and one of the members, Cuba, has broken away. The North Atlantic, the South East Asia, and the Central Treaty Organizations (NATO, SEATO and CENTO) all cluster around the United States while the Warsaw Pact is their Eastern European counterpart developed by and clustering around the Soviet Union. All of them are instruments of the Cold War.

The Commonwealth and the various attempts at organizing the non-committed Third World states are not limited to a geographical region but, on the contrary, cut across continents and races. Interesting as they are as unique attempts to foster cooperation across formidable geographical and other barriers, they need not be considered in any detail as they have not fulfilled their early promise of achieving some degree of integration of member-states.

Regional organizations in which no Superpower participates have not been a great success either. Attempts in South East Asia have so far failed, while the Arab League and the Organization for African Unity exhibit little solidarity and lack real unity of purpose in action. Common enemies constitute the cement holding these organizations together – the Arab states are united against Israel while the African states confront the white-dominated countries of southern Africa. The common enemies are therefore excluded from these organizations although geographical and economic logic calls for their inclusion. Certainly a Middle Eastern organization including Israel and embracing a Jordan waters development agency would be extremely advantageous to all participants, as would be an all-African organization embracing southern Africa. Political hostility, however, prevails over economic considerations and it is difficult to envisage fundamental changes within foreseeable time.

The only large-scale attempt at functional regional cooperation which has taken place in Western Europe does not inspire confidence that economic and social considerations would eventually prevail over politics. The Western European communities started with the political unification of the region as an avowed ultimate objective. All their members participate in the anti-communist North Atlantic Treaty Organization, but the communities themselves are not directed against the Soviet Union or communist East Europe although they enjoy the support of the United States. Established during the fifties, the three communities – the Coal and Steel Community, the European Economic Community and EURATOM – were aided in their initial stages by the Western European solidarity established during the common utilization of the generous Marshall Aid programme which had made possible European recovery in the late forties, as well as by the rising surge of prosperity which, to some extent at least, was due to the communities themselves. In a rapidly worsening economic climate and under the stress of a deep rift between the French and the other five members regarding the fundamental issues of attitudes to the United States and to the British application to join, by 1968 the communities were facing a severe crisis. Their momentum is likely to carry them across this crisis but is bound to be greatly reduced in the process. Instead of becoming – as had seemed quite likely – a new type of supra-national organization, to a large extent the communities have now reverted to the traditional type of inter-governmental institutions. In the past the famous 'community method' allowed the European Commission, which is the major community organ, a considerable power of initiative and left to it the elaboration of detail after the Council of Ministers had agreed upon principles. Since the 1965 constitutional crisis and the subsequent Luxembourg Compromise, the Commission's power of initiative has been curtailed and arrangements of a kind previously delegated to it are now negotiated by inter-governmental committees at which the Commission is only represented. No wonder the communities seem incapable of meeting creatively the many problems facing them. Again, once the immediate economic benefit dwindles, cooperation slackens; politics is clearly predominant over economics. It is, however, possible that the hopes of the members are justified that an enlargement of the communities through the inclusion of Britain, Denmark, Ireland and Norway, negotiated in 1971, would lead to another *relance européenne* and would instil new dynamism into the situation.

On the global level, regional organizations tend to foster conflict rather than cooperation. If the world were effectively divided into highly integrated regional organizations, in all likelihood rivalries among these would replace the rivalries among states and, being between larger units, would be even more dangerous. It is impossible to regard regional organizations as logical stepping-stones towards a world organization. On the contrary, even when brought into a relationship with the world organization, they tend to develop an autonomy which weakens the latter. Although in the inter-war period regional security arrangements were to complement the imperfect collective security system, after 1945 they have clearly replaced collective security altogether. The U.N. Charter does, indeed, provide for subordinate regional security arrangements but in fact such post-war arrangements were brought into being on the basis of the self-defence escape clause in Article 51, which ensures their complete autonomy.

The United Nations has, of course, deeply disappointed those who had optimistically believed that it would become an effective guardian of world peace through a system of collective security. Ingenious law drafts exist to cover even the most complicated and delicate issues and contingencies. If only the major powers wished this, peace could be secured through the United Nations and the rule of law, but it is extremely hard to expect that the states will forgo the traditional prerogatives of their sovereignty.

Although lacking success in its major objective, the United Nations has not been a complete failure. The Organization has helped the Superpowers in the evolution of their relations through 'preventive diplomacy' which contains minor conflicts and prevents their escalation, and through the provisions of a debating forum in which political legitimacy has to be obtained and which consolidates and ratifies the major customs of the Cold War and the subsequent *détente*. It has presided over relatively peaceful decolonization, the most gigantic political process ever recorded. Despite several acute crises, no member has permanently left the United Nations and nobody appears to envisage its demise; on the contrary, in 1971 it included communist China and it seems now likely that it will become fully representative by including also the divided countries.

The United Nations often served as an instrument of conflict. During its period of predominance, the United States used its huge voting majorities as a stick to beat the Soviet Union; likewise, the now dominant Afro-Asian bloc uses its majority to castigate the imperialist and racialist members. The American majorities, however, disappeared in the late fifties and colonialism is being rapidly liquidated. United Nations involvement in conflicts is, therefore, likely to diminish and the Organization will probably continue and develop its hitherto modest cooperative politics. As Inis Claude puts it, we have not produced a 'synthetic great power' but we have at least established a 'synthetic neutral'* commensurate with the gigantic size of the present-day Superpowers.


## World Government and the Transformation of Man

The logic of the situation is inescapable – only a world government would be capable of controlling man's destiny. Such a government, however, is scarcely thinkable without the transformation of the nature of man, which, in turn, is difficult to conceive outside a world government. We are up against the old vicious circle again. Even those who firmly believe that there is

*Inis L. Claude, Jr, *The Changing United Nations*, New York, Random House, 1957, p. 121.

promise in attempting to bring about the necessary changes whether in man, or in the system, or in both, do not expect these changes to become effective within the foreseeable future. And yet, are the so-called 'realists' more realistic? Undoubtedly our international system is more stable than those we have known previously in history and, despite their obvious shortcomings, the existing states seem more assured of continued existence than were their predecessors in the last century which, on the face of it, was much more peaceful.* But can this system continue indefinitely on the brittle basis of nuclear deterrence?

Regarding international organization, which is clearly much more readily attainable than a world government, M. Jean Monnet, the father of the European Communities, spoke as follows: 'We are in a world of rapid change in which men must learn to control themselves in their relations with others. To my mind this can only be done through institutions. Human nature does not change, but when people accept the same rules and the same institutions, their behaviour towards each other changes. This is the process of civilization itself.'† The date of the speech is 1961; since then, with the crisis of the European Communities, M. Monnet's expectations must have become attenuated.

It is difficult to draw a clear boundary between attempts at strengthening regional organizations, or the United Nations, and those at establishing an international police force which implies a world political authority, or a straight-out world government. All these have been the subject of many an ingenuous analysis but also of much muddle-headed and unrealistic writing. Many responsible statesmen, including heads of governments and foreign ministers, are on record, too, in support of one or more of these solutions. Being, however, practical men immediately responsible for the interests of their respective countries, they do not explain how the transition will proceed and one frequently doubts whether they expect that it will ever be achieved at all.

If the history of the functional approach is any guide, slow

* cf. F. H. Hinsley, *Power and the Pursuit of Peace*, Cambridge University Press, 1963.

† Quoted by E. Plischke, ed., *Systems of Integrating the International Community*, Van Nostrand, 1964, p. 82.

evolutionary changes are, indeed, much easier than a fundamental transformation but cannot, unfortunately, be relied upon to lead to the latter. We are undoubtedly facing a formidable 'thought barrier' before we transcend the boundaries of the national territorial state and free ourselves from the traditional thinking in terms of threat systems and of power politics. Possibly the only way of overcoming this thought barrier lies in a frontal assault upon it, in a complete transformation of our outlook. Some writers are quite optimistic about the prospects. Although through liberating himself from the thraldom of nature man has become a slave of the environment he himself had made, his contriving mind which has been so far devoted to the mastery of nature has now turned to the mastery of society. If he devotes himself as diligently to the new task as he did to the old one, he will eventually emerge triumphant.*

Even if these hopes are justified, for the time being peace must remain uneasy and be disturbed by threats and breaches of the most dangerous nature. The immediate danger of a nuclear war is great and is perhaps growing – in January 1968 the hands of the symbolic clock upon the cover of the *Bulletin of the Atomic Scientists* were moved five minutes closer to Doomsday, from twelve to seven minutes to midnight, although a year later, following the progress of the non-proliferation treaty, they moved it back; the instruments of biological and chemical warfare are being assiduously developed. Further ahead loom the dangers of the population of the world increasing to the point of starvation; no solution is in sight for many conflicts as acute as those between the Arabs and the Israelis, the Indians and the Pakistanis, or the Greek and the Turkish Cypriots. However, even as intractable problems as those of the United States involvement in Vietnam and of the exclusion of communist China from the international

---

* For interesting analyses of this view, see Herbert Rosinski, *Power and Human Destiny*, Pall Mall, 1965, or Kenneth Boulding, *The Meaning of the Twentieth Century*, Allen & Unwin, 1965. Such views about the future of mankind can be held by rationalists, far remote from the mysticism of Teilhard de Chardin, who likewise sees this future as being determined in the 'noosphere' and not on the material plane.

system, have finally moved towards some form of resolution. Therefore it is not unreasonable to remain moderately optimistic in our outlook, whether we envisage the continuation of the present international system of national territorial states, or a world government, or some in-between arrangement. Our position affords no more rational justification for pessimism than for optimism and, as the two views affect the nature of reality, it seems well worth while being as optimistic as our information and understanding allows us.

At all levels and from all approaches it is possible to envisage ways and means of mitigating conflict and of fostering coopera- tion. We can endeavour to develop flexibility, we can try to move, if necessary unilaterally, towards harmony in the hope of reciprocity on the part of others. We can think about the various schemes for fundamental transformation with a view to seeing how feasible they may eventually become in the future rather than how un- realistic they are now. At the same time, however, sheer prudence demands from the statesmen that their optimism does not become unrealistic and dangerous, that they do not lower defences to the point of jeopardizing the states they are responsible for.

A colossal intellectual and social effort will be necessary in order to leave the world to succeeding generations in a shape even slightly better than it is today, let alone to open the road towards its ultimate fundamental transformation; it will be an achievement if we avoid a nuclear war and leave them any world at all. What then can we positively do? While keeping in mind the possible avenues for cooperation in the future and pursuing policies that would secure them, we must, at the same time, somehow cope with the threats of the present and do this in a way that will not jeopardize future prospects. To concentrate ex- clusively on the one or the other could nullify, in the long run, any chance of success with either.

Constant vigilance, unrelenting effort and a clear vision of the direction in which our efforts must be made may bring us nearer the peace we all desire, which some hope for and others despair of. However sceptical we may be about our prospects, we have no choice but to proceed. It is healthier to do so with moderate optimism; for to expect the worst is to invite the worst.

# INDEX

# MORE ABOUT PENGUINS
# AND PELICANS

*Penguinews*, which appears every month, contains details of all the new books issued by Penguins as they are published. From time to time it is supplemented by *Penguins in Print*, which is a complete list of all available books published by Penguins. (There are well over three thousand of these.)

A specimen copy of *Penguinews* will be sent to you free on request, and you can become a subscriber for the price of the postage. For a year's issues (including the complete lists) please send 30p if you live in the United Kingdom, or 60p if you live elsewhere. Just write to Dept EP, Penguin Books Ltd, Harmondsworth, Middlesex, enclosing a cheque or postal order, and your name will be added to the mailing list.

Note: *Penguinews* and *Penguins in Print* are not available in the U.S.A. or Canada

# POLITICS AND SOCIAL SCIENCE

*W. J. M. Mackenzie*

For as long as politics has been a human activity, it has also been a subject of serious study. Such names as Machiavelli, Hobbes, Montesquieu, and de Tocqueville have exercised enormous influence in the history of politics.

In our generation the study of politics has developed dramatically in new and fascinating directions. New ideas and techniques in the fields of philosophy, psychology, biology, sociology, and mathematics have all played a part in revolutionizing the world of academic politics and giving meaning to its new name of political science. In this new Pelican, Professor Mackenzie briefly reviews the history of the academic study of politics from Plato and Aristotle to Bagehot and Marx. But the most important contribution of his book is to give the ordinary reader the first opportunity to read a complete survey of the incredible diversity of modern political science in a book which never loses sight among the technicalities of method of the prime aims of the study of politics.

In effect, Professor Mackenzie ably interprets political science to the social scientist, and social science to the student of politics. In so doing he makes both clearer to the intelligent man in the street.

# VOTERS, PARTIES, AND LEADERS
## *The Social Fabric of British Politics*

### *J. Blondel*

Are we witnessing the end of class-barriers in the political behaviour of the British voter? Does the businessman vote like the railwayman, the white-collar worker like the unskilled labourer?

Of course they do not. But how different are their voting habits? Trade unions are Labour-inclined, but all trade unionists are not Labour men. Are these non-Labour trade unionists exceptional? And, at the other end of the scale, are Labour-inclined professional people, managers, and executives rare but interesting exceptions?

These are some of the questions which the newly appointed Professor of Government in the University of Essex attempts to answer in this original book. In examining the background, outlook, and interests of voters, party members, politicians, civil servants, and party leaders, and endeavouring to trace some of the subtle threads that tie certain individuals to certain organizations, he presents an anatomy of the political world. And he asks: 'What is the "Establishment" we talk of? Does it exist? And if so, does it rule?'